Arab Folklore

A Handbook

Dwight F. Reynolds

Greenwood Folklore Handbooks

GREENWOOD PRESS
Westport, Connecticut • London

Library of Congress Cataloging-in-Publication Data

Reynolds, Dwight Fletcher, 1956–
  Arab folklore : a handbook / Dwight F. Reynolds.
    p. cm. — (Greenwood folklore handbooks, ISSN 1549–733X)
  Includes bibliographical references and index.
  ISBN-13: 978–0–313–33311–8 (alk. paper)
  1.   Arabs—Folklore.   I. Title.
  GR268.A73R49   2007
  398.208992'7—dc22   2007026931

British Library Cataloguing in Publication Data is available.

Library of Congress Catalog Card Number: 2007026931
ISBN-13: 978–0–313–33311–8
ISSN: 1549–733X

First published in 2007

Greenwood Press, 88 Post Road West, Westport, CT 06881
An imprint of Greenwood Publishing Group, Inc.
www.greenwood.com

Printed in the United States of America

The paper used in this book complies with the
Permanent Paper Standard issued by the National
Information Standards Organization (Z39.48–1984).

10   9   8   7   6   5   4   3   2   1

Copyright Acknowledgments

The author and the publisher gratefully acknowledge permission to excerpt material from the following sources:

From *The Arabian Nights: The Thousand and One Nights,* translated by Husain Haddawy. Copyright © 1990 by W. W. Norton & Company, Inc. Used by permission of W. W. Norton & Company, Inc.

Reprinted from Issachar Ben-Ami, *Saint Veneration Among the Jews in Morocco,* pp. 105–110, with the permission of Wayne State University Press.

Reprinted from, Haya Bar-Itzhak's *Jewish Moroccan Folk Narratives from Israel,* pp. 93–97, pp. 129–131, with the permission of Wayne State University Press.

Excerpts from *Romancing the Real* by Sabra Webber. University of Pennsylvania Press, 1991: pp.102–108. Reprinted by permission of the University of Pennsylvania Press.

Excerpts from Earle H. Waugh, *Memory, Music, and Religion.* Copyright © 2005. University of South Carolina Press, 2005: pp. 27–28. Reprinted with permission.

This book is dedicated to
'Abd al-Hamīd Hawwās,
teacher, mentor, and friend.

Contents

Preface

This addition to the Greenwood Folklore Handbook series follows the basic structure of earlier volumes, adapted, however, to fit its regional, rather than genre-based, focus. As a resource for students and interested members of the general public, it is designed to provide an overview of Arab folklore by means of selected miniature case studies, rather than extensive lists of genres, forms, and types. In a volume this size it would be impossible to provide a comprehensive survey of the folk culture of some 20 countries, many of which encompass multiple regional folk cultures as well. So the examples examined here have been chosen to serve not only as illustrations of a particular genre of Arab folklore, but also as demonstrations of some of the main themes that lie at the heart of modern folklore studies. The reader will find some examples presented primarily for their formal characteristics, others for their social function, and still others as demonstrations of performance interaction, historical continuity, modern innovation, individual creativity, the impact of the mass media, variation by region or by ethnic or religious community, gender differences, questions of identity, interaction between oral and written transmission, techniques of memorization and improvisation, political aspects of folk culture, and many other issues. At the end of each chapter appears a list of suggested Further Readings, all of which, along with many other works, appear in the extensive Bibliography at the end of the volume. In addition, a Glossary of Arabic terms has been provided, though every effort has also been made to explain these terms wherever they appear in the text.

Chapter One provides a basic introduction to Arab culture, complete with brief discussions of the history, religions, ethnicities, languages, and geographical features of the region that Westerners usually refer to as "the Arab world." Chapter Two provides a short discussion of the definitions and classifications of folklore by modern scholars and presents the classification scheme used to structure the remainder of the volume. Chapter Three presents some three-dozen examples of Arab folklore from Algeria, Egypt, Iraq, Israel, Jordan, Kuwait, Lebanon, Morocco, Oman, Palestine, Saudi Arabia, Sudan, Syria, Tunisia, the United Arab Emirates, and Yemen. These are organized into four broad categories: (1) verbal arts, (2) musical arts, (3) material arts, and (4) customs and traditions. Chapter Four provides an overview of some of the most important approaches and methodologies that have been used in the study of Arab folklore, and Chapter Five examines some of the contexts in which Arab folklore can be found—oral traditions, written historical sources, in modern literature, film, and theater, and in the mass media.

It is my hope that this volume will provide readers with a glimpse of the diversity and richness of Arab folk culture, a world that seems remarkably distant from western media portrayals of Arabs. Yet for anyone who has lived in the Arab world, it is obvious that the two views are related—there are indeed religious and political conflicts in the Arab world, but by viewing Arabs only through the lens of television news cameras, Westerners severely limit any chance they have of ever coming to understand one of the world's most remarkable cultures, a culture that historically, religiously, economically, politically, and socially is deeply intertwined with our own.

Acknowledgments

This volume is an attempt to open up the incredibly rich world of Arab folklore to English-speaking students and scholars. As such, it is a reflection not only of the many scholars whose works are quoted and cited within its pages, but also of all of the teachings and information I have received from scholars, performers, and other individuals over nearly three decades of exploring folk traditions of the Arab world. First and foremost, I wish to thank my teachers of Arab folklore and ethnomusicology—'Abd al-Rahmān al-Abnūdī, 'Abd al-Rahmān Ayyūb, 'Abd al-Hamīd Hawwās, A. Jihad Racy, Yusuf Shawqī, and Muhammad 'Umrān—whose love of, and insights into, Arab folklore and music have continued to inspire and inform my own.

In addition, I would like to express my gratitude to my professors and mentors at the University of Pennsylvania who offered me such remarkable training in the field of folklore and in Middle Eastern studies—Roger Abrahams, Roger Allen, Dan Ben-Amos, Henry Glassie, Kenneth Goldstein, Dell Hymes, Virginia Hymes, George Makdisi, Margaret Mills, and Don Yoder—in what can now be seen as a truly remarkable, even historic, confluence of scholars.

A survey of this nature necessarily draws on the work of many different scholars, so I could not present this volume without thanking the authors who have allowed their research to appear here in various forms: Kamal Abdelmalek, Lila Abu-Lughod, Clinton Bailey, Haya Bar-Itzhak, Janice Boddy, Glenn Bowman, Pierre Cachia, Steven Caton, Anis Frayha, Husain Haddawy, Valerie Hoffman, Sharif Kanaana, Aida Kanafani, Scott Marcus, 'Afaf Marsot, Sadok Masliya, Ibrahim Muhawi, Edward Ochsenschlager, Dilworth Parkinson, Edward Reeves, Jonathan Shannon, Samir Shehata, Aliza Shenhar, Andrew Shryock, Susan Slyomovics, Saad Sowayan, 'Abd Allāh al-Tābūr, Samir Tahhan, Earle Waugh, Sabra Webber, and Mourad Yelles-Chaouche.

I also wish to give thanks to those friends and colleagues who have read and commented on portions of this work: Sandra Campbell, Patricia Kubala, Scott Marcus, and Shawkat Toorawa. Any errors that remain reflect my own shortcomings, not theirs.

Additional thanks go to Scott Marcus for the use of musical instruments from his personal collection; these appear in figures 9, 12, 13, 14, and 15.

And finally, my deepest thanks go to the inhabitants of the village of al-Bakātūsh, Egypt, for the hospitality and generosity they have shown me over a quarter of a century, and to all of the other individuals in the Arab world who have so graciously housed me, fed me, entertained me, and taught me over the years.

One

Introduction

WHO ARE THE ARABS?

Arabs originally inhabited the Arabian Peninsula and a few adjacent regions, but in the wake of the Islamic conquests in the seventh century C.E., they soon came to govern a vast region that extended from Spain in the west to China and India in the east.[1] The Arabs were the dominant social class in this new Islamic empire, but they were at first very thinly spread over the recently conquered territories and constituted only a small percentage of the total population. Over the course of several centuries, however, the indigenous populations in what is now known as "the Arab world" adopted the Arabic language as their mother tongue and embraced many aspects of Arab culture as their own, a process that was facilitated by frequent intermarriage among Arabs and local populations, as well as widespread conversion to Islam. Eventually, nearly all the peoples living in the region from Morocco to Iraq grew to consider themselves Arabs, with a handful of exceptions such as the Berbers of North Africa, the Nubians of southern Egypt, and the Kurds of northern Syria and Iraq. In the 1950s the president of Egypt, Gamāl ʿAbd al-Nāsir (Nasser), responded to the question "Who is an Arab?" by saying that an Arab is anyone whose mother tongue is the Arabic language and who identifies with Arab culture, and this remains the most common definition of the term today.[2]

---

1. The abbreviations C.E., for "common era," and B.C.E., for "before the common era," are used by scholars as a nonsectarian alternative to "before Christ" (B.C.) and "anno Domini" (A.D.).

2. When the Arab League was established in 1946, it adopted the following definition: An Arab is a person whose language is Arabic, who lives in an Arabic-speaking country, and who is in sympathy with the aspirations of the Arabic-speaking peoples.

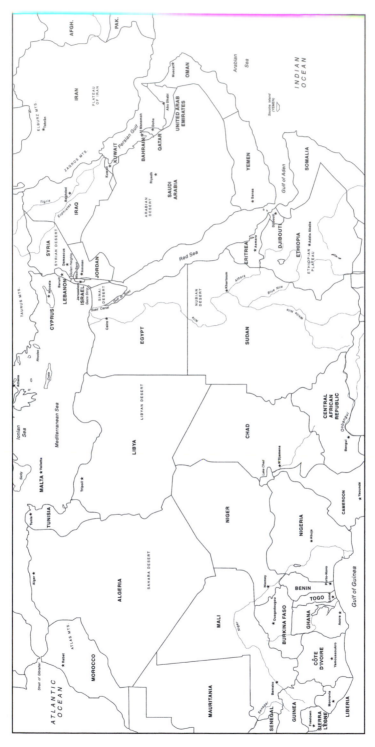

The contemporary Arab world.

Arabs now number some 300 million and are the majority population in over 20 countries of the Middle East. As a result of several waves of emigration beginning in the mid-nineteenth century, substantial Arab immigrant communities also exist in North America, Latin America, and Europe. Arabic is one of the six official languages of the United Nations and is also the sacred language—the language of the Qur'ān (Koran) and of daily prayer—for over one billion Muslims around the world. Though Arabs are united by a common written language and history, their culture is also extremely diverse, differing greatly from region to region, which is one reason why Arab folklore is such a rich and fascinating topic.

A Brief History

Arabs first lived primarily in the Arabian Peninsula (modern Yemen, Oman, Saudi Arabia, Kuwait, Bahrain, Qatar, and the United Arab Emirates) and its northern hinterlands (modern Palestine, Syria, and southern Iraq). They are mentioned in ancient texts of several different cultures. In Akkadian they were known as the *Aribi;* in ancient Persian the land of the Arabs was known as *Arabaya;* and in biblical lore the Arabs are associated with the descendants of Ishmael, whom God promised to make into a "great nation" (Genesis 17:20, 21:18) and also with the descendants of Esau, who ruled the Holy Land before the Israelite kings (Genesis 36:9–43). During the Roman period, the northwestern portion of the Arabian Peninsula (Palestine, Jordan, and southern Syria) became a province of the Roman Empire and was known in Latin as *Arabia Petrae* (that part of Arabia ruled from the city of Petra). Yemen, far to the south, was known as *Arabia Felix* (Fortunate or Prosperous Arabia) because of its flourishing agriculture and rich trade in frankincense and myrrh, in contrast to *Arabia Deserta,* which referred to the interior desert regions. After the fall of the Roman Empire in the fourth century C.E., the Arabs found themselves sandwiched between two other great empires: Persia (now Iran) to the northeast and Byzantium (the Greek-speaking Eastern Roman Empire that had its capital in Constantinople, now Istanbul) to the northwest.

During this pre-Islamic period, a number of independent Arab kingdoms emerged for various periods of time, the most famous of which was in Sheba (Saba) in Yemen, the kingdom of the Queen of Sheba known for her celebrated visit to King Solomon. Another Arab kingdom, that of the Nabateans, was located in Petra, the city cut into stone, located in modern Jordan.

Two other important Arab kingdoms were the Lakhmid and Ghassānid kingdoms, which acted as buffer states or client states between the more powerful forces of Byzantium and Persia. These Arab kingdoms developed into thriving cultural centers that attracted merchants, scholars, poets, musicians, and travelers from foreign lands. Several have left behind impressive architectural and archaeological remains, such as those at Madā'in Sālih in modern Saudi Arabia, about which there are many legendary tales in the folklore of the Arabian Peninsula.

The Treasury in the rock-hewn city of Petra in Jordan. Courtesy of Shutterstock.

Although some Arabs in this early period were desert-dwelling nomads, or *Bedouin,* most Arabs lived in small settlements, towns, or cities that were linked together via prosperous trade routes. These trade routes stretched northwards into Central Asia, eastward across the Indian Ocean, southward into sub-Saharan Africa, and westward toward the Mediterranean. The constant flow of caravans and merchants brought goods and ideas from far-off places and provided contact with many other cultures and religions. Archeological remains show that it was not uncommon to encounter luxury goods from throughout the Mediterranean, Africa, India, and even China in the urban centers of the Arabian Peninsula.

Whether they lived in towns or as desert nomads, Arabs were linked together by two key characteristics in this early period: (1) the Arabic language and (2) a shared tribal social structure.

Arabic is a Semitic language related to Akkadian (the earliest attested Semitic language used by the ancient Assyrians and Babylonians), Phoenician, Hebrew, Aramaic, Syriac (a Christian liturgical language derived from Aramaic), and more distantly to Amharic (Ethiopia). The Semitic language family is completely unrelated to the Indo-European family to which English and most European languages belong. Arabic existed as a purely oral language until the fifth and sixth centuries c.e. when a modified form of the Phoenician alphabet began to be used for writing it. Although Arabic was one of the last languages in the eastern Mediterranean to become a written language, linguists believe that it has retained some of the oldest features of the Semitic language family, features that were already disappearing in Aramaic and Hebrew when those languages were first written down. To better understand problematic phrases in Hebrew or Aramaic, such as interpreting difficult passages in the Bible, scholars of comparative Semitics often turn to Arabic for possible explanations.

Tribal social structure in its simplest form is a manner of organizing society into genealogies that show who is related to whom, not just through individual family trees, but also through membership in various interrelated social groups: families, clans, tribes, and tribal confederations. For the nomadic Bedouin, one very important aspect of this system is that each of these various social groups had their traditional migration routes as well as recognized grazing rights in different regions for different seasons of the year. This division of the sparse resources of the Arabian Peninsula was what allowed camel nomadism to function as a social system.

Arabian tribal structure also included a number of key concepts and customs in which people were understood and dealt with not just as individuals but also as members of their family, clan, and tribe. For example, if an individual were to steal or commit a murder, the family or clan could be held responsible for this crime and would either have to surrender the offender to the clan of the victim, or, if an agreement could be reached in the case of a killing, would have to pay a large amount (often in livestock or camels) called a *bloodwit* to the victim's family (the *bloodwit* or *wehrgeld* tradition was also common in many parts of Europe at this time). Other examples of important social behaviors linked to tribal structure are the act of seeking refuge and the offering of hospitality: If an individual or group sought and received refuge from a stronger group, the hosts were obliged to defend them at all costs and the refuge seekers might even be absorbed eventually into the protecting group through intermarriage. One of the most famous ancient Arab legends about defending a refuge seeker is that of the Jewish Arab al-Samaw'al ibn 'Ādiyā' with whom Imru' al-Qays, a famous poet, sought refuge while fleeing from the Lakhmid King al-Mundhir. Imru' al-Qays left his daughter, a rich set of armor, and his inheritance in the protection of al-Samaw'al. An army sent by King al-Mundhir besieged the castle of al-Samaw'al and eventually captured al-Samaw'al's son. Rather than break his vow as protector and give in to their demands that he turn over Imru' al-Qays's daughter and property, al-Samaw'al was forced to see his own son put to death before his eyes. His name is famous even today for having upheld his role as host and protector of refuge seekers, and is preserved in the proverbial phrase *awfa min al-Samaw'al*—"more loyal than al-Samaw'al."

Tribal social structure and the pooling of resources also provided substantial advantages for survival in the harsh desert environment of the Arabian Peninsula and in the sometimes very risky venture of caravan trading. If a caravan met with ill fortune or a drought struck a particular region, related clans provided the "safety net" that would allow a social group to survive hard times. In return, they would provide similar aid in the future. In this context it is also easy to understand why hospitality, particularly to travelers and strangers, came to be considered one of the primary virtues of desert life, along with generosity, keeping promises, and protection of the weak. Traditionally, hospitality must be offered to all comers, and to avoid possible friction caused by intertribal rivalries, three full days and nights of hospitality were given without asking the stranger his name or tribal affiliation. Thus even enemies could seek and receive hospitality from each other to survive, if need be. One traditional saying in Arabic even today is: "The guest is to be treated as the guest of God" *(al-dayf dayf Allāh)*. To refuse hospitality or to insult someone as inhospitable were two of the worse offenses a person could commit in early Arabia. In modern times the offering and acceptance of hospitality are considered by Arabs to be among the most important and distinctive aspects of their culture. Many of the customs of the ancient Arabs of the Arabian Peninsula were preserved in proverbs and traditional sayings that together provide a fascinating map of their values and manners. These were written down in large anthologies in medieval times, and many are still used in common parlance even today.

Strong social bonds to the family or clan did not mean, however, that there were no individuals who rejected the tribal system. Some of the most famous oral poems of the fifth and sixth centuries were composed by the outcast or brigand poets *(sa'ālīk)*, who threw off all bonds to their families and tribes to eke out an existence alone in the wilderness or with fellow loners. In one of the most famous of these poems, the poet al-Shanfara (fifth or sixth century C.E.) declares that he is leaving his tribe to dwell alone among the wild beasts of the desert:

> I have in place of you, other kin: the wolf, unwearying runner,
>   the darting sand leopards, and the bristle-necked hyena.
> These are my clan. They don't reveal a secret given in trust,
>   and they don't abandon a man for his crimes [...]

I have but three friends: a brave heart, a bare blade,
    and a long bow of yellow wood.
Smooth and taut, sonorous,
    Bedecked with jeweled tokens, secured with a crossbelt.
When it lets the arrow slip, it twangs,
    Like a child-bereft mother, grief-struck, who moans and wails

(Sells 1987, 24–25)

Thus, almost paradoxically, the virtues vaunted in ancient Arabian oral poetry included both staunch loyalty to one's tribe and a fierce sense of individualism and self-reliance. These same contradictory values are expressed in many modern Arab folktales, epic poems, and proverbs.

Religion in Ancient Arabia

Until the beginning of the seventh century, most Arabs were pagan, but there were also sizable communities of Christian and Jewish Arabs. Pagan Arabs worshipped a variety of gods and goddesses, as did the Greeks and Romans, each of whom had one or more shrines or sanctuaries. One primary element of these various cults was the act of pilgrimage to these sacred places. Mecca, in particular, was the site of several of the most popular of these shrines, and pilgrimage constituted a significant source of income for the city along with trading. One of the most strongly enforced customs of the pagan period was the maintenance of two holy months each year during which it was prohibited to raid the livestock of other tribes, kill, take vengeance, or in any way disturb the peace. This provided periods when people could travel on pilgrimages without fear and attend the large markets that were held during these months of truce. The markets provided venues not only for the buying and selling of goods and livestock but also for listening to performances of poetry and storytelling. The market of 'Ukāz was particularly well known as a center for the public recitation of poetry.

The Christian and Jewish Arab communities were composed both of Christians and Jews who had immigrated into the Arab lands from elsewhere and of Arabs who had converted to these religions. For example, King Yūsuf Dhū Nawās of Yemen (ruled 515–25 C.E.) is said to have converted to Judaism and promulgated a number of Judaizing laws. He waged war against the nearby Christian Arab kingdom of Najrān and conquered it but later was himself defeated by invading Ethiopian Christians. Both the Lakhmid and Ghassānid kingdoms further north were largely Christian and the Kinda tribal federation is said to have been largely Judaized.

Christianity and Judaism were not, however, highly unified, homogenous religions in this period: Christians in the fourth and fifth centuries, for example, were in the process of separating into many different churches (Nestorian, Jacobite, Monophysite, Arian, and so forth) because they differed on many basic questions about their religion: Was Jesus entirely divine or entirely human or a mixture of both? Was he co-equal with God or a secondary figure of lesser status? Was he co-eternal with God or had God created him? Could Mary be referred to as the "Mother of God" if she was a mere mortal? Who or what was the Holy Spirit? How could God be One, Two, and Three all at the same time? There were many different answers to these questions, each with its own adherents. At the Ecumenical Councils (or Synods) of Nicea, Chalcedon, Ephesus, and Constantinople, the majority of those present declared the opinions of the minority to be heresy and excommunicated those bishops and their followers. In essence, whichever doctrine got the most votes became dogma. Many of the most ancient Christian practices and beliefs were voted down and rejected, and the people who upheld those beliefs were cast out of the fold. Those communities did not cease to exist, however, but rather developed independently. Many of the Eastern Christian Churches of the modern Arab world have their origins in those early schisms and to this day maintain liturgies and doctrines that predate those of the Western churches. The majority of Arab Christians still celebrate their religious services in the original languages of the early Christians: Aramaic, Coptic, Greek, and Syriac.

In this same period, Judaism was also undergoing tremendous change. Rabbinic Judaism was in the process of establishing itself, but a more traditional branch, Karaite Judaism, rejected the innovations being added to scripture in the second to sixth centuries. The Karaites did not accept the oral law (Mishna) or Talmudic traditions and instead relied entirely on the original Hebrew Bible (Tanakh) as scripture. The Karaites at one point probably included up to 10 percent of all Jews; in recent centuries Egypt and Istanbul have been the homes of the largest Karaite populations.

Another religious community, the Samaritans, is known to many people only through the parable of the Good Samaritan in the New Testament. Samaritans claim to be the descendants of the northern Judean Jewish kingdom who were not removed to Babylon by the king of the Assyrians in what is called the "Babylonian captivity." They possess their own version of the Torah, their religious practices are derived from ancient Jewish practices, and the center of their spiritual life is Mount Gerizim, near Nablus, rather than Jerusalem. They see their version of Judaism as the true form and, like the Karaites, reject the texts and institutions of Rabbinic Judaism. In modern times Samaritans have numbered only a few hundred souls and speak Arabic or modern Hebrew as their mother tongue.

An additional set of influences in the pre-Islamic era came from the Iranian religions Zoroastrianism, Mandeanism, Manicheaism, and Mithraism, all of which share a basically dualist vision of the universe as a struggle between the forces of good and evil, darkness and light. Mithraism contributed to Christianity the date for Christmas (December 25), which was originally celebrated as the birth of the god Mithra. The earliest Christians believed that Jesus was born in March, and the establishment of December 25 as a Christian festival several centuries later appears to have been a move by the Church to combat the popularity of Mithraism among Roman soldiers and to align the celebration of Christmas with the winter solstice, which was celebrated by many pagan societies.

In short, the pre-Islamic period in the Arabian Peninsula was marked by a lively interchange among pagan, Jewish, and Christian faiths, and Arabs practiced all of these religions. There were pagan Arabs, Jewish Arabs, and Christian Arabs. The entire period of history up to the beginning of the revelation of Islam to the Prophet Muhammad is known among Muslim Arabs as the *Jāhiliyya,* which means the period of "ignorance" (i.e., of right religion) or of "lawlessness."

The Advent of Islam

Muhammad was born sometime around 570 C.E. and lived his early life as an ordinary human being. He was orphaned very young and was consequently raised first by his grandfather and then by his uncle. He worked with trading caravans and, having acquired a reputation for honesty and fairness, was entrusted with the goods of a widow named Khadīja. After he had worked as her agent for a period, the two were married. Muhammad, however, began experiencing doubts and dissatisfaction with pagan life in Mecca and began to seclude himself to reflect and meditate. Then, in the year 610 C.E., at the age of 40, Muhammad had an experience that was to change his life. He heard a voice that said to him, "Recite!" To which he responded, "I am not a Reciter."[3] The voice again commanded him, "Recite!" And he again answered, "But I am not a Reciter." Again the voice spoke and this time he replied, "What shall I recite?" And the voice spoke to him the first portion of the Qur'ān to be revealed to humankind (Q 96: 1–5):

Iqra' bismi Rabbika lladhī khalaq
Khalaqa l-insāna min 'alaq
Iqra' wa-Rabbuka l-akram
Alladhī 'allama bi-l-qalam
'Allama l-insāna mā lam ya'lam

Recite in the name of thy Lord God who created,
Who created Man from a clot of blood,
Recite! For thy Lord is most Generous,
He has taught by the pen,
He taught Man what he knew not.

---

3. Some scholars interpret the Arabic to mean: "Read!" to which Muhammad replied, "But I do not know how to read" (lit. "I am not a reader"), for he was illiterate.

Here is an alternative translation that gives a stronger sense of the rhyme found in the original Arabic:

> Recite in the name of your Lord, Who did create
> Did create humanity from coagulate
> Recite for your Lord is Magnanimous
> Who, through the use of the *calamus* [pen],
> Has taught humanity that of which it was ignorant.[4]

For Muslims this moment marks the beginning of Muhammad's accession to the rank of prophet and the beginning of the revelation of Islam, which literally means "submission (to God's will)." From this point onward Muhammad's actions (Ar. *sunna*) and his words (Ar. *hadīth*) are considered to be a model for all humans, and Muslims actively seek to imitate him in many ways. Over the rest of his life, piece by piece, the text of the Qur'ān was revealed to Muhammad through the voice of the angel Gabriel, and after his death it was assembled and codified into the Qur'ān as it is known today.

One of the primary messages of Islam was the absolute unity of God—Jesus was recognized as one of the prophets, but not as divine—which for many people helped resolve the constant arguing among Christian theologians about the almost incomprehensible doctrine of the Trinity (Q 112: 1–4):

> Qul: huwa Allāhu ahad
> Allāhu samad
> Lam yalid wa-lam yūlad
> Wa-lam yakun lahu kufuwwan ahad

> Recite: God is One,
> God is Eternal.
> He begets not, nor is He begotten
> Unto Him there is no equal.

Or, in a translation that preserves more of the rhythm and rhyme of the Arabic:

> Affirm: He is God, Matchless
> God, Ceaseless
> Unbegetting, Birthless
> Without a single partner, Peerless[5]

This belief in the absolute unity of God is the first of the five Pillars of Islam that define the basic responsibilities of a Muslim: (1) bearing witness to the unity of God and that Muhammad is His Messenger; (2) praying five times a day; (3) almsgiving to the needy; (4) fasting during the holy month of Ramadān;

---

4. Used by permission of Shawkat Toorawa.
5. Used by permission of Shawkat Toorawa.

and (5) completion of the pilgrimage to Mecca if one is able. When Islam first began to spread throughout the Middle East, the form of the religion that was encountered by the earliest converts was probably not much more complex than these basic tenets—a religion that was straightforward and, in its simplest form, understandable by all believers. This was a sharp contrast from the complexities of Jewish law and Christian theological debates. Later, of course, a sophisticated body of Islamic law was created to handle the needs of the community, but the fundamentals of the religion have remained surprisingly clear and consistent.

Early Islam's great religious campaign was the eradication of polytheism (the worship of multiple gods) and idolatry (the worship of statues and images). Although it was relatively tolerant toward Jews and Christians, whom it recognized as worshippers of the One True God and as People of the Book or People of Scripture, it was completely opposed to paganism. Neither Jews nor Christians were forced to convert, and Muslim men could marry Jewish or Christian wives. Paganism, however, was not allowed to continue in any form, nor could a Muslim man marry a pagan woman, in part for fear of the influence she might have over their children.

Muhammad first preached this new revelation in his hometown of Mecca. Although he attracted only a small band of followers there, the authorities of the city saw him as a threat, not least of all to Mecca's role as the most prominent site of pilgrimage in the Arabian Peninsula and to the many pagan shrines located there. An attack on Muhammad's life was planned, but he was forewarned and was able to slip out of Mecca by night and travel north to the city of Yathrib (later renamed Medina). The residents of Medina had invited him to come to their town to act as a mediator among the various feuding tribes there, for he had already achieved a reputation as a judicious figure. Muhammad's flight *(hijra)* from Mecca became the starting point for the Islamic, or *Hijri,* calendar that is sometimes abbreviated with the letters A.H. for *anno hejirae,* parallel to the use of A.D. for *anno Domini* (the year of our Lord) to indicate the Christian calendar. (In this book, as in most modern scholarly works, all references to the Christian dating system are marked C.E. for *common era* in recognition of the fact that it is used by many non-Christian cultures as well.) A song of welcome traditionally believed to have been sung by the inhabitants of Medina at the arrival of Muhammad, "The Full Moon Has Risen Before Us" *(Tala' al-badr 'alaynā)* is a common folk song in many parts of the modern Arab world even today, and the events of the flight from Mecca to Medina are memorialized in narrative folk ballads, particularly in modern Egypt.

Muhammad proved to be an able administrator and statesman, as well as a skilled military leader and a peacemaker. A number of battles were fought between the Medinans, led by Muhammad, and the Meccans, but eventually, as more and more people converted to Islam and began to follow the revelation preached by Muhammad, his hometown of Mecca surrendered without a final battle or siege. Soon thereafter Muhammad died. Though there was at first great consternation among the members of the new community, Abū Bakr, who succeeded Muhammad as leader of the Muslims, came forward and stated (so that none should confuse the mortal humanity of the Prophet with the eternal divinity of God):

"O you who worship Muhammad, Muhammad is dead. But you who worship God, God is Alive!"

Each of the three monotheistic religions has contributed to the richness of Arab folklore. Each has its own official religious rites and rituals, of course, but each also possesses many folk beliefs and practices, religious folk music, legends of saints and miracles, pilgrimage practices, and the like. Surprising to some outsiders is the degree to which Muslim, Christian, and Jewish Arabs have shared pilgrimage sites over the centuries, often asking favors and blessings from saintly figures belonging to the other religions. Where these communities have interacted over time, they have developed many shared practices at the folk level that are not at all apparent from the more "official" versions of their faiths (see Customs and Traditions in Chapter Three).

The Arabization of the Middle East

During the first century after Muhammad's death, the Islamic community underwent a tremendous expansion, spreading within a few short decades westward as far as Spain and southern France, and eastward as far as western China and India. In short, the Arabs quickly conquered a territory larger than the Roman Empire at its apogee. Over the ensuing centuries, the populations of Iberia (modern Spain and Portugal), North Africa, and the Middle East as far as Turkey in the north and Iran in the east became almost entirely Arabized, that is, they began increasingly to speak Arabic as their mother tongue and eventually lost knowledge of the languages that had previously been spoken in their areas. In addition, neighboring languages such as Persian and Turkish were deeply influenced by Arabic, and even today a large percentage of the vocabulary of those languages is made up of Arabic loanwords. The Coptic language (the last form of the Ancient Egyptian tongue) died out in everyday use by the eleventh and twelfth centuries, and Latin disappeared even more rapidly from North Africa. In Palestine, Lebanon, and Syria, where the population had previously spoken Greek and Aramaic, Arabic was soon adopted as the language of daily life and of intellectual exchange, and the older languages rapidly became restricted to liturgical uses. The disappearance of Aramaic, Coptic, Greek, and Latin, and their replacement by Arabic, constitutes a vast and truly astonishing language shift and eventually led to an enormous increase in the number of people who would come to call themselves Arabs.

In the region from Morocco to Iraq, only a handful of indigenous languages still survive among non-Arab minority ethnic groups: the Berber languages are spoken as a primary language in certain regions of Morocco, Algeria, and Tunisia; Nubian is spoken in southern Egypt and northern Sudan; Kurdish is spoken in northern Iraq and Syria; some members of the Assyrian/Chaldean Christian communities of Iraq and Syria speak neo-Aramaic (modern Aramaic); and in the southernmost regions of the Arabian Peninsula, another Semitic language is spoken by a few tens of thousands of people, which in English is sometimes confusingly referred to as "South Arabic" even though it is a language completely separate from Arabic; most scholars prefer to call it Mehri or Socotri.

Along with the gradual linguistic and cultural Arabization of the region also came increasing numbers of conversions to Islam. By about the tenth century, Islam had become the majoritarian religion throughout the Arab world and today approximately 90 percent of all Arabs are Muslim. Like Judaism and Christianity before it, Islam also developed internal divisions, particularly into two main branches—Sunni and Shi'i—both of which are found in the modern Arab world, as well as one smaller but important group that broke away in the Middle Ages, the Druze. The largest Shi'i communities in the modern Arab world are located in Iraq, Lebanon, and Bahrain where they may constitute as much as 60 percent of the population (though reliable figures are hard to come by), with smaller communities in Saudi Arabia and elsewhere. The Druze hold that one of the medieval Shi'i rulers of Egypt, al-Ḥākim, brought divine revelation and is even held to be himself divine. The Druze see themselves as a reforming sect within Islam, but most Muslims see them as heretics and do not accept them as Muslims. They are found primarily in Lebanon, Syria, Israel, Palestine, and Jordan.

Christianity remains strong in Egypt, Palestine, and Lebanon, with smaller but still important communities of Christians in Syria and Iraq. Some Arab Christians belong to churches that are in communion with Rome or are branches of Western Protestant churches, but most belong to the ancient Eastern Churches. The Coptic Orthodox church of Egypt, for example, is descended from the See of Alexandria and has been independent since the Council of Chalcedon in 451 when it opposed the interference of Emperor Marcianus in church affairs and the doctrine adopted in that council that declared that Jesus had two separate natures, one human and the other divine. The Coptic Church instead held that Jesus had a single nature and is sometimes referred to by outsiders as a "monophysite" church (a characterization that the Coptic Church, however, rejects). The Coptic Church still uses Coptic (the last surviving form of the Ancient Egyptian tongue) as their liturgical language. The Assyrian and Chaldean Christians of Iraq, descendents of the See of Babylon, have a complicated history but are usually considered to have become independent after the Ecumenical Council of Ephesus in 431 in the wake of the discussions about whether Mary could be called the "Mother of God" or more literally, "God-Bearer" (*theotokos* in Greek). The Chaldeans split from the Assyrians and reunited with the Roman Catholic Church in the eighteenth century and are therefore referred to as one of the Eastern "Uniate" churches. Both churches use Syriac, a form of Aramaic, for their liturgical language, and some members of these communities speak neo-Aramaic as their mother tongue. Other Eastern churches present in the modern Arab world include the Armenian Orthodox, Greek Orthodox, Maronite, Melkite, and Syrian Orthodox churches.

Significant Jewish communities existed in Morocco, Algeria, Tunisia, Syria, Iraq, Yemen, and Egypt, but most of these groups left their homelands in the wake of the 1948 war in which Palestinians and neighboring Arab states attempted to resist the seizure of Palestinian land to create the Jewish state of Israel. For nearly 1,400 years, Arabic-speaking Jewish communities existed, and indeed thrived, within the Arabo-Islamic Middle East, and many great medieval Jewish writers, including, for example, the famous philosopher Maimonides, wrote primarily in Arabic. Al-Andalus (Islamic or "Moorish" Spain) was home in the early Middle Ages to over half of the world's Jewish population. In other words, there was a time when the majority of Jews in the world spoke Arabic as their mother tongue. It was during the Golden Age of al-Andalus that Jews adopted the structures of Arabic poetry, including its meters and use of end rhyme, and adapted them for use in Hebrew. The very first rhyming poems ever composed in Hebrew were calques, or imitations, of Arabic poems. Likewise, Jewish scholars adapted the categories and terminology that Arab grammarians and linguists had developed for analyzing Arabic and applied them to Hebrew to write the very first grammars of that language.

The oppositional dichotomy made between Arab and Jew, now so common in the Western mass media, in fact only came about in the twentieth century, primarily as a result of the creation of the Jewish state of Israel. This was a move strongly opposed by the Arab nations who saw it as an injustice forced upon the Palestinians by Westerners who were trying to atone for the horrors of the Holocaust and for centuries of European anti-Semitism. The Arab objection was quite simple: Why should Palestinians have to give up their homeland to make up for crimes that had been committed by Europeans? Although that disagreement has strongly shaped political views in the twentieth and twenty-first centuries, these clashes are of relatively recent origin compared with the earlier and much longer period of co-existence. Recently, some scholars have attempted to remind the world of this historical relationship by highlighting that extensive shared past in contrast with the relatively short period of conflict, however bitter and irresolvable it may at times appear (see, for example, Alcalay 1993).

In addition to the spread of the Arabic language and culture along with the Islamic religion, another key element aided greatly in the demographic expansion of Arabs throughout the Middle East: In Arab culture, children inherit the ethnicity of their father. Thus a child born to an Arab father and a non-Arab mother is Arab. Furthermore, Islam allows Muslim men to take Jewish or Christian but not pagan wives and considers their offspring Muslim. In addition, if a Muslim man has enough money to care for them and has the ability to treat them equally, he can marry up to four wives (though this has never been a very common practice except among the rich and in a few specific regions). During the early Islamic conquests and the rapid expansion of Arabo-Islamic culture, Arab men serving in the military traveled far from their native lands and often married local women. If an Arab soldier married a local Christian or Jewish bride and had five sons, they were all Arab and Muslim; if each of them in turn married local Christian or Jewish women and had children, all of their children would also be Arab and Muslim, and so forth. So in addition to processes of acculturation and of conversion, there was a natural demographic process that aided in the eventual Arabization of most of the region.

In summary, initially Arabs lived primarily in the Arabian Peninsula and in some adjacent regions to the north. Starting in the seventh century with the expansion of Islamic rule, intermarriage, conversion to Islam, and adoption of Arabic as a primary language all contributed to a dramatic increase in both the territory under Arab rule and the number of people who considered themselves to be Arabs. At first there were pagan, Christian, and Jewish Arabs, and then, after the advent of Islam, paganism rather rapidly disappeared (though in various folk traditions explored in this volume we shall encounter traces of pagan practices), and the majority of Arabs became Muslims; however, significant numbers of Christians are found in several of the eastern Arab countries. Like Christian Arabs, Jewish Arabs have existed for 2,000 years or more, and it is only in the wake of the Israeli-Palestinian conflict that it has come to seem paradoxical to refer to Arabic-speaking Jews as Jewish Arabs.

Geography

Traditionally Arabs have referred to the main regions of the Arabic-speaking world with four terms: the *Maghrib* ("where the sun sets," including modern Morocco, Algeria, Tunisia, and Libya); the *Mashriq* ("where the sun rises," comprising modern Egypt, Palestine, Lebanon, Syria, Jordan, and Iraq); the *Jazīra* ("the Peninsula," containing Yemen, Saudi Arabia, and the Gulf States); and *Bilād al-Sūdān* ("the Lands of the Blacks" including Mauretania, Niger, Mali, Chad, and Sudan). In addition, the term *al-Andalus* is used to refer to Muslim Spain (or "Moorish Spain"), which lasted from the Arab conquest of the Iberian

Peninsula in 711 to the fall of Granada, the last Muslim kingdom in Iberia, in 1492.

Though the Arab world is geographically dominated by two large desert areas—the Sahara (from the Arabic word *sahārā,* meaning "deserts") in northern Africa and the desert zone of the Arabian Peninsula—only a small percentage of Arabs live in these regions. The vast majority of Arabs live in river valleys such as those of the Nile River in Egypt or the Tigris and Euphrates rivers in Iraq, coastal areas such as the eastern and southern Mediterranean, or in mountainous regions such as in Yemen, Lebanon, or Morocco. Nevertheless, the desert-dwelling Bedouin have played a cultural and historic role for centuries as an often romanticized source of "pure" Arab customs and traditions, such that they are many times accorded a greater importance than their actual numbers might otherwise warrant: Bedouin hospitality, Bedouin coffee, and Bedouin poetry all play a significant role in the construction of Arab identity even today. There is, however, also a negative view of the Bedouin in Arab folklore that portrays them as dirty, uncouth, and prone to banditry. These contradictory images of the Bedouin exist side by side and have done so for centuries.

On the other hand, a major portion of Arabo-Islamic culture has always been urban, and a large percentage of Arabs live in the great cities of the Middle East including Cairo, Damascus, Baghdad, Medina, Mecca, Fez, Tunis, Mosul, and others, some of which are thousands of years old, while still other Arabs inhabit rural agricultural areas. This broad spectrum of ways of living—ancient cosmopolitan cities, small towns, agricultural villages, coastal fishing ports, high mountain farms, and desert encampments—makes it almost impossible to speak of an "average Arab" or even of a "typical Arab lifestyle." An Egyptian whose family has lived in Cairo for a thousand years, a Yemeni tribesman from a small mountain village, an Iraqi fisherman living in the marshes of the Euphrates River, a Moroccan living in Marrakesh at the edge of the great Sahara desert—all of these are "typically Arab."

Colonialism and Its Aftermath

In 1798 Napoleon invaded Egypt with an army of 38,000 men and initiated a century and a half of European invasions, military occupations, and colonization that eventually reached most regions of the Arab world. Algeria, for example, was occupied by the French for 132 years (1830–1962). The French outlawed the use of Arabic in schools, instituted a French government, imposed the French legal code, and expropriated the most fertile lands in the country and redistributed them to French colonists to entice them to move to Algeria. Algeria was eventually annexed to France—it was not considered a colony but rather was declared to be fully and eternally an integral part of France. In the 1950s the Algerians fought a bitter and bloody war of independence against the French, the "War of a Million Martyrs," in which nearly one in seven Algerians died either in the fighting or from disease and hunger in the refugee and concentration camps set up by the French. The American president John F. Kennedy is honored even today in Algeria for his statements in support of Algerian independence. Algeria finally won its independence from France in 1962.

Morocco and Tunisia also came under French control, though neither of these countries was annexed to France. Italy invaded Libya in 1911 and claimed it as a colony. The English took control of Egypt first through financial means (by offering enormous loans to the Egyptian government and demanding the right to determine Egypt's financial and foreign policies in return) and then by military occupation beginning in 1882. Egypt did not achieve full independence from Great Britain until the 1952 revolution that eventually brought Gamāl 'Abd al-Nāsir (Nasser) to power. After World War I (WWI), Palestine and Iraq were placed under British Mandates, while Syria and Lebanon were awarded to France by the League of Nations. Great Britain also maintained various forms of control over Kuwait and other Gulf states.

The political shape of the contemporary Arab world was thus, to a very large extent, forged by rivalries among France, Great Britain, and, to a much lesser extent, Italy. The boundaries of modern Arab countries were drawn according to the will of the European powers in the wake of WWI, and the Arabs themselves were given little to no opportunity to represent themselves in that process. There is, therefore, little cultural or historical validity to a number of the boundaries that now exist. Many of the conflicts in the modern Middle East are the direct result of the boundary disputes created by the Western powers nearly a century ago.

Another result of the colonial period is that the various Arab countries have different linguistic "orientations" in their choice of a second language as well as in their political and cultural affiliations: In North Africa French is the most common second language and is still largely the language of university education; in Egypt, Palestine, Jordan, and the Gulf, on the other hand, English is far more common; in Lebanon and Syria, French was the most common second language for several generations, but English has recently overtaken it in many domains. Each of these countries has also had a general political orientation to either the English or French legal system, which has also contributed to their respective current political structures as modern nation states. This situation also affects scholarship about the Arab world: The majority of Western scholarship about North Africa, for example, is in French, whereas Western scholarship about the Eastern Arab world is primarily in English, and scholarly writings about Lebanon and Syria are divided between the two.

The Arabic Language

No single element of Arab identity is more important than the Arabic language: It is, quite simply, the glue that holds Arab culture together. The language itself, and anything primarily defined by the language, is referred to in English as *Arabic* (hence Arabic poetry, Arabic grammar, etc.), whereas a person or anything related to the Arabs as a people is more correctly referred to as *Arab* (an Arab woman, Arab cooking, Arab music, etc.). The term *Arabian* in modern English is now only used in reference to the peninsula of that name (Arabian tribes, Arabian horses, and so on). In some sense, however, it is misleading to refer to Arabic as a single language, for it exists in many different forms. The most prestigious form, often referred to in English as *Classical Arabic* or *Standard Arabic*, is used primarily as a written language and in certain formal speaking events, but is not spoken by anyone as their mother tongue. Although the vocabulary of this standard language has changed over time, its basic structures have remained remarkably stable. An Arab reading the newspaper in a Cairo café over his morning cup of coffee is reading nearly the same grammatical forms as are found in the Qur'ān and in oral poetry dating from 1,500 years ago.

In contrast, what people actually speak at home, at work, and in the rest of their daily lives are regional dialects of *colloquial Arabic*. All of the dialects are historically related to Classical Arabic, but some of them differ from one another as much as Spanish, French, Italian, and Portuguese (all of which are descended from Latin) differ from each other. If the Arabic dialects were written languages, they would almost certainly be referred to as separate languages, but since the dialects have remained almost entirely oral forms of communication, we continue to refer to Arabic in the singular, in recognition of the single written form of the language.

Folklore is usually an oral, and often a very local, phenomenon, and it is nearly always created and performed in one of the colloquial dialects. Thus there is a problem in writing down folklore in Arabic because dialects are not normally written down, but this is not an irresolvable problem. When Arabs write colloquial dialects down, the result is a bit odd—as if we were to write English as it is actually pronounced rather than "az we ar yust tu seyin it ritin." With practice, it can be fairly easy to read a colloquial text if you know the dialect in question; but if you do not, then it is very difficult to know exactly how to pronounce the words (as in the preceding English example). This is sometimes true of English as well where, for example, one cannot know solely from a written text if the word *house* in a ballad collected in Great Britain should be pronounced <haws> (rhyming with *mouse*) with an English accent or <huus> (rhyming with *noose*) with a Scots accent. But because folklore is most often written down by persons who speak the dialect in question, and those texts are most often read by scholars or people from that region, they in fact have little difficulty because it is the form of the language most familiar to them.

As a Semitic language, Arabic is completely unrelated to English or the other Indo-European languages. Perhaps the single most interesting aspect of the Semitic languages is that most words are formed from triliteral (i.e., three-consonant) roots, and all words from the same root will have related meanings. The root letters *K—T—B*, for example, have to do with writing and, by using a regular set of rules, we can generate dozens and dozens of words from that one root. The form of each word in the following list tells whether it is a basic action, a causative action, the person who does the action, the result of the action, a place for doing that action, and so forth (a dash over a letter represents a long vowel):

kataba	(basic verb) to write
kattaba	(causative verb) to cause someone to write (to dictate)
kitāb	(result of writing) a book, a written message
maktūb	(something written) written (as opposed to spoken)
kātib	(someone who writes) an author, writer, or secretary
maktaba	(a place/institution for writing) bookstore or library
takātub	(action between two parties) correspondence

These same forms can be used with hundreds of different roots, such as *D—R—S*:

darasa	(basic verb) to study
darrasa	(causative verb) to cause someone else to study (to teach)
dirāsa	(result of studying) a study, report
madrūs	(something that has been studied) studied
dāris	(someone who studies) researcher, investigator, or student
madrasa	(a place for studying) a school
tadārus	(action between two parties) to study carefully together

Once students have mastered the morphology (word forms) of Arabic, they are able to understand an enormous amount of vocabulary, including words they have never seen before. They might know, for example, that the form of a particular word means "a place for doing *X*" and that the root letters *L—'—B* are associated with the idea of "to play," so *mal'ab* is "a place for playing," that is, a playground, playing field, stadium, or even a game board. Every word form and every triliteral root is like a philosophical idea—the root gives the basic concept and the form tells us if the word is a verb, noun, or adjective, and other aspects such as whether the action is simple, done with someone else, done to oneself, and so forth.

Another major difference between Semitic languages and Indo-European languages is that the latter are characterized by complex systems of verb tenses and modes: *speak, spoke, have spoken, had spoken, am speaking, was speaking, had been speaking, would speak, would be speaking, would have spoken, would have been speaking, will speak, will be speaking, will have spoken, will have been speaking,* and so forth. Standard Arabic, on the other hand, uses only two primary tenses: past and present. The future is formed simply by putting a particle in front of the verb, but without changing the form of the verb, and the pluperfect ("I had spoken") is communicated by the use of another particle (*kataba,* "he wrote," and *qad kataba,* "he had written," for example). Overall, the tense system of Arabic is exceedingly simple. Instead, as demonstrated, it is the morphology (word-form system) of Arabic and the other Semitic languages that enable these languages to express highly complex ideas, some of which are very difficult to translate into English. The forms themselves, however, are not very difficult. With the two roots previously listed, for example, it can be seen that with a basic action such as *kataba* or *darasa,* one can simply double the middle consonant—*kattaba* or *darrasa*—to create a verb which means to cause someone else to do that action, and one can do this with nearly every verb in the language. (The double consonant is held longer than a single consonant, as in italian.) Thus "to write" generates "to dictate" and "to study" generates "to teach" simply by doubling the middle consonant.

All in all, Arabic is a constant interaction between forms and roots, creating fascinating connections between ideas. One favorite example among students is that the Arabic words for "bed" *(sarīr),* "secrets" *(asrār),* and "happiness" *(surūr)* are all formed from the same root: S—R—R. To study a Semitic language is to learn an entirely different way of conceptualizing language, and this special structure of Arabic has contributed a great deal to the Arab love of poetry, for the structure of Arabic makes it easy to create rhymes.

The use of rhyme became common in European languages starting in the tenth and eleventh centuries, so many people think of rhyme as a natural part of European poetry. But in fact, neither ancient Greek nor Latin used rhymes at the ends of verses, nor did biblical Hebrew, Aramaic, Persian, Egyptian, Assyrian, Babylonian, or Sumerian. In Arabic, on the other hand, end rhyme has been the basic structure of poetry since the earliest known writings in that language. It is pervasive in the Qur'ān and still plays a very strong role in Arabic poetry today, particularly in folk poetry. Because Europeans did not adopt rhyme until nearly three centuries after the Arabs had conquered Spain and Sicily, many scholars conclude that the Arabs probably introduced the concept of end-rhymed poetry to the Europeans.

In sum, Classical Arabic forms a link among all Arabs, but this classical form has to be learned in school because no one speaks it naturally. At the same time, everyday life, and thus almost all forms of Arab folklore, are in dialectal or colloquial forms of Arabic, some of which are as different from each other as modern European languages differ from one another.

Pronunciation Guide

Though it can be difficult to learn to pronounce Arabic proficiently from a written description, the following guidelines should make it possible to pronounce most of the Arabic words used in this book relatively easily from the English transliterations.

Arabic has a fairly simple vowel system. All of the Arabic vowel sounds are also found in English and can be either short or long. When they are long, this is indicated in the English writing system with a macron over the letter: ā, ē, ī, ō, ū.

\<a\>	short as in *but* or long \<ā\> either "light" as in *can* or "dark" as in *father*
\<e\>	short as in *get* or long \<ē\> as in *gate*
\<i\>	short as in *bit* or long \<ī\> as in *beat*
\<o\>	short as in *port* or long \<ō\> as in *boat*
\<u\>	short as in *put* or long \<ū\> as in *moon*

There are also several diphthongs (combinations of two vowels together) as in English:

\<aw\>	as in *house*
\<ey\>	as in *hay*
\<ay\>	as in *my*

The Arabic consonant system possesses a fascinating feature, which it shares with the other Semitic languages but which is very different from English—most of the consonants have two forms, front and back (also referred to as "light" and "dark" or "normal" and "emphatic"), and these are considered completely separate sounds. In English we can get a sense of these contrasting sounds by saying the pairs of words in the following list. In each case the initial consonant in the first column is pronounced further forward and "lightens" the vowel sound, while that in the second column is pronounced further back in the mouth and "darkens" the following vowel. Feel how the position of your tongue changes when pronouncing these words:

cap	cough
dapper	dawdle
sat	sought
tap	taught

In Arabic the initial sounds in the second column (pronounced further back in the throat) are considered to be completely distinct letters from those in the first column: There are two *S*'s, two *D*'s, two *T*'s, and so on. There are also two contrasting <h> sounds in Arabic: One is like the English <h> in *hello*, and the other is further back in the throat and is breathier, resembling the sound people make when they breathe on their eyeglasses to clean them. For most of these letters, it is customary to put a dot under the letter to indicate that it is the dark or back form, but the dotted forms will not be used in this volume. You will, however, encounter them in many publications about Arab culture. For the two <k> sounds, it is common to use *k* to represent the front sound and *q* to represent the back sound, and this convention will be used here.

Since English uses the letters *th* to represent two completely different sounds (as in the words *this* and *thin*), when transliterating Arabic the letters *dh* are used together to represent the <th> sound in the word *this*, and the letters *th* are used to represent the <th> sound in *thin*, so that they can be distinguished from each other.

Arabic also uses one sound that exists in English but which in English is not considered a separate letter—the little break in the flow of air used to separate syllables that begin with vowels such as in the exclamation "Uh-oh!" Linguists call this a *glottal stop,* because the flow of air is stopped briefly at the glottis, deep in the throat. This is usually represented in English transliteration with an apostrophe—so the word *sa'ala* (to ask) is pronounced with three separate syllables: <sa—'a—la>, while the word *sāla* (to flow) is pronounced with only two syllables, a long syllable followed by a short one: <sā—la>.

Finally there are three sounds in Arabic that do not occur in English: <kh>, which is pronounced like Scottish *loch* and German *Bach;* <gh>, which is pronounced like the French guttural <r> in *Paris;* and the letter *ayn,* < ' >, which is pronounced deep in the throat and really doesn't have an equivalent in English or other European languages. It is indicated by a single quotation mark. This letter, which is very distinctively Arabic, is also the first sound in the word *'arab,* which is Arabic for *Arabs.*

When pronouncing Arabic from an English transliteration it helps to remember that in multisyllabic words, the long vowel usually receives the stress.

FURTHER READINGS ON ARAB CULTURE AND HISTORY

Alcalay, Ammiel. 1993. *After Arabs and Jews: Remaking Levantine Culture.* Minneapolis: University of Minnesota Press.

Allen, Roger. 2000. *An Introduction to Arabic Literature.* New York: Cambridge University Press.

Bowerstock, G. W. 1983. *Roman Arabia.* Cambridge, Mass.: Harvard University Press.

Elias, Jamal. 1999. *Islam.* Upper Saddle River, N.J.: Prentice-Hall.

Fromkin, David. 1990. *A Peace to End All Peace: The Fall of the Ottoman Empire and the Creation of the Modern Middle East.* New York: Avon Books.

Gerber, Jane. 1994. *The Jews of Spain: A History of the Sephardic Experience.* New York: Free Press.

Hourani, Albert. 2002. *A History of the Arab Peoples.* Cambridge, Mass.: Belknap Press of Harvard University Press.

Hoyland, Robert G. 2000. *Arabia and the Arabs: From the Bronze Age to the Coming of Islam.* New York: Routledge.

Irwin, Robert, ed. 2002. *Night and Horses and the Desert: An Anthology of Classical Arabic Literature.* New York: Anchor Books.

Kennedy, Hugh. 2004. *The Prophet and the Age of the Caliphates: The Islamic Near East from the Sixth to the Eleventh Century.* Harlow, England: Pearson/Longman.

Lamb, David. 2002. *The Arabs: Journeys beyond the Mirage.* New York: Vintage Books.

Mansfield, Peter. 2004. *A History of the Middle East.* New York: Penguin Books.

Newby, Gordon Darnell. 1988. *A History of the Jews of Arabia: From Ancient Times to Their Eclipse under Islam.* Columbia: University of South Carolina Press.

Nicholson, Reynold A. 1930. *A Literary History of the Arabs.* Cambridge, England: Cambridge University Press.

Pacini, Andrea, ed. 1998. *Christian Communities in the Arab Middle East: The Challenge of the Future.* New York: Oxford University Press.

Schippmann, Klaus. 2001. *Ancient South Arabia: From the Queen of Sheba to the Advent of Islam,* trans. Allison Brown. Princeton, N.J.: Markus.

Sells, Michael. 1999. *Approaching the Qur'ān: The Early Revelations.* Ashland, Ore.: White Cloud Press.

Two
Definitions and Classifications

Folklore is one of the richest and yet least-studied aspects of human culture, for although it is constantly present in the lived experience of everyday life, it is not usually written down or recorded but is more typically passed from one person to the next through direct communication. Because it is not set down in one official or correct form, folklore tends to change from one context to the next, from one performance to the next, and that variation is often one of its most prized qualities—its ability to seem both familiar and new at the same time. Folklore is rarely associated with a known writer, composer, or artist but is far more likely to be thought of by those who transmit and perform it as traditional or anonymous.

Folklore is the songs we sing without reference to printed music, the bedtime stories we tell our children without reading from a book, the family histories or experiences we recount at the dinner table over and over through the years, the jokes we hear and pass on at work, the games children learn from other children on the playground without reference to rules or to adults, the way we celebrate our holidays and the foods we cook time and again, the way we decorate our houses for various types of celebrations, our family cures for sore throats and colds, the scary stories we tell around the campfire, superstitions that we may not believe but still repeat when the occasion arises, the campus legends we tell in university dorms, proverbs and riddles heard we know not exactly where but still remember. In short, folklore is all of the many different ways we express who we are as members of a particular group—a family, an ethnic group, a fraternity, a religious community, and so on—but which we have learned directly from other people rather than from books, television, or movies. One way of conceiving of and defining folklore is to think of it as *the multitude of artistic forms of communication that we learn directly from other people and then perform and transmit repeatedly over time.*

Arab culture, like all human cultures, is permeated and held together in many different ways by its folklore. Whether living in villages or big cities, whether members of the working class or the elite, almost all Arabs are familiar with examples of verbal arts (such as proverbs, tales, and poetry), with different customs and beliefs (such as wedding practices, birth rituals, and pilgrimages), and with a wide variety of different musical and material art forms, the origins of which can be located in Arab folklore. Western scholars of folklore have demonstrated in recent decades that nearly all interacting social groups develop and maintain folklore in various forms no matter what social class they are associated with (opera fans, university campuses, officemates, church choirs, country clubs, sports teams, chambers of commerce, etc.) because interacting social groups constantly develop customs, in-group jokes, rituals, narratives, oral histories, and so forth, as a means of creating and maintaining a group identity. These more contemporary forms of folklore, however, have as yet been little studied in the Arab world, in part because these phenomena are not part of the Arab concept of *folklore.* This volume will focus on what Arabs themselves call *al-turāth al-sha'bī* (folk heritage) or *al-funūn al-sha'biyya* (the folk arts), meaning that the Arab concept of folklore will be the measure for what is included here, rather than the most recent definitions that have emerged in Western scholarship.

For the purposes of this handbook, Arab folklore has been divided into four broad categories:

1. **Verbal Arts** (oral poetry, folk tales, epic poetry, proverbs, riddles, classic comparisons, jokes, and so forth)
2. **Musical Arts** (folk songs, musical instruments, dances, etc.)
3. **Material Arts** (vernacular architecture, dress and jewelry, folk painting, crafts such as metalwork, woodwork, glasswork, tilework, and so forth)
4. **Customs and Traditions** (weddings, birth rituals, games, festivals, pilgrimages, folk medicine, fortune-telling, beliefs about the supernatural, popular entertainments, and so forth)

With the exception of the fourth category, "customs and traditions" (Ar. *'ādāt wa-taqālīd*), these are all artificial categories created for the purpose of studying this material and are not indigenous terms or concepts found within Arab culture. Scholars in the social sciences have adopted the term *etic* to refer to views, concepts, or categories that are imposed from outside a culture and *emic* to refer those found within a culture. These terms derive from the twin terms *phonetic* and *phonemic* in linguistics: Phonetics is the study of all sounds of a language that can be distinguished scientifically, whereas phonology is the study of how speakers perceive the sounds of a language. For example, when English speakers say the words *dagger* and *dog* the initial <d> sounds are different, but English speakers perceive them to be the same sound—*phonetically* they are different, but *phonemically* they are the same because English speakers think of them as being the same sound. In Arabic, on the other hand, those two sounds are considered to be completely different sounds and are written with different letters of the Arabic alphabet—so in Arabic they are both phonetically and phonemically distinct, that is, they are not only demonstrably different using electronic technology and analysis, but they are also perceived as being different within the culture itself.

In the early days of Western folklore scholarship, it was deemed important to develop a system of classification and definition that would allow scholars to make cross-cultural comparisons (see Chapter Four). Thus even today scholars often use etic terms for many genres of folklore: folktale, fairy tale, epic, proverb, legend, myth, riddle, joke, and so forth (the *Greenwood Folklore Handbook* series includes volumes that provide excellent introductions to many of these genres). The definitions of these genres have been much debated over the years, but a general consensus has emerged among most Western researchers about the scholarly use of these terms in folklore research. These genres, however, were all derived from European models, and researchers working in non-Western cultures have often had great difficulty making this matrix fit the traditions they were studying in other parts of the world. A major shift in the field of folklore came about with the call for researchers to set aside the international system of folklore genres and to study the nomenclature and classification system of each individual society (Ben-Amos 1969/1976). Rather than arguing about whether a particular Arabic tale was a folktale or a legend, for example, the focus now turned to eliciting the terminology used by the storytellers themselves and how *they* defined and classified the tale. There was a clear shift towards studying the emic view of folklore genres. The generic terms such as tale, proverb, legend have remained in use because they provide a simple means of talking about folklore genres across languages and cultural boundaries, but in the field of folklore scholarship there is a newer, parallel emphasis placed upon understanding the "ways of speaking" of a particular group in its own terms (see, for example, Gossen 1971).

To provide a sense of how Arab folklore genres relate to folklore from other cultures, the international categories in the preceding list will provide the framework for Chapter Three, but an attempt has also been made to present each example within the context of the genre system of the community of its origin. This allows us to see how one form of poetry differs from another, how one type of tale is distinguished from other tales, and so forth. These questions are critical because it turns out that the genre distinctions made by cultures often involve much larger and very significant concepts about society, time, and the nature of the universe. Some genres are performed only by men and others only by women. It may be acceptable for prepubescent children to perform some genres but thought necessary that they stop performing them when they become full-fledged adults. Some genres might only be performed at a specific time of the year, or of the day or night, or in specific places. In other words, the different concepts people use when they make distinctions among folklore genres are critical to understanding the concepts that underlie their understanding of their community and society. Although examining the difference between types of poetry or types of narrative in detail may at first seem merely a question of form, folklorists have discovered that the issues involved are often deeply rooted in concepts of womanhood, manhood, childhood, distinctions between religious, ethnic, and regional identities, beliefs in the supernatural, and so forth. Exploring a culture's understanding of its genres of folklore is one way in which the study of folklore helps us to understand human culture and identity.

Two problems immediately present themselves, however, when dealing with indigenous genres in the Arab world. First, the nearly infinite variety of regional cultures within the larger Arab culture becomes quickly apparent—there are literally hundreds of genres of folk poetry in the Arab world, each with their different name, structure, and social distinctions, to say nothing of the genres of folk narrative, folk song, vernacular architecture, wedding customs, and so forth. Second, many of the terms are used in different regions to mean different things—in one region a *salfeh* may be a truthful historical account and a *qissa* a fictional story, while in a neighboring region the *qissa* may be considered factual and *hikāya* might be the term used for a fictional tale. The examples presented in this handbook should therefore be viewed as but a tiny selection from the "sea" *(bahr)* (as one would say in Arabic) of Arab folklore genres, and the reader should be aware that some terms appear in this volume with different meanings in different places. Every effort has been made, however, to make those local meanings clear whenever they occur. In addition, a Glossary of all Arabic terms used is found at the end of this volume.

The examples that appear in the following chapter have been selected to give an overview of the richness and diversity of the folk cultures of the Arabic-speaking world. Because it would not be possible in a volume of this size to offer examples from each region in every category, representative selections from several areas in the Arab world have been chosen for each type. The choice, however, has also been guided by the availability of publications in English, or at least in modern European languages, so that further readings are accessible to the interested reader. In a handful of instances, however, this has not been possible, and examples of traditions and genres that have been written about only in Arabic have been included for the sake of completeness.

Three
Examples and Texts

VERBAL ARTS

Oral Poetry

No art form is more closely intertwined with Arab culture and identity than poetry. It is generally considered to be the most typical and most highly regarded form of both verbal art and written literature in the Arab world. One distinctive characteristic of Arab culture and folklore is the great variety of different types of poetry that are used to fulfill many different social functions in both public and private life. In different times and places poetry has acted as an important means of preserving oral history; it is used in some regions as a medium for testifying in tribal courts and making statements in other solemn contexts; in some regions poetic duels are waged as entertainment at weddings; it is often used as a means of expressing one's deepest personal feelings; the ability to improvise poetry of the right style and form on public occasions is considered in some communities an important mark of one's level of education, intelligence, or even of manhood and tribal solidarity; lengthy epic poems preserve the memory of the lives and exploits of ancient heroes; religious narrative poems sung as ballads are one of the main ways that some individuals learn about and come to understand their faith; and spontaneously improvised verses are used in daily life for everything from criticizing government policies to cracking jokes among friends. This is a far cry from the comparatively limited role poetry plays in most modern Western societies.

To understand the richness and the force of poetry in Arab society it is necessary for outsiders to abandon the common western stereotype of poetry as a marginal, effete artistic activity and re-imagine it as a powerful form of "social action" or "cultural practice." We must also understand something of Arabic poetry's history to understand its importance in modern Arab folklore.

The History of Arabic Oral Poetry

In ancient Arabia, before the advent of Islam and of Arabic writing, poetry was an important means of communication because it could be memorized and transmitted with fewer changes than ordinary speech. Arabic poetry is composed in poetic meters of intricate patterns of long and short syllables, and it is sometimes organized into equally complex rhyme schemes as well. Ancient Arabic poetry was typically composed with a single rhyme repeated at the end of every verse, but folk poetry has developed many different rhyme patterns over the centuries. These structures—meter and rhyme—make it easier to memorize poetry than to memorize a passage of prose or a normal conversation. The rhyme makes it easy to remember the last word of each verse, and the regular meter makes certain words "fall into place" and also makes it clear if a word has been skipped or a substitution has been made. One ancient Arabic term still in use today for prose is *kalām manthūr* (scattered words) because prose has no structure or pattern, whereas poetry is referred to as *kalām manzūm* (organized words) because the words are carefully ordered by both meter and rhyme. These terms ultimately derive from the ancient Arabic image of poetry being like pearls strung onto a necklace, whereas prose was thought of as loose pearls with nothing to hold them together.

We can sense something of the power of meter and rhyme for holding words together in modern English by thinking of the limerick—the pounding accents of the verses and the final rhymes make it simple to memorize, and if a word is dropped or substituted, that change is immediately detectible. Arabic poetry is not usually organized by stress accents, like the limerick, but rather by patterns of long and short syllables, but the principle is similar. In an oral society, poetry could therefore be transmitted through time and space with far less change than prose and was thus considered more reliable and more truthful than normal speech.

It was a great advantage to a tribe in ancient Arabia to have good poets in their midst because they acted as the public spokespersons of the tribe. If the men of the tribe committed acts of heroism in battle, it was their poets who immortalized those deeds in poetry both for people within the tribe and as a means of vaunting the tribe's victories and the valor of its men to other groups. When someone died, it was the poets who eulogized them in poetry and caused their memory to live on among later generations—many of the women poets of ancient Arabia were particularly well known for this type of elegiac poetry. If another group insulted or satirized a tribe, the tribe's poets were the ones who responded to the jibes and defended its honor. In the huge markets held in the pilgrimage towns such as Mecca during the two truce months of each year, one major activity was the public recitation of poetry. Listeners would memorize the best poems and carry them back with them to all corners of the Arabian Peninsula. It was thus that news of raids and battles, deaths and marriages, spicy tales of romantic encounters, and beautiful descriptions of the desert landscape and its flora and fauna were spread far and wide. A well-known phrase in Arabic is that "poetry is the registry [*dīwān*] of the Arabs," that is, where all memorable historical events were stored.

With this in mind, it is easy to understand the statement of Ibn Rashīq (d. 1063 or 1071) about life in ancient Arabia: "When there appeared a poet in a family of the Arabs, the other tribes round about would gather together to that family and wish them joy of their good luck. Feasts would be got ready, the women of the tribe would join together in bands, playing upon lutes, as they were wont to do at bridals, and the men and boys would congratulate one another; for a poet was a defence to the honour of them all, a weapon to ward off insult from their good name, and a means of perpetuating their glorious deeds and of establishing their fame for ever. And they used not to wish one another joy but for three things—the birth of a boy, the coming to light of a poet, and the foaling of a noble mare" (Nicholson 1930, 71).

Even if this description is somewhat exaggerated, the importance of poets to early Arab culture is clear. In addition, there were secondary figures, known as a "reciter" *(rāwī)* rather than as a "poet" *(shā'ir)*, who were attached or apprenticed to the more prominent poets. Their work consisted of memorizing all of the compositions of their master poet, and often as not they were the ones who publicly performed these poems in marketplaces and other forums.

This ancient poetry was folklore in the sense that it was a completely oral tradition and was transmitted in live performance. In later centuries, however, much of this poetry was written down from oral tradition and the poems became "literature." Because the Arabic language continued to change over time and Arab society spread far beyond the Arabian Peninsula, the vocabulary of this poetry eventually became archaic and almost incomprehensible to normal people, so in the Middle Ages scholars wrote commentaries explaining the old vocabulary and clarifying difficult-to-understand references to places, animals, and ancient Bedouin customs. Nowadays these same poems, which were oral folklore 1,500 years ago, are thought of as the most classical works of Arabic literature and are taught to all Arab schoolchildren, who are often frustrated by the difficulty of the language and the alien nature of the culture the poems describe. A similar pattern of transformation from oral to written and finally to literary classic can been seen in the cases of great works in other cultures such as Homer's *Iliad* and *Odyssey* in Greek and *Beowulf* in English.

A groom attired in traditional wedding dresses during a group wedding ceremony. Collective weddings have become more popular in the poor country because of high dowry trends in some towns. © Yahya Arhad/epa/Corbis.

Although in modern times desert Bedouin and transhumant pastoralists (populations who move between traditional grazing areas with changes in the seasons, often in mountainous regions) constitute less than one percent of the Arab world's population, they have played an important role in defining Arab culture over the centuries. Arab and non-Arab scholars alike have turned to these communities to study customs and traditions that have sometimes been preserved with little change over long periods. Of particular interest to folklorists has been the documentation of the various social functions of oral poetry and other forms of verbal art. So let us begin our survey with three cases of poetry among modern Bedouin and tribal groups and then move on to examine oral poetry in rural and urban contexts in the Arab world.

Oral Poetry in Tribal Contexts

Yemen: The Practice of Poetry in Everyday Life. In his book *Peaks of Yemen I Summon* (1990), anthropologist Steven Caton documented and analyzed different uses and styles of poetry in the Hawlān al-Tiyāl region of northeastern Yemen. Children who grow up in a traditional environment in this region are exposed to the art of poetry from an early age in many different forms: many children's games are accompanied by rhyming lyrics, work songs with poetic lyrics are frequently sung, and poetry is constantly being recited and composed at celebrations and public events. There is typically no formal instruction in the art of poetry; rather, young people learn to compose poetry by imitating what they hear, and their early attempts are usually well received and enthusiastically encouraged. One important type of poetry for men in this region is the *bālah,* which is a short, improvised poetic form performed at weddings and at other social occasions. As part of the celebration, men take turns stepping into the center of the gathering and composing short poems either in response to a theme already addressed by earlier participants or tossing out a new idea to which others can respond. One exciting aspect of this type of poetry is its extemporaneous nature; it is not prepared in advance but rather is composed in performance in a competitive, agonistic context.

When the moment has come for a *bālah* performance, a half dozen to a dozen men move to the center of the gathering and form a circle. They are known in Arabic as the "two lines" *(saffēn)* and it is their job to act as the chorus: One group will chant the refrain and the other will echo part of the verse. These men are often young, even adolescents, who perhaps do not yet have the skill to compete in the *bālah* on their own. Hovering outside this inner circle are the men who are about to compete in the *bālah,* the poets waiting on the wings preparing to jump in and take their turn:

The poets, whoever they turn out to be, shut their eyes as they listen to the chanting, their faces tense with the effort of composition, their lips silently forming the lines that spring from their imagination. Confident that they have composed a well-formed verse, their faces brighten, and one among their number (which varies from two to five or even more) moves decisively toward the circle and breaks through the linked arms of the choristers, who close ranks behind him [. . .] He walks half of the circle's circumference and at the same time chants the first hemistich *(harf)* of his turn. Depending on the particular chant, the chorus might intrude at this juncture with a choral refrain, but in any case, the poet finishes his turn by chanting the second hemistich and continuing around to close the circle [. . .] He then immediately exits from the middle of the circle, and the chorus meanwhile picks up the chanting of the last hemistich of the poet's turn, alternating it with the refrain line. Now it is up to his rivals to continue building the poem. (Caton 1990, 82)

The performance thus consists of three concentric circles: At the center is the poet who chants his improvised verse in two half-lines (hemistichs), around him are the chorus who echo his verse and chant the refrain line, and around them are the audience members voicing their approval or disapproval of each verse as it is revealed. The competing poets must not only match the meter and rhyme of the previous lines, but the substance of each new verse must engage that of the earlier verses. Even more demanding is that the poets are not allowed to use a rhyme word that has already been used (at least not in the same sense of the word), so the competition gets more and more difficult the longer it goes on.

The verses of the *bālah* often have a formulaic quality about them, in part because of the limited repertory of traditional themes (greetings to the guests, congratulations to the hosts, compliments to the men of the tribe and region, religious statements about the glories of God, and so forth) but also because many of the key motifs in this genre of poetry can be expressed with slightly different words to fit different metrical and rhyme schemes. Lines of *bālah* verse are composed, performed, and forgotten all in a single evening—they are not created to be committed to memory, critiqued in detail, and recited years later. The focus is on the performance and the competition, not on the crafting of verses that will endure.

Following are a few selected lines from a wedding performance that opened with mention and praise of God, and then moved to praise of the Prophet Muhammad. Eventually four different poets alternated at the center of the circle, and the subject matter moved to a series of greetings to those present, the exchange of proverbial wisdoms, and felicitations to the bridegroom and his family.

Poet 1

Verily, I begin with Him who causes the lightning to flash and Him who makes it appear,
Verily, whosoever prays to God, the Generous One, [he] will not be disappointed!

Poet 2

Verily, I invoke God who was at the beginning [of creation] and [will be] at the
   end,
Verily, I praise God millions of times that we count.

Poet 1

Verily, Preserver of ships on whose waves one is brought to safety,
Verily, I mention Muhammad, God's blessings on *al-Tayyiba* [the city of Medina]

Poet 2

Verily, I mention Muhammad since his mention is a duty,
Verily, he intercedes for us on our behalf [with God, to keep us from] Hell, whose
   heat is blazing.

Poet 1

Verily, O God, we implore You to spare us from calamities.
Verily, I say good evening, I am of men who love war.

Poet 2

Verily, good evening to you, verily, you are the fanged lions.
Verily, O men of the *hadhramī* blades [i.e., from the region of the Hadhramawt],
   sharpen the fine cutting edge.

Poet 3

Verily, long life to all of you, and may you not see any calamities [in life],
Verily, O thousands of welcomes, innumerable.

Poet 4

Verily, O blessed evening when a friend meets his friend.
Verily, O welcome to the guest far and wide.

Poet 1

Verily, I serve the happy groom fine perfume.
Verily, and [I serve] the foreign [i.e., from outside the village] guest melon and
   grapes.

Poet 3

Verily, O welcome to the guests as a group whose honor is precious.
Verily, and the groom—we will even add to all he wants...

(Adapted from Caton 1990, 90–92)

In contrast to the spontaneous competitive performances of the *bālah* are
the more stately, powerful performances of another genre known as the *zāmil.*
Whereas the *bālah* is a collective genre and can only be performed by multiple

poets in collaboration, the *zāmil* is composed by a single poet, often acting as the spokesperson of a group. One of the most fascinating contexts for this genre of poetry is in the negotiation of tribal disputes. When problems arise over grazing lands, raids, boundaries, and the like, a type of tribal court or assembly can be convened in which those involved in the dispute argue their cases in front of neutral outsiders—but they must couch their most important statements in poetry. This requirement has a number of advantages: First, it keeps the dialogue calm and controlled since the participants must stop to mold their thoughts into well-formed verse (anything less would be seen as a shameful lack of self-control). Second, because poetry is easily memorized and transmitted, these statements must be in the most eloquent and persuasive form possible (bad verses would be recalled ever after as demonstration of a lack of poetic talent). Finally, the remembered poetry acts as a public record of the case for later reference. This formal language, the carefully controlled turns at speaking, and the overall decorum required in the tribal assembly are at times surprisingly reminiscent of the ritualistic behaviors seen in modern Western law courts.

Following are a few verses of *zāmil* poetry from a tribal dispute. One tribe was using disputed territory to graze its sheep when members of another tribe, which claimed that territory as their own, shot the grazing sheep. This act of aggression sparked a declaration of war from the first tribe, but nearly as soon as the first shots had actually been fired, calls for mediation and negotiation were made throughout the region. These verses, each by a different participant, offer greetings to those who have come and state clearly the purpose at hand.

> Greetings to those who have come from the tribes of the Khawlan as experts
>   in tribal law // and who respect the traditions of the Bakīl;
> He who comes intending to reproach every wrongdoer [is welcome]
>   Otherwise, he can continue on his way.

> O Banī Shadād, O A‘rūsh, solve the problem // provide something as evidence
>   that will speak about *ash-shaghāb* [the name of the tribal boundary].
> Each person has prepared a complete and absolute denial // he has said it was his
>   property before [God] revealed the fourth sacred book [= the Qur’ān, which
>   was revealed after the Torah, Psalms, and New Testament].

> Greetings, O men of the assembly // O you who are striving earnestly to stop the
>   tribes from fighting.
> Negotiate with us these important matters // let us not be like the locust that
>   wanders away from the swarm.

In the end, the most important qualities of a *zāmil* are that it be persuasive and memorable rather than beautiful per se. But the rhetorical and aesthetic dimensions are deeply intertwined in the *zāmil*, for a beautiful well-formed poem is also more likely to be persuasive and memorable: "Art" and "action" are inseparable.

(Adapted from Caton 1990, 163, 167)

Yet a third type of poetry common to this region is the formal ode or *qasīda*. This type of poetry perhaps most closely resembles the modern Western concept of a poem, and it is also the form closest to classical Arabic poetry. The ode is usually many verses long with a single end rhyme, it is composed by an individual poet sometimes over a period of many days or weeks, and it may even be polished and improved over time by the poet in reaction to suggestions by friends and listeners, but eventually it is performed publicly as a completed work and the poet's name is always associated with the poem. In modern times these finely crafted poems are often recited on radio or television, and some even circulate on cassette tapes (Miller 2007). From these mass media sources, however, they are frequently memorized and then recited orally by listeners, thereby achieving a second existence in live oral performance—from oral transmission, to the mass media, and back to oral performance. These intricate poetic creations are often dozens of verses long and many of them in more recent times contain political arguments, messages to rulers about how to govern, complaints of ill treatment on the part of people from a particular tribe or region, or other matters of current interest.

In sum, these three genres of men's poetry from the same region of northern Yemen represent a spectrum of poetic practices. The *bālah* is a communal, spontaneously improvised form performed inside, at night, at weddings and other celebrations, in a charged competitive atmosphere where the audience loudly voices its approval or disapproval of each new verse, but the verses are then quickly forgotten. The two-line *zāmil* on the other hand is composed by a single poet, is performed outside and often in solemn circumstances expressing opinions or even (as we saw previously) arguing in a tribal court, and is meant to be remembered by the audience, who in general listen intently to the proceedings. Finally, the *qasīda* is a lengthy, intricately crafted poem by a single poet, which is composed over a period of time, but eventually circulates as a finished product and at times achieves national or even international fame. All of these, Steven Caton has argued, are closely tied to the performance of manliness *(muruwwa)* and of one's identity as a tribal *(qabīlī)* man in this region of Yemen. Poetry in Yemen is not just an art form but rather a social practice.

Egypt: Poetry and Honor among Bedouin Women. A rich and fascinating tradition of Bedouin women's poetry from the northwestern desert of Egypt is explored in Lila Abu-Lughod's *Veiled Sentiments: Honor and Poetry in a Bedouin Society* (1986). In particular, the author analyzes the role of poetry as a counter-discourse

An undated photo of an Egyptian Bedouin woman baking
bread on a sag. Courtesy of Shutterstock.

to action and direct communication, one in which women can express their most
personal feelings by couching their words in traditional, oblique images. Part of
the concept of honor among the Awlad 'Ali Bedouin tribe is a form of emotional
stoicism that considers it shameful to complain publicly about one's personal
life, especially about intimate matters such as relations between spouses or family members, nor should one openly express deeply felt emotions such as pain,
grief, vulnerability, and love. Women, in particular, must also avoid mention
of anything that might imply sexual desire, in adherence with the strict code
of Bedouin modesty. Instead, the desired public demeanor is to be forbearing,
stalwart, and strong. Poetry, however, allows female members of the Awlad 'Ali
tribe, and occasionally men as well, to express those emotions that cannot be
expressed in regular speech and to send "veiled" social messages with at times
powerful results.

This genre of poetry is called the *ghinnāwa* (lit. little song). These are short, almost haiku-like compositions of one or two verses that can be performed in two very different manners. One way to perform them is simply to recite the verses in a straightforward manner in a regular speaking voice:

Tears increased, Oh Lord
The Beloved came to mind in the time of sadness

A very different mode of performance, however, is achieved when women chant these verses to a repetitive, mournful melody in which the verse is revealed, one image at a time, until it finally appears in complete form at the end of the song:

In the time
In the time
In the time of sadness
In the time
The beloved in the time of sadness
In the time
In the time
The beloved in the time of sadness
In the time
In the time
In the time [my] tears
[My] tears increased oh Lord
In the time
In the time
The beloved came to mind
The beloved came to mind in the time of sadness

(Abu-Lughod 1986, 179)

In these poems, people are never mentioned by name, nor are there usually specific details that would make it possible to identify the participants. Instead, persons and situations are portrayed in generic forms that preserve anonymity. Abu-Lughod found that members of the tribe could rarely interpret a poem until they knew who had composed or recited it, at which point they would immediately apply their knowledge of that person's situation to the situation described in the poem. In effect, this verbal art form allows people to complain without complaining and to express their most private emotions anonymously without incurring the disapproval of their peers:

More than anything else, the subject matter of this much-loved genre distinguishes it from other genres of poetry and song and accounts for its special place in Bedouin society. The *ghinnāwa* is the poetry of personal sentiment. It is about feelings people have, feelings about situations and human relationships. Even a cursory look at the poetic vocabulary of the *ghinnāwa* betrays this content. The simple formulas, so prevalent that they practically define the genre, are the terms for the self and the beloved. (Abu-Lughod 1986, 181)

Some of these poems are composed entirely afresh by the singer, some are variations on common themes, and others have remained almost unchanged over generations and are recited or sung by women as a reflection of their situation. Most deal with issues of modesty, gender, sexuality, personal life, sentiment, vulnerability, loss, pride, death, honor, and love. Because these poems are typically revealing of intense emotional states, their beauty is tied to their ability to move the listeners. An oft-repeated phrase among the Awlad 'Ali is "Beautiful poetry makes you cry" (Abu-Lughod 1986, 177).

Following are several examples of *ghinnāwa* poems with brief descriptions of the contexts in which they were composed and performed:

Rashīd married a second wife but his bride ran away after only a brief stay in her new home. Publicly he expressed no affection for her or any concern at her departure, which would have been seen as a sign of weakness on his part. Instead he angrily demanded to know who had "ruined her" (i.e., caused her to be unhappy). The family saw this as a family, not an individual, crisis and talk soon turned to the possibility of sorcery. A local holy man confirmed this suspicion and the accusation rapidly spread with Rashīd directing the blame at his first wife. Eventually, however, the new bride was convinced to return to her husband. When asked privately how he felt about the situation, Rashīd responded in poetry:

Cooking with a liquid of tears at a funeral for the beloved
Her bad deeds were wrongs that hurt yet I won't repay them,
    still dear is the Beloved (189)

The feelings of pain and his affection for his new wife, neither of which could be acknowledged publicly, were only revealed in his poem.

Migdim, an elderly paternal aunt, came to visit the household of her nephew. She was usually received with hospitality and kindness, but that particular evening she was first invited to sleep in the bedroom of her nephew's wife; he returned unexpectedly, however, and she had to get up and move to another room. She went to sleep with her grandnieces using bedding offered by the wife of her other nephew, but then he too came home and the bedding had to be taken back for his use. Eventually, she spent the night alone in an uncomfortable room with almost no bedding. The following morning she recited this poem:

I never figured you'd do wrongs like these, oh they hurt
Forced by drought in the land to seek refuge among people of twisted
   tongues (196)

The reference to "people of twisted tongues" was explained as evoking a time when a tribe has to seek pasturage in such distant lands that they encounter people who speak languages they do not understand.

When a young man was killed by members of a neighboring tribe, his family publicly expressed only anger and their desire for revenge. Privately, however, many of them expressed their grief in poems. His mother recited these verses:

Dear ones deprive me of sleep
Just as I drift off, they come to mind

A cousin expressed similar feelings of loss:

Caught by a memory unawares
Brought tears in the hour of pleasure

And his widow recited verses of her struggle to control her despair:

Ill and full of despair
Show me what medicine could cure this malady

Drowning in despair
The eye says, 'Oh my destiny in love!' (203–4)

Among the Awlad 'Ali, what is expressed in the *ghinnāwa* is deeply embedded in, or is perhaps the counter-discourse to, a code of public behavior that requires members to demonstrate strength, endurance, and control over one's emotions and a high level of sexual modesty. Combined, these characteristics create honor, while the breaking of that code brings shame to the individual and, by extension, to the family group, clan, and tribe. Yet somehow poetry is allowed to express those emotions about which one cannot speak openly or act upon publicly, and it is perhaps precisely the process of controlling these wild, uncontrolled emotions by forcing them into verse that allows this counter-discourse to exist:

By channeling such powerful sentiments into a rigid and conventional medium and delimited social contexts, individuals demonstrate a measure of self-mastery and control that contributes to honor. (245)

This type of poetry, then, is both an act of release and of self-discipline, a form of artistic communication that is powerful precisely because it has been controlled, and beautiful because it moves us.

An undated photo of an elderly Jordanian Bedouin man.
© Judy Lawrance/Alamy.

Jordan and Saudi Arabia: Poetry as Oral History. One of the most enduring uses of poetry in Arabic oral tradition has been in the transmission of oral history. The earliest known historical narratives of the Arabs, written down and gathered together in early medieval times into anthologies called *Ayyām al-'Arab* (lit. The Days of the Arabs) after having been transmitted orally for centuries, are prose narratives from the pre-Islamic era punctuated with short poems to mark the key points of the account. A similar *prosimetric* (mixed poetry and prose) genre is still found in the Arabian Peninsula and in regions of Jordan, Palestine, Syria, and Iraq, where tribal histories are often narrated as prose embedded with poems. The poem acts not only as an artistic moment within the performance but also as a type of attestation that the prose narrative is true, for it is often assumed (as we have seen in the preceding discussion) that the poetry has been transmitted with little or no change due to its strict meter and rhyme scheme and is therefore historically more reliable than the prose account it accompanies. This idea was succinctly summed up by a Jordanian Bedouin shaykh, discussing the relationship between oral history and poetry with anthropologist Andrew Shryock, in his statement: *il-gissa illay ma 'ind-ha qasīd kidhib* ("The story that doesn't have a poem is a lie") (Shryock 1997, 258).

Saad Abdullah Sowayan notes in *Nabati Poetry* (1985), his remarkable study of oral poetry in Saudi Arabia:

Although nomadic poetry deals mainly with tribal raids and forays, it is not straightforward historical narrative. Poets make only allusions and cryptic references to the incidents celebrated in their poems. Therefore, a poetic reference usually alternates with a prose narrative which recounts the raids and battles celebrated in the poetry and serves to put the poetry into its proper context and to illuminate its allusions. The poetry does, however, serve as an authentic document substantiating the incidents in the narrative and enhancing their circulation and preservation in public memory. (Sowayan, 52)

Thus there is a symbiotic relationship between the two parts: the prose carries the mundane details and explains the allusions in the poetry, while the poetry lends authority to the prose account as well as making it more memorable and more enjoyable.

Following are selections from a series of poems, most of which are from 10 to 20 verses long in their complete form, from a chain of events that took place in the first half of the nineteenth century. Si'dūn al-'Wājī, the shaykh of the Wlād Slēmān tribe in the Najd region of what is now Saudi Arabia, had two valiant sons named 'Gāb and Hjāb, but he had quarreled with their mother and she had returned with her sons to her own tribe in southern Syria. One of Si'dūn's cousins named Shāmikh then wrested the leadership of the tribe from him and forced him to live as a miserable outcast at the edge of the tribe's encampment. So Si'dūn sent the following poem to his eldest son:

My heart is set ablaze by anxieties; it simmers as if on glowing embers.
O, treacherous fate, how quick it turns! My happy days suddenly changed to
  adversity.
I was far ahead of misfortune before, but now it tramples upon me with its
  shod hooves.
I used to wear a badge of distinction, and led the troops astride a noble steed.
When enemy horsemen attacked, I was the first to meet them and cover the
  retreat of my kinsmen.
But today, I have no mount on which to carry my baggage. Oh, how shameful!
  I have been humbled and subdued.
Oh, how painful is misfortune! Gone are the glorious days.
I have often asked, where is my son, who spills the red blood of the enemy?
  I have often wondered, where is my beloved son?

> Enemy horses flee when they hear his thunderous voice; he terrifies the mares
>   on the battlefield.
> He chases them like an eagle; vultures dine on the flesh of his enemies. (54)

Having received this poem, his two sons rode to their father's aid and with their
assistance Si'dūn regained the chieftainship of the tribe. The sons then decided to
reside with the tribe of their father, rather than with that of their mother. Later
the grazing lands of their tribe are stricken with drought so Si'dūn decides to
invade the territory of a certain Mislit, a shaykh of the Shammar tribe. He sent
the following poem as a warning to Mislit that he must either abandon the lands
willingly or face Si'dūn and his men in battle. The poem is addressed to his messenger who rides in a delegation of eight men mounted on identically colored
camels, and the poet underlines the bravery of his tribe by noting that their camels are ones that they have raided from other tribes:

> Hail, you rider on a barren mount whose breasts were never suckled by a calf;
>   one of eight identical camels, she is not alone.
> Their chests are wide, their legs are spotted with white, thoroughbreds of Omani
>   origin.
> You will alight by the camp of Mislit, the scion of noble ancestors; tell him to
>   quit his land, we wish to take possession of it.
> We wish to graze our camel herds there—sweet to the ear is their growling;
>   we fatten them on coveted pastures.
> We herd them bearing long lances to protect them against enemy tribes.
> We did not inherit them from our ancestors; they are the milch camels of our
>   adversaries, which we took by force [...] (57)

Not surprisingly, Mislit does not give up his tribal grazing lands without a fight,
and leads a dawn attack on Si'dūn's camp, but Si'dūn in the end defeats him and
the Shammar are forced to cede their grazing rights to the stronger tribe. To an-
nounce this victory and make sure that the neighboring tribes all know who has
won the rights to this land, Si'dūn composed and had circulated the following
poem, which boasts of their victory and, in particular, praises his eldest son, 'Gāb,
for his heroism. The poem is once again addressed to the messenger who is being
sent out to recite it in the camps of the neighboring 'Anazah tribe; again we see
that praising the quality of a man's mount is by extension praise not only of the
man himself, but of his tribe:

> Hail, you rider on a speedy mount that runs like a terrified ostrich on level plains,
> A handsome mount with erect hump and arched neck, a purebred of noble
>   ancestry—
> Not a common pack animal—it is a wild beast that has never been ridden before.
> You will alight at the camps of the 'Anazah, who adorn their sharp spears with
>   gallant deeds.

When you join their assemblies in the tents of their chiefs, and my faithful friends
    among them question you,

Tell them multitudes that cannot be counted attacked us at dawn; the people of
    the mountain attacked us in the early morning.

Praise the Lord, they were vanquished and their stragglers sought refuge in [the
    distant provinces of] Gfār and Hāyil.

Many bodies fell to the ground, their heads severed by our sabers; with our
    swords we demonstrate our anger at our foes.

Many enemy horsemen were thrown down; they fell from their horses and rolled
    in the dust.

Intoxicated by his multitudes [of followers], Mislit attacked us in the morning,
    and 'Gāb, the wild eagle, met him on the field, riding his fiery horse.

[Mislit] threw down his sword and ran away; he spurred his mare and hid behind
    the dunes.

He left behind [his slain cousin] Jrēs in Zawāgīb; woe to him, he will bemoan this
    gallant lad.

['Gāb] sits in his tent, dignified and clad in war attire; he is still young, but he is
    already renowned for his glorious deeds. (58)

From these examples, we can see that poetry is not just a passive tool for recording history, but rather is active in the making of history itself: Petitions for
help, challenges to battle, announcements of victory, in short, every major step
in a tribe's history are couched in poetry so that it may be memorized, recited,
transmitted, and preserved. As the Jordanian shaykh said, "A story that does not
have a poem is a lie!"

Similar studies have been conducted among the Bedouin of the Negev desert
(Bailey 1972, 1981), in Central Arabia (Kurpershoek 1994–2002), northern Arabia (Ingham 1982, 1986), and Jordan (Shryock 1997), all of which have documented a remarkable consistency in the use and conceptualization of poetry
among nomadic Bedouin. To explore different aspects of the role of oral poetry in
Arab societies, let us now turn to rural and urban contexts to examine traditions
of oral poetry from villages and towns.

Rural and Urban Traditions of Oral Poetry

Egypt: Proverbial Wisdom in Intricate Rhymes. Throughout village Egypt, one
of the most popular forms of poetry is the *mawwāl*, a short poem that usually
features proverb-like statements about fate, love, honor, human behavior, and life's
tribulations. These poems are often in five- or seven-verse patterns, but are also
sometimes strung together and used as the vehicle for long narrative poems (see
Religious Ballads). The most distinctive characteristic of the *mawwāl*, however,
is that most of its verses end in intricately rhymed puns, sometimes so difficult
to catch that listeners have to struggle to extract the meaning of the poem and

may even disagree in their interpretations. In performance the *mawwāl* is usually recited or sung so that all of the rhyme words are pronounced almost exactly the same and the listeners must themselves figure out which words are intended. The following brief example gives some sense of how the *mawwāl* works; it is composed in English (not translated from Arabic) and uses one of the stock motifs of Arabic folk poetry, the hunter and the gazelle (substituting the word *deer* for gazelle), the gazelle being a common metaphor for the beloved, or for any beautiful young man or woman. Read through the poem pronouncing each rhyme word in the same manner—*dēr*—halfway between the English words *deer* and *dare*:

> The heart is a hunter who seeks to catch *dēr*
> But after a single glance, his prey strikes him as *dēr*
> Its beauty and voice please the eye and *dēr*
> So instead of capturing his prey, he himself is captured *dēr*
>> For the heart is a hunter,
>> But also the hunted
> A man's strength is his weakness—so hunt only if you *dēr!*

The rhyme words, all pronounced the same way in performance, must be replaced in our minds with the words *deer, dear, the ear, there,* and *dare* for the poem to make sense. This communicative process is very different from that of most puns in English. In English a pun usually consists of the listener recognizing the similarity between two words or phrases and the process of making the connection produces a humorous response, in part because of the random relationship between the two, which sound alike but mean very different things. In the paronomasia (wordplay) found within the *mawwāl,* however, the listener hears "meaningless" repetitions of a single syllable, word, or phrase, and has to "crack open" that string of sounds over and over again to create different words. The meaning is hidden within the sounds—it is concealed and must be revealed. We can also see that the *mawwāl* is a distinctively oral form of poetry, for if one writes the intended words (*deer, dear, the ear,* etc.) on the page, the cleverness of the *mawwāl* is lost and the poems are much less interesting, whereas if one were to write the same sounds over and over again at the end of each line, the poem would become gibberish. A *mawwāl* can only be committed to writing by eliminating one of its most distinctive characteristics.

Interestingly enough, one of the common motifs of the *mawwāl* genre is precisely the act of concealment: One should conceal one's troubles and not show them to everyone thereby giving people something to talk about; one must conceal any romantic feelings one has, as well, to avoid provoking gossip; and one should let no one know if enemies have insulted or wounded one. Instead, one must be stalwart and forbearing *(sābir),* one should be like a male camel *(jamal)* and bear one's burdens and wounds stoically, and above all, one must submit to the will of God *(hukm Allāh).* The world of the *mawwāl* is a world of stock symbols from the folk imaginary: A king or ruler is a lion *(asad),* the raven *(ghurāb)* is an omen of death or separation, the mosquitoes *(nāmūs)* are petty interlopers, the eye *('ēn)* stands for the self or the soul, and fate and destiny are represented by figures such as Time *(al-zaman)*, the Days *(al-ayyām)*, the Era *(al-dahr)*, the Nights *(al-layālī)*, and other images. Although these symbols are found in other forms of folk poetry as well, the *mawwāl* is unique for being conducted almost entirely in this symbolic discourse.

Because the *mawwāl* is itself so short and so complex, it is rare to have a performance just of this genre. Instead, it is performed in tandem with other larger genres such as epic poetry *(sīra)*, religious singing *(inshād dīnī)*, or the singing of narrative ballads, all of which are examined in some detail later. The *mawwāl*, however, usually produces a very distinctive mood from the rest of the performance. First of all, the audience must remain quiet during the *mawwāl* so that they can catch the words and decipher the poem; and second, many singers use the *mawwāl* as a moment to demonstrate vocal artistry and therefore sing in a highly embellished manner with a great deal of *melisma* (stretching a single syllable over several musical notes). Whereas audiences of epic poetry often shout out encouragement to the poet or reactions to the story during the performance ("Bravo, that's it!" "Heavens!" "Oh no!" etc.), they typically fall silent during a *mawwāl* and voice their approval only when it has been completed. It is not uncommon for an audience to demand to hear the *mawwāl* again to better grasp its meanings, and if a poet feels the poem is still not being properly understood, he may pause at the end of each verse and cue the audience with the right words ("Its beauty and voice please the eye and *dēr...*" [aside to the audience] "The ear!").

Following is a *mawwāl* that was sung as part of an evening of epic poetry in the village of al-Bakātūsh, Egypt, by Shaykh Biyalī Abū Fahmī in February 1987. The syllables in boldface type were pronounced almost identically with only the slightest differentiation between the sounds <gh> and <kh>:

> *Qāl: il-'ajab 'alā jamal majrūh wi-mi**ghattī***
> *Yifūt 'alā l-i'ād mihammil ghulb wi-mi**ghattī***
> *Yiqūl: anā fī zamānī kunt ashīl ahmāl wi-a**khadtī***
> *Yā 'ēnī, khudī lik rafīq zēn min khiyār in-nās wi-law **khadtī***
> > *Yibqā dā khēra wi-law*
> > *Hakam al-zaman wi-māl*
> *Yuq'ud yidamdim 'alā l-'ibād wi-yi**ghattī***

He said: What a wonder is the camel who is wounded but **conceals it**
He passes by his enemies bearing misfortune and is **covered by it**
He says: "I, in my time, used to bear burdens and **travel on**"
O my eye, take a fine companion from good people, if you must **take one**
> This will be good and if
> Fate judges and "leans" [on you]
He will sit with you and say to others only "hmmm" and **"hurrumph"**

(Reynolds 1995, 151–53)

Translated into plain prose, the poem praises individuals who are as strong as camels, which bear their burdens and troubles and do not complain, but instead simply get on with their lives and work. If one must have a close friend in whom to confide, one should be sure to choose well, from among the best of people, so that when you have troubles you can count on your friend not to gossip about you with others, someone who will respond to people's comments or inquiries about you with nothing more than a "hmmm" or "hurrumph."

Later that same evening, Shaykh Biyalī inserted another *mawwāl* with similar imagery into his performance:

> *Wi-yikūn jamalī 'ind shēl il-himl **khatābī** [khatā biyya]*
> *Mā kān ghurāb il-naya shālnī wa-**khatābī** [khatā biyya]*
> *Yā nār qalbī 'alēhum qidīnī **hatābī** [hatabī]*
>   *Anā as'alak ya rabb [2x] yā mugrī l-laban fī l-**bizz***
>   *tita'ta' il-bakr min taht il-himūl wi-yi**fizz***
>   *wi-tsaltan il-'**izz***
> *wi-layālī il-'izz bitdūm lī lakin il-layālī ma'a l-ayyām **hatābī** [hatta biyya]*

> My camel at the carrying of the burden **wronged me**
> In spite of the Raven of Separation, [Fate] bore me and **carried me**
> O Fire of my heart, against them light **my kindling**
>   I ask of you, O Lord! [2x], O you who cause milk to flow in the **breast**
>   You stir the young camel 'neath his loads and he **springs up**
>   And you have authority over all **prosperity**
> Let the nights of prosperity continue for me—But the nights, along with
>   the days, **push down on me** [humble me]

(Reynolds 1995, 153–54)

A translation of these images might give us the following interpretation of the poem: As a strong man, when the time comes, I should shoulder life's burdens, but I sometimes fail; Fate seized me, despite my good intentions, and bore me away from what I had hoped my life would become; O my heart, strengthen yourself against the difficulties of life (or: against your enemies); I ask you, O Lord, You who cause milk to flow in the breast, you give the young hope despite their troubles, you who have power to grant prosperity; let me continue to prosper—yet all of the forces of the world seem to be working against me!

The *mawwāl* is thus a poetic form that communicates by means of a language of symbols and forces its listeners to engage in a willful act of interpretation of the poem through the untangling of its complex wordplay. Additionally, although these poems can also be recited in a standard speaking voice, they are more often sung, usually to lyrical and embellished melodies, creating a distinctive moment in an evening's entertainment for aesthetic appreciation. It is extremely difficult to translate a *mawwāl* for the images of the poem allow multiple interpretations both at the level of which rhyme word is intended and then again at the level of deciphering the symbols used in the poem. A translation of a *mawwāl* is in reality but one of a number of possible interpretations.

Algeria: Love and Romance in Women's Poetry. The city of Tlemcen, now with a population of about 150,000, is located in westernmost Algeria, almost on the Moroccan border. During the Middle Ages, it was one of the most important urban centers of North Africa and was the capital city of the Ziyanid dynasty from the thirteenth to sixteenth centuries. It is equally noteworthy, however, for its remarkable music culture, for it is the heartland of many different types of traditional music ranging from classical art music to popular and folk genres. Tlemcen is first of all home to one of the great traditions of classical Andalusian music (descended from the court music of medieval Moorish Spain) called *gharnātī* (Granadan) or *san'a* (art) music. From this tradition, two other genres developed sometime after the fifteenth century: The first, the *inqilābāt,* are local compositions in the Andalusian style that use the classical Arabic language of the medieval repertory; the second, *hawzī,* is composed in local Tlemcenian dialect to a lighter, more upbeat musical style. *'Arūbī* is a folk song genre with roots in the hinterlands, and *gherbī* is a genre associated with Tlemcen and the Moroccan cities of Oujda and Fez. Just north of Tlemcen, in the region of Oran on the Mediterranean coast, lies the birthplace of *rai* music (for all of these genres, see *The Garland Encyclopedia of World Music,* vol. 2, *The Middle East* [New York: Routledge, 2002], 427–77). In addition to all these traditions, there is a remarkable genre of women's folk poetry and song, *hawfi,* which is performed outdoors, only by women, in a very special manner and has been most carefully studied and documented by Mourad Yelles-Chaouche (1990).

Hawfi poetry is sung by women in gardens, on picnics, on all-women pilgrimages to saints' tombs and other outdoor occasions in association with the act of swinging in swings (in Tlemcenian dialect, *joghlīla*) usually near some body of water such as a spring, stream, or small cascade. Although similar forms have been documented in a handful of other locations in North Africa, the *hawfi* tradition is most commonly associated with the city of Tlemcen. The swings are extremely simple and consist of nothing more than a rope, both ends of which are tied to a sturdy tree branch, often a fig tree, with a sheepskin or a small cushion of some sort forming the seat. Typically three women or girls participate with one sitting on the swing and two others pushing her. The girl in the swing intones the poetry in a simple, slow chant. When her turn is over, another takes her place, but traditionally the youngest girls go first and older ones go later. The poems are all anonymous, entirely oral, and are learned by young girls by hearing older girls and women sing them. The songs are composed in the distinctive dialect of the town of Tlemcen, which differs in a number of key features from the dialects of the surrounding countryside.

Even more remarkable than this ritualistic style of performance is that the women of Tlemcen also preserve a legend about the origin of *hawfi*, and whenever they gather to swing and sing, they begin the session by chanting what is, according to the legend, the first *hawfi* ever sung. The legend says that one day, long ago, the sultan of Tlemcen proclaimed to all his subjects that it was forbidden, on pain of death, to go near the pool at the bottom of the waterfalls of Mefrouch because the women of his household were going to bathe there. A hermit or mystic named *Rūh al-gharīb* (lit. Spirit of the Stranger) disobeyed the royal decree by not leaving his usual dwelling near the pool. When he was discovered, the sultan's soldiers seized him and cut the tendons behind his knees (hamhocked him). While he lay suffering from the great pain of this punishment, he is said to have pronounced the very first poem of the *hawfi* genre (English translations are from the Arabic and French texts in Yelles-Chaouche 1990):

āsh 'āl rūh al-ghrīb	*bi-jlājlū yadwī*
Neskun f-jaw es-samā	*we-n'āned l-arwī*
We-l-yūm yā sāhbī	*l-arkāb khānūnī*
na'fes 'lā būghyūl	*f-l-ard yesba'nī*

What did he say, Rūh al-gharīb, he who with his bells did shine?
"I was dwelling in the heavenly abode, competing with the sheep,
But today, my friend, my knees have betrayed me,
When I want to stomp a sowbug into the ground, it is faster than I" (109, 226)

In the city of Blida, Algeria, however, where *hawfi* singing is also known, a rather different story is told: A spirit named Duwākhkha, who causes dizziness, is said to have taught the game and the songs of the swing to a princess who had befriended her, by tying cords of silk to form a swing suspended from the branches of a sacred tree.

Many of the images of these two etiological myths (tales of origins) are tied to the sacred and to the practice of magic. The heavenly abode and the sacred tree are clear indications of the spiritual realm. Sheep are common animals of sacrifice, particularly in Islamic culture where they are slaughtered each year at the feast that marks Abraham's near sacrifice of his son (in Islamic tradition it is Ishmael the eldest son, rather than Isaac, who is nearly killed and for whom a ram is substituted at the last moment). The hocking of an animal such as a camel or a young bull before slaughtering it by cutting its throat is a practice known in Arab culture from ancient times and references to this appear frequently in pre-Islamic poetry. Bells are also associated with magic and are sometimes used to ward off evil spirits, and perhaps even more so in this case because the bells the hermit wore caused him to "shine." Combined with the fact that the swings are usually suspended near bodies of water, which also often carry the aura of magic and of secret practices, the whole constellation of swings, water, songs, and images of the sacred suggest that *hawfi* may have historical roots in ancient popular beliefs and rituals, perhaps now long gone, that combined Islamic religious and pagan magical elements.

The themes of *hawfi* songs collected in the past century include many that are purely Islamic and deal with praise for the Prophet Muhammad and thanks to God. But many other motifs in this song repertory are placed in the mouths of unmarried girls who sing to their mothers or their aunts about the men they are in love with, the men they will or will not marry, and even the men with whom they plan to run away. Far from the strict modesty of the Bedouin women's poetry examined previously, many *hawfi* songs speak openly of love and young women's attraction to handsome young men. As with women's lyrics in many cultures, these are filled with metaphorical references to plants and flowers. There are also numerous references to the Arab tradition of marrying a girl to her paternal cousin, but in these songs the singer often rejects the traditional match in favor of marrying a handsome stranger or neighbor:

I have planted jasmine in the courtyard [lit. heart] of our house
Its roots are of ginger and its branches of verdigris
Mother, O mother, is anything more powerful than love between neighbors?
Desire is in my eyes and in my heart there burns a fire! (233)

I met a handsome youth who was climbing to the citadel
In his hand a silk handkerchief, to wipe away his tears.
I said to him, "O handsome youth, what has caused these tears?"
He replied, "O mistress, what a sad Friday I have had!
Saturday is for the Jews, and Sunday for the Christians,
And Friday is for girls to gather, but none have come to me!" (245)

I was sitting in the garden, hiding behind the almond tree
And there passed by me a handsome youth holding a blue staff
His cap was cocked to one side and his hair was gleaming.
For him I would abandon my children, for him I'd be divorced,
For him I would destroy the town and turn it into a caravanserai (246)

My daughter is on the swing, her hair is hanging loose
Go tell her paternal cousin to crack open [the lock] on his chest;
Have him place one hundred upon one hundred [pieces of gold]
    and yet one hundred more, in her silk scarf
Have him place a hundred and [supply] a servant to raise the children (253)
My aunt, O my aunt, keep your son in your house

While I was watering the basil, he was tossing lemons at me.
Your son I will not marry, even if he covers me in riches
I will marry a handsome youth whose figure pleases me! (285)

But within the *hawfi* repertory are also traces of the social pressures and constraints unmarried women face in traditional communities—not all the songs are daydreams of marrying handsome strangers. Young women live with the constant threat that their reputations will be ruined by gossip and slander, or that the young men they care for will betray them:

O my mother, O mistress, I will certainly die betrayed
The people of our quarter are all in league against me
When I go out they discuss me like a bull [for sale]
When I return they cry out, "[Come here] you who want your part!"
O my mother, O mistress, my flesh is too dear for envious dogs [such
    as these] (328)

With my tears I have washed a room and a chamber
With my tears I have washed a student's cloak
You will not have to dig me a grave, nor make me a coffin
I will cast you to the bottom of the sea, there your bones for fish will be (235)

I cut the meat with my own hands and then I added the spices
I've heard the slander with my own ears and I know who said it
O you who spread such ugly gossip, what good can it do you?
The lion keeps his place in the jungle and lets the dogs bark (236)

I have written a message, O dove, fly off and carry it
As far as the tomb of the Prophet, ply your wings towards him
Whoever has a tender heart will read what it contains
And whoever has a heart of stone will tear it up and throw it away (237)

Hawfi poetry from the city of Tlemcen provides a glimpse into the real-life desires and fears of girls and women, albeit couched in traditional poetic imagery. Many of these songs are reminiscent of women's poetry from various regions of the Mediterranean, and even of certain English ballads. Rather than a discourse of veiled allusions and metaphoric images, the all-female performance context of the *hawfi* seems to create a space, within a game-like activity, for giving voice to feelings and desires that might be deemed unacceptable and even scandalous by the dominant male society.

Oral Epic Poetry: The Epic of the Banī Hilāl. Arab culture possesses a particularly rich tradition of epic poetry; there is historical documentation for more than a dozen distinct epic poems, each of prodigious length and complexity. Arabs do not seem to have composed epic poems in pre-Islamic times, however, and written references to these massive poetic narratives first begin to appear in historical sources around the eleventh century; the earliest surviving written texts of the poems date to two or more centuries later. M. C. Lyons's three-volume work *The Arabian Epic* (1995) provides not only a guide to the history of these different epic poems, but also detailed summaries of the plots, which makes it an indispensable tool for both the study of Arabic epic traditions and of epic traditions in cross-cultural perspective. Selections from several of these epics have appeared in translation including the Epic of the Black Knight 'Antar ibn Shaddād (Hamilton 1820; Richmond 1978), the Epic of the Pre-Islamic Hero Sayf ibn Dhī Yazan (Jayyusi 1996), and the Epic of the King of Egypt al-Zāhir Baybars (Bohas 1985–98). All of these are translations of written versions of the epics rather than from live performances for the simple reason that only one of the Arabic epics has survived in oral transmission and performance until the present: the Epic of the Banī (or Banū) Hilāl Bedouin Tribe *(Sīrat Banī Hilāl)*. Fortunately this last surviving oral epic has been studied by a number of different scholars from many different angles, focusing, for example, on the social context of the epic, the process of transmission, variations in performance, regional differences, audience reactions and interpretations, musical dimensions of the performance, and so forth (see Connelly 1986; Reynolds 1989, 1995, 2006b; Saada 1985; Slyomovics 1987a, 1987b; 'Umrān 1999).

Until the early twentieth century the story of the Banī Hilāl was performed in a variety of forms across the breadth of the Arab world from Morocco to Iraq—as folktale or local legend recounted in prose or in poetry or in a combination of the two, in proverbs, in riddles, but most famously as epic poetry. (A folktale recounting part of the epic is available in English translation in Hurreiz 1977, 96–103.) By the second half of the twentieth century, however, the only regions where live performances of the epic poem could still be found were northern and southern Egypt. In several other regions, notably Morocco and Syria, a tradition of public storytelling still exists in which storytellers read epic poems from printed books and improvise additional material as commentaries and explanations.

The gist of the Hilālī epic's story is historically true. The Banī Hilāl Bedouin were native to the Najd region of the Arabian Peninsula, but did not participate in the early Islamic conquests of the seventh and eighth centuries. In the tenth century, for reasons that are not entirely clear from historical sources, this enormous tribe began to migrate westwards. When they reached Egypt, they nearly toppled the ruling Fatimid dynasty, but instead were forced further west into what are now Libya, Tunisia, and Algeria. By the end of the eleventh century the Banī Hilāl had conquered most of the major cities in the region, and they proceeded to rule over North Africa (minus Morocco) for just over a century. Then, however, the Almohad dynasty of Morocco began to expand eastward and in two cataclysmic battles in 1153 and 1160, the Banī Hilāl were utterly and completed destroyed. The once powerful tribal confederation splintered into small groups and disappeared from history, but the stories of their heroes, their conquests, their romances, and their deaths spread far and wide, embellished and elaborated by countless generations of storytellers and poets until ultimately being unified into one enormous coherent narrative. When this epic is performed by a master poet in Egypt, it may take from 100 to 140 hours to sing it in its entirety—a full month of nightlong performances.

Historical sources about the Banī Hilāl are few, and for the most part they recount only the conquest of various cities and regions of North Africa. The epic poem, on the other hand, spends a great deal of time recounting their history as seen from within the tribe: the births of the various heroes, their exploits in raids and battles, their wooing of maidens and eventual marriages, the various tensions and power struggles among the tribal leaders, and so on, all set within the larger narrative of the Banī Hilāl's conquest of North Africa and their eventual annihilation. Unlike some epics that recount the life and deeds of a single hero (Beowulf, Roland, and El Cid, for example), the Banī Hilāl epic has a complex cast of main heroes and in this regard is similar to the Iliad or the King Arthur cycle. In addition, the heroes of the Banī Hilāl epic are not perfect heroes, unidimensional, idealized figures of bravery and honor, but rather each also possesses weaknesses and faults, which lends to the overall story a psychological complexity not found in some epic poems.

The most important characters of the epic include (1) Abū Zayd, who is a strong warrior and a man of intelligence and fine words, but also a man of cunning and wiles, so that he at times behaves in ways that are questionable, ambiguous, and might even be interpreted as dishonorable; (2) Diyāb, who is a truly great warrior, indeed almost invincible, but who is also prickly and thin-skinned, and is so hyperconscious of his honor that when left to his own devices he at times makes foolhardy decisions that endanger the whole tribe (such as when he is challenged by an overwhelming enemy force but for the sake of his honor commits the tribe to battle); and (3) Hasan, who is a man of diplomacy, politics, and peacemaking—he eventually becomes the leader of the tribe—but who is neither as sharp-witted as Abū Zayd nor as powerful a warrior as Diyāb. Finally, there is al-Jāzya, who is simply the most beautiful and wisest woman in the world, but who is also a skilled warrior who sometimes rides into battle with the men. Each of these characters has their strengths and their flaws, and the epic, as well as telling the historical tale of the conquest of North Africa by the Banī Hilāl, portrays the never-ending tensions and interactions among these three versions of manhood—brains, brawn, and politics—and an idealized image of womanhood represented in the figure of al-Jāzya.

A poem of this length can only be preserved and performed by persons who have devoted years of their life to learning it as children. Most of the epic singers in Egypt are from families of professional epic poets where the one and only occupation of the males of the household has been to sing the epic of the Banī Hilāl. They usually began their apprenticeship as children at five to seven years old, and mastering the entire epic often took more than a decade. Many then spent several years as "second string" poets accompanying older, more accomplished singers to their performances and taking over for short periods when their master poet took a break. The arrival of obligatory public schooling, however, while certainly good for Egyptian society as a whole, has decimated the ranks of the epic singers, for nowadays their children attend school rather than learn the epic poem sung by their fathers and grandfathers.

The epic singers do not memorize a text, however, and then sing it over and over again verbatim. Rather they learn the complex narrative in infinite detail and at the same time learn a process that has been dubbed "composition in performance" (see Lord 1960). This process allows the poets to perform the episodes of the epic with greater or lesser detail depending upon how enthusiastically the audience responds to the performance. If the audience is enjoying a battle scene, the poet will expand it with descriptions of the horses, the harness, the swords, and a blow-by-blow account of each contest. If the audience seems bored with the battle scene, however, he may wrap that up quickly and move on to a scene that is more romantic, or humorous, or religious.

The following selected passages are drawn from a performance by Shaykh Tāhā Abū Zayd recorded in the village of al-Bakātūsh in June 1987. The poet's name, Tāhā, is also one of the poetic epithets of the Prophet Muhammad, so it occurs in the text at several points with that meaning, and his "second name" (i.e., the name of his father) is Abū Zayd, the name of one of the central heroes of the epic. Taking the names of heroes from the epic is but one of many ways in which the poets link themselves directly to the poem they sing. This episode is "The Birth of Abū Zayd," which is considered in some regions the beginning of the epic, although in others there are episodes about the history and genealogy of the tribe that come first. The scene opens with the lament of Rizq the Valiant, son of Nāyil, wishing for a son to carry on his family name. He has previously married a series of wives, but they have borne him only daughters. To give a sense of the traditional interaction between poet and audience members, comments from the listeners have been included in brackets. Note that each time a character in the epic begins to speak there is a strict sequence followed for moving from the narrative voice to the quoted speech that includes a formulaic reference to the Prophet Muhammad, then a phrase that tells us who is speaking, and finally a reference to their emotional state. During the sections of sung poetry, the poet

Shaykh Tāhā Abū Zayd singing epic poetry. Photo credit: Dwight Reynolds.

accompanied himself on the Egyptian two-string spike fiddle *(rabāb)*, the most common instrument for epic singing (see the section on Musical Instruments under Musical Arts).

[Spoken]

After praise for the Prophet of the tribe of 'Adnān, and we do not gather but that we wish God's blessings upon him, for the Prophet was the most saintly of the saintly, and the seal of God's Messengers, and on the Day of Resurrection he shall smile on the faces of all who wish God's blessings upon him!

The composer of these words tells of Arabs known as the Banī Hilāl Arabs. Their Sultan at that time and that era was King Sarhān and their [foremost] warrior was Rizq the Valiant, son of Nāyil, for every age has its nation and its men. The guardian of the maidens was a stalwart youth, his name was Prince Zayyān, and the protector of the Zaghāba clan was the courageous Ghānim, a warrior among warriors.

Now Rizq had married of women eight maidens, but had not yet sired a male heir. He sat in his pavilion and some tykes passed by him (the tykes of the Arabs, that is, the little boys, if you'll excuse me).[1] His soul grew greatly troubled over the lack of an heir, so Rizq sat and sang of his lack of a male heir, words which you shall hear—and whosoever adores the beauty of the Prophet increases his wishes for God's blessings upon him:

[All: May God bless and preserve him!]

[Music]

[Sung]

I am the servant of all who adore the beauty of Muhammad,

[All: May God bless and preserve him!]

Tāhā [Muhammad] for whom every pilgrim yearns.

Listen now to what Rizq the Valiant, son of Nāyil, sang,
  While tears from the orb of his eye did flow:

"Ah! Ah! The World and Fate and Destiny!
  All I have seen with my eyes shall disappear!

I do not praise among the days one which pleases me,
  But that its successor comes along, stingy and mean.

O Fate, make peace with me, 'tis enough what you've done to me,
  I cast my weapons at thee, but my excuse is clear.

My wealth is great, O men, but [I am] without an heir;

[Voice: Allāh!]

Wealth without an heir after a lifetime disappears.

I look out and catch sight of Sarhān when he rides,
  His sons ride [with him], princes and prosperous.

---

1. The poet first uses an archaic term *ghilmān* (tykes) and then glosses the word for his audience with the more colloquial *al-'ayyāl al-sughayyara* (young boys). According to village etiquette, when a man addresses other adult men, he excuses himself at the mention of children, women, certain animals, and objects of daily life (such as shoes) that are considered private, unclean, or are associated with common insults.

I look out and catch sight of Zayyān when he rides,
   His sons ride [with him] and fill the open spaces.

I look out—Ah!—and catch sight of Ghānim when he rides,
   And his sons ride [with him] and are princes, so prosperous.

But I am the last of my line, my spirit is broken,
   I have spent my life and not seen a son, prosperous.

I have taken of women, eight maidens,
   And eleven daughters followed, princesses true!

This bearing of womenfolk—Ah!—has broken my spirit,
   I weep and the tears of my eyes on my cheek do flow."

[*Plot summary:* Eventually is it suggested that Rizq ask for the hand of the daughter of Qirda, the Sharīf (i.e., ruler) of Mecca, whose name is Khadra (lit. green, verdant, fertile). So Rizq leads the entire tribe to Mecca to ask for Khadra's hand. Following is a speech made by the religious judge, or Qāḍī, of the Banī Hilāl tribe, Fāyid, to the ruler of Mecca during the negotiations.]

[Spoken]

Qirda said to them, "Welcome to you, O Arabs of Hilāl, you have honored us and graced us in our land and our country." Then he moved them to his own area [and settled them] in tents of honor and hospitality. And the Qāḍī, came forth, Fāyid, who was the father of Badīr. And [Sarhān] said to him, "Speak, Qāḍī, and speak of the brideprice for the maiden." [Poet's aside to audience: "The brideprice, that is, the dowry"] See now what the Qāḍī, will say—and whosoever adores the beauty of the Prophet wishes God's blessings upon him:

[All: May God bless and preserve him!]

[Music]

[Sung]

I am the servant of all who adore the beauty of Muhammad,
   Tāhā, who requested [the power of] intercession and obtained it.[2]

---

2. In Islamic tradition, the Prophet Muhammad, on his "Night Journey" *(isrā')* to Jerusalem and his Ascension *(mi'rāj)* up through the Seven Heavens, asked and received the right to intercede with God on behalf of the nascent Islamic community. His first act of intercession was to have the number of daily prayers that God wished to require of all Muslims reduced from 50 to 5.

Listen now to what the Qāḍī, Fāyid said and what he sang!
"[My eye] aches and sleep frequents it not in this state.[3]

It goes to sleep with [good] intentions but awakes filled with caution,
As if the hooks of life were in [sleep's] domain.

If my burdens lean, with my own hand I set them straight,
But if the world leans, only God can set it straight.

Happy is the eye which sleeps the whole night through,

[Shaykh Ṭāhā: Ah yes, by God!]

It passes the night in comfort, no blame is upon it.

But my eye is pained, it keeps vigil the whole night through,
It passes the night telling me of all that has befallen it.

Listen to my words, O Qirda, and understand,
These are the words of princes, not [mere] children.

We wish from you a maiden, high-born,
Of noble ancestry from both grandfathers, paternal and maternal uncles [too].

We shall give her a dowry, a dowry [worthy] of nobles, O Hero,
We shall dress her in the finest and purest of silks.

Perhaps she'll bear a son, a prince awe-inspiring,
He shall emerge from the vessel whose waters are pure [the womb].

If he comes and speaks a word in the mosque the men will say,
'That is the son of Rizq who came to us and said it.'

We'll not take the fair maid for the fairness of her cheek,
If the fair one goes astray her menfolk are blamed.

[Voice: True!]

We'll not take the dark maid for the greatness of her wealth,
If your wealth decreases she'll blame you for her loss.

[Laughter]

---

3. The eye in Arabic tradition is the locus and symbol of deep-felt emotions similar to Western images of the heart and soul.

We'll not take the foolish maid or the daughter of a miser,
    Flustered on the feast-day, we won't join families with her.

We'll not take one who scrapes [lit. licks] the pot with her hand,

                [Laughter]

If a few days of want come she'll vie with her own children [for the food]!

                [Laughter]

We shall only take the high-born princess,

            [Voice: Allāh!]

Who honors the guest of God, yes, when he comes to her.[4]

She who receives the guest of God with welcome and greetings,
    So that her man may sit honored among men.

We shall give you, O Qirda, a hundred horses, and a hundred sheep,
    And a hundred concubines, and a hundred camels.

And a hundred slaves, O Kindest of the Arabs,
    And a hundred fair slave girls to serve their men.

And on top of all this and that, one thousand [pieces] of gold,
    For wealth is useful and the years are long.

This is our dowry, O Paternal uncle, in our country,
    We are Arabs, the poorest of its men.

             [Laughter]

Have pity on us—Ah!—O Son of Hāshim [Qirda],

           [Voice: Allāh!]

Nobles are not thanked except for their deeds."

This one [Qirda] said,
    "Write such and such, O Qāḍī, of the Arabs,
    From me [I give] its equal for the Lady Khadra.

---

4. The "guest of God" *(dayf Allāh)* is a central concept in Arab hospitality and refers to the idea of treating every guest as if they were sent from God and also to the idea that all sustenance and wealth is given by God.

Perhaps Fate will change towards her,
   And if she sets aside her wealth,

[Voice: Allāh!]

Even if Fate and Destiny and Time change towards her,
   She need not rely even on the least of her menfolk."

[Laughter]

The Courageous One signed her wedding contract—Wish God's blessings on the
   Prophet!

[All: May God bless and preserve him!]

They slaughtered young camels and they invited all her men.

[*Plot summary:* The wedding takes place and Khadra goes to live with the Banī
Hilāl tribe, but for seven years she does not bear a child. People begin to talk and
many urge Rizq to divorce her and marry another who will bear him a son. Rizq
and Khadra quarrel over the lack of a child. She leaves their tent in tears, but then
she meets Shamma, the wife of Sarhān, who also has not yet given birth to a son,
and the two of them, along with a servant woman named Saʿīda wander out into
the desert along the edge of the sea.]

It was Friday morning—Wish God's Blessings on the Prophet!

[All: May God bless and preserve him!]

God hears the prayers of the oppressed.

She said to Khadra:
"Let us go, you and I, to the sea in the wilderness,
   Let us go calm our blood in its emptiness.

When you look at the salten [sea] you shall encounter wonders,
   You shall encounter wonders, by the will of God."

They set out, the two of them with her slave, Saʿīda,
   The wife of Najjāh [one of the tribe's slaves], oh so beautiful.

Suddenly a white bird . . .

[Voice: Yes!]

                    . . . from the distance came to them,
   It was a white bird, beautiful to behold.

It landed and did not take flight again, that bird in the wasteland,
    All the other birds flocked round him.

Said Shamma, "O Lord, the One, the Everlasting,

[Voice: Allāh!]

Glory be to God, there is no god but He!

Grant unto me a son, like unto this bird,
    May he be handsome and kind[5] and the Arabs obey his [every word]."

Her request was completed, O Nobles, and the bird rose up,
    The bird took flight and climbed to the heights.

Suddenly a dark bird from the distance came to them,

[Laughter—Voice: This is Abū Zayd!]

A dark bird . . .

[Voice: Yes!]

. . . frightful to behold!

[Voice: Heavens!]

He beat his wings at the other birds,
    And each one he struck did not [live to] smell his supper!

Said Khadra . . .

[Voice: Yes!]

. . . "O how beautiful you are, O bird, and how beautiful your darkness!

[Voice: Allāh!]

Like the palm-date when it ripens to perfection.

O Lord, O All-Merciful, O One, O Everlasting,

[Voice: May God be generous to you!]

---

5. The term *hasan* in Arabic denotes both physical beauty and kindness of personality.

[Shaykh Tāhā: May God reward you!]

Glory be to God, Veiled in His Heaven!

[Audience member places cigarettes in front of Poet]

[Shaykh Tāhā: May you always have plenty!
May you always have plenty, we wish you!]

Grant unto me a son, like unto this bird,
  And may each one he strikes with his sword not [live to] smell his supper!"

[Voice: My heavens!]

[Voice shouting: That's Abū Zayd!]

Thus did the two of them make their requests [from God].

Then Saʿīda [the slave] said:
"O Lord, grant unto me a son as well, like unto my mistresses.
  He who addresses his supplication to God, God fulfills it!"

[*Plot summary:* Each child is born according to his mother's prayers to God. Shamma's son is born handsome (lit. *hasan*) and is named Hasan, and Khadra's son is born jet black, like the bird she wished upon. Soon the tribe is abuzz with whisperings of adultery—how can a black child be born to white parents? At first Rizq believes her but then, tragically, he weakens before the ever more malicious gossip, repudiates his wife, and casts her and their infant son out into the desert. God sends them a guide in the form of a Sufi mystic, a dervish, who leads them to the camps of the greatest rivals of the Banī Hilāl, the Zahlān tribe. There they are welcomed and the leader of the Zahlān raises the boy as if he were his own son. As an infant he is named Barakāt (lit. blessings), but as he grows up he becomes the strongest warrior of the tribe and is renamed Salāma (lit. peace or safety) for his prowess on the battlefield assures the tribe's safety. Eventually, however, the two tribes end up in battle against each other, and each tribe sends in its greatest hero—father and son face each in battle unknowingly, but God and Fate intervene to keep them from killing each other. Only poor Khadra, driven nearly insane by this battle between her husband and his child, understands what it going on and what tragedy could result.]

[Spoken]

Rizq drew out his sword and he was the Valiant of the Banī Hilāl Arabs and their warriors. And as soon as he approached Salāma the two of them both charged. The Raven of

Separation[6] cawed directly over their heads and the Lady Khadra looked out over the two sides and she felt as if her mind had lost its balance. Look at what Khadra will say—and he who loves the beauty of the Prophet wishes God's blessings upon him:

[All: May God bless and preserve him!]

[Music]

[Sung]

O Listeners to this speech, wish God's blessings upon the Prophet!

[All: May God bless and preserve him!]

Tāhā, the pilgrims peregrinated and came [to him].

Said Khadra, "Ah! from Fate and Destiny!
O woe is he whose forces Destiny has destroyed!

O woe is he whose enemies are from among his own relatives!
A wound which festers, for which he finds no cure.

The hard-palmed [stingy] one will never know generosity,
The evil one, all his life, his lord [God] does not help him.

If he has walked two days on an unjust path,
The treacheries of Destiny must eventually overtake him.

O Lord, O All-merciful, the One, the Everlasting,
Glory to God, there is no god but He.

O Lord, O All-merciful, I have no lord save Thee,
O Lord, All-powerful, may the will of God [be done].

O Lord grant victory, grant victory to the hero,
O Lord protect [him], O Lord protect [him].

O Lord protect the father from his son,

[Voice: God is great!]

Lest they say that Khadra from adultery begot him.

[Voice: God is great!]

---

6. The raven is an omen of death or lifelong separation in Arabic folklore.

[Voice: There is no god but God!]

O Lord protect the father from his son,
  Lest they say that Khadra from slaves begot him.

O Lord protect [him], Glory to God,
  Glory to God, veiled in His heaven!

O Creator of creation and Reckoner of their numbers,
  And if I have said something, may it be the will of God."

Salāma and his father, O Nobles, they clashed together,
  The singing [swords] sang and their minds from them strayed.

They unsheathed their sword-tips, the lances did not waver,
  None can repulse the boy except for his father.

[Voice: Heavens!]

Ten nights the battle [continued] between them,
The Son of [Khadra] Sharīfa in the encounter was fierce.

He attacks his father in a terrifying attack,
  [But] by Fate his hand was diverted!

Then Rizq attacked his son,
  [But] by Fate his hand was turned aside.

[Voice: God is great!]

Then [his son] said to him, "O Uncle Rizq, you are blessed,
  Your path is blessed, O how beautiful!

You are blessed, so let's go home,
  A truce, a truce, and [later] to the field we shall return."

Salāma went home, he complains, O Nobles, and he weeps,
  He complains and he weeps to his mother tears like hot embers.

"The likes of my Uncle Rizq the warriors have never seen,
  A staunch hero, the Arabs fear his encounter.

[Voice: Allāh!]

Perhaps, O Mother, death has drawn nigh,
  At the hand of my Uncle Rizq, O how dreadful."

[Voice: Heavens!]

[*Plot summary:* Salāma refers to Rizq as his "uncle" only as a term of respect, for he does not yet know that he is related to this man. After 10 days of battle, it is Shīha, Rizq's daughter (and thus Salāma's half-sister), who begins to suspect the truth. She waits at the edge of the battlefield and quizzes Salāma about his father and his tribe, and then tells him to go demand that his mother tell him the truth. When pressed, Khadra recounts to him the story of his birth, the accusations of adultery, and their expulsion from the Banī Hilāl tribe. He then confronts his father on the field and Rizq, recognizing his son at last, begs his son's forgiveness and that of Khadra, and all are finally reconciled. Having surpassed all the Arabs in battle, Salāma is renamed Abū Zayd (lit. father of superiority), the name he bears for the remainder of his life.]

The epic of the Banī Hilāl goes on to tell of the birth and youth of each of the main heroes. When they are still young men, however, tragedy strikes. They go off to Mecca to fight off an enemy force that is attacking the Holy City, but while they are gone the 'Uqayla Bedouin tribe treacherously attacks the Banī Hilāl at night. Since only the old men are in the camp, and they have been caught by surprise, all but one are slaughtered during the attack. The young heroes return from Mecca victorious, only to discover their fathers have been killed during their absence, and that they are now responsible for the fate of the tribe. Eventually they seek revenge and successfully establish themselves among the tribes of the Najd region. A number of episodes recount the youthful adventures of the individual heroes as they go about doing acts of gallantry, often falling in love with beautiful maidens in the process, and then returning with their newly won brides to the tribe. At one point, however, there is a horrendous drought that lasts seven years during which "not a drop of rain or dew did fall." The tribe is desperate because all of their livestock are dying, so they decide to send out a reconnaissance mission in search of a new homeland and pasturelands for the tribe. The reconnaissance group consists of the hero Abū Zayd (whose birth was recounted in the preceding verses) and his three nephews. They wander the world seeking pasturelands for the tribe—they travel through Syria, Iraq, Jerusalem, Ethiopia, Cyprus, and many other regions but eventually find their way to "Tunis the Verdant," which they decide would make the perfect homeland for the tribe. Before they can return with this news to the Banī Hilāl, however, the three nephews are imprisoned (or, in some regional variants, one is imprisoned, one dies of a snake bite, and one is killed). Abū Zayd returns alone to the tribe and the tribe prepares to leave its homeland, now not only in search of pasturelands for their livestock but also to rescue their three young men.

This part of the epic is known as the "Westward Journey" (Ar. *taghrība*). The tribe follows an equally circuitous route back to Tunis, encountering obstacles and adventures at every stage of their journey. When they finally arrive in Tunis they rescue the surviving nephew(s) from prison and prepare to conquer Tunisia. The ruler of Tunis, al-Zanātī Khalīfa, knows that he will die in the encounter but rides into battle anyway to meet his fate. The epic, curiously enough, does not end with the battles against the Moroccans that history books recount but rather with internecine battles among the fractious clans of the Banī Hilāl. Thus the epic ends with what is perhaps an even more tragic scene, the once mighty tribe destroying itself in a tribal civil war.

Epic poetry is a very special form of poetry, for it can only be performed by a small number of highly skilled individuals, and then only if they have spent years practicing and mastering the material and the poetic form. It is also unique in its almost encyclopedic portrayal of a culture (at least in an idealized form), for through an epic poem we observe daily behaviors, customs and traditions, super-stitions and folk remedies, ways of eating and dressing, stereotypes about ethnic groups, religious groups, social classes, genders, and many other aspects of folk culture. What makes the epic of the Banī Hilāl particularly rich is that various images (such as manhood and womanhood) are presented in a constant state of tension, at times one version of the hero (or heroine) wins and at times another. Richer still are the audience discussions, during tea breaks and after performances, about the complex twists of the story they have heard and their varying judg-ments and interpretations of those events. Reynolds (1995) has argued that these live epic performances and the resulting discussions between the poets and their audiences constitute an ongoing dialogue among listeners, poets, and the epic heroes themselves about critical social issues such as religion, ethnicity, gender, morality, honor, and shame, and that it is this ongoing conversation that has kept the Banī Hilāl epic such a rich and vibrant tradition for so many centuries.

Popular Ballads of Egypt: Tales of Honor, Murder, Love, and Scandal. On the boundary between folk and popular, and between oral and written traditions, are the lengthy ballads that recount stories of star-crossed lovers, crime and punish-ment, and catastrophic events (religious ballads will be dealt with separately in this chapter). In Egypt many of these ballads circulate for decades, and the tales they tell are often familiar to listeners of all classes. Scholars believe, however, that many of these traditional song tales were originally composed by literate authors who then sold their texts to professional singers (many of whom, particularly in the past, would have been illiterate) to be performed at saints' festivals, harvest celebrations, weddings, and other occasions. Once they entered oral performance, however, they were imitated by other singers and became well known among rural and lower-class urban populations alike. Pierre Cachia (1989) has gathered some of the best-known examples into a collection that provides not only a superb historical introduction to the genre but full translations and explanatory notes as well. Perhaps the single most famous of these songs in Egypt is the ill-fated love story of "Hasan and Na'eema." The ballad opens with the historical setting:

> O Master of the [*rabāb*]-cord [Poet], give us your attention
> As we tell of an event that took place in 'forty-nine
> At the start of [the month of] Rajab, which ends with the new moon
>   of [the month of] Sha'bān,
> Concerning a lad called Hasan the singer,
> In whose father's name forty-five acres were registered, his father
>   being headman of [the village of] Bahnasa l-Gharra . . .

Despite the respectability of his family, their land-holdings, and his father's position as a shaykh in the village, Hasan becomes a singer (a somewhat disreputable occupation) and travels up and down the Nile valley performing. One evening Na'eema hears him sing and the two fall instantly in love:

> There is nothing tougher than love that forms between two at first sight
> The fair one went out and brightened the whole universe
> The village girls went down to fill their water-jars
> They walked shaking their buttocks and everything else—how sweet
>   their upper parts!
> As she walked Na'eema said: "Hasan,
> Take two of your friends and go to my father, Abu Huneyn, at his home
> My father is a good man and will not shame a guest over a lawful request . . ."

But Na'eema is wrong and her father rudely rejects Hasan's request for her hand, thinking him merely an itinerant singer:

> In anger the lad went out of the village
> He met Na'eema swaying like a young camel.
> "What news, O singer? When is my nuptial henna-staining due?
>   tonight or tomorrow?"
> He answered, "Your father does not consent, Na'eema,
> Maiden, since yesterday my woes have multiplied! . . ."

She urges him not to give up and together they arrange for Na'eema to run away from her father and live with Hasan's mother while they prepare for their marriage. Hasan spends the days in the local café and the nights in a guesthouse so that there should be no reproach or gossip. But after 15 days her father finds her and takes her back to their village against her will:

> Abu Huneyn is taking her home in bitterness
> As soon as he brought her back to his village
> He was picked on by his kinsfolk and dull-witted people:
> "So you've brought us back Na'eema after she has stayed away fifteen days,
> And been ruined by the singer in this exploit of his?"
> He said: "I have brought you Na'eema blameless in her honor and in duty.

Some man he is, and none among us is his peer.
Who in the village is man enough to work me a plot against him?"
He reached agreement with Sālih and Mahmūd, those friends of his.
They said: "We are the ones to plot his end for you."
He agreed to pay them thirty Egyptian pounds,
Giving them ten and holding back the twenty.
They took a car from the garage,
Reached a speed of eighty,
And got down in Bahnasa l-Gharra . . .

The two henchmen meet Hasan and tell him that Naʿeema's father has reconsidered and that their whole village is waiting to celebrate the engagement. Hasan joyfully tells his friends and his mother that he is off to be betrothed and follows the men to his beloved's village. There a fake celebration has been arranged with food and drink. But then the men seize Hasan and confront him:

[T]hey said, "Hasan, the end of your lifespan is due."
Naʿeema stepped in saying, "My father gave you thirty,
Here is a full count of a hundred."
But they said: "Naʿeema, if he is such a lover he should have loved in his own
    village!"
[The Poet here interjects the moral of the story]
O You who would love, love on your home ground
And you shall live happy and gratified;
Others too will rejoice at what you have been given.
But if, out of stupidity, you love an outsider,
You shall die a stranger, and men shall see you ever weighted down!..."

The men kill Hasan by cutting off his head, which Naʿeema manages to scoop up and then run off and hide. His corpse is thrown into the Nile and floats to his natal village, where his family soon realizes that Hasan has been murdered. A police detective disguises himself as a woman and goes to Naʿeema's village, finds her, and listens to her tale. Her male family members are arrested and taken to court. She begs the judge not to hand out the sentence until he has seen how handsome Hasan was, and she brings out the head, which she has kept washed and scented, shows it to the court, and then collapses:

The judge said: "Stand up, Naʿeema, I shall sentence them for your sake,
And my judgment shall cause distress."
He announced: "The Court passes these sentences:
On Salih—five times five, a whole twenty-five years.
On Mahmud—five times five, a whole twenty-five years.
On her brother—three times five, fifteen years hard labor."
He said to her: "Now then, whose ward will you be, Naʿeema?"
"I shall be the ward of Hasan's father.

If only the food that was served to [my father] had had a serpent squirt in it!"
"What of your mother, Na'eema?"
She said: "The spread of dissension all started with my mother.
But she must be honored in that she bore me for nine months,
    and for two years she tended me, carrying me on her hip.
She is to be honored for having reared me."
So Ali d-Daramalli [the detective] was made an officer in the Department of
    Investigations,
And Na'eema went home with Hasan's father.

(Adapted from Cachia 1989, 323–50)

The murder of Hasan the singer is riddled with complex issues of class and honor. Although he is a singer, we are told he is in fact from a good family, the son of a powerful father, and the heir to large landholdings. Nevertheless, his abduction of the unmarried girl, even with her consent, is an act that no traditional family could accept. There is no surprise among Egyptian listeners that her father should have plotted an honor killing (in fact, it is almost more surprising that she herself was not killed by her father and brothers). In the mid-twentieth century, many Egyptian villagers were still unfamiliar with the British-style court system and laws that had been adopted in the wake of the British occupation of Egypt in 1882. Thus the denouement of the story involves not only the tragic story of the main protagonists, but also the tension between traditional ideas of honor, the imposed British court system, and, of course, the extraordinary power of love. On one hand Na'eema goes to live with Hasan's father in a final act of loyalty to his memory, but on the other, the performing poet sends his own message to his listeners in the passage (cited previously) where he advises his listeners to love close to home and not to fall in love with strangers. Yet in Egypt, as in many other cultures, part of the tremendous allure and excitement of such tales of romance is precisely because they contain accounts of such openly transgressive behavior.

Another very well-known ballad recounts the incident at Danshaway, where British troops fired upon Egyptian peasants on June 13, 1906 (see Cachia 1989). A fight broke out between some British soldiers who were out in the countryside shooting doves and local villagers who considered the doves to be the property of the village. There were injured parties on both sides, but one British soldier eventually died, in part due to sunstroke. The court sentenced 4 of the village men to death by hanging, 4 more to life in prison, and 17 more to lesser penalties. The hangings and floggings were carried out in public and the incident rocked the country and became a *cause célèbre* in the Egyptian and international press. Eventually, the remaining men were pardoned. Many Egyptians know this event primarily from the many versions of the ballad that are sung even today. In many ways these narrative ballads of famous murders, court cases, kidnappings, and love affairs functioned like an oral version of the tabloid press for literate audiences.

Muslim and Christian Religious Ballads of Egypt. Religious narrative ballads sung among Coptic Christians and Muslims constitute a closely related genre of folk and popular poetry in Egypt. In form and structure they are almost indistinguishable from the ballads examined in the preceding section, which deal with current and historical events. The religious ballads, however, provide a rich entrée into the folk religious worldviews of these closely interrelated communities of Muslims and Coptic Christians. In many ways the folk practices of these two groups are far more similar to each other than they are to their own official theologies and dogmas. Folk (or popular) Christianity and Islam, for example, both embrace the working of miracles, the recognition of holy persons (saints) believed to have special powers, the efficacy of asking holy figures for intercession with God, the merit of doing pilgrimages or visitations (Ar. *ziyāra*) to the tomb or shrine of a holy person, the merit of attending a saint's festival (Colloq. Ar. *mūlid,* Class. Ar. *mawlid*), and a wide variety of folk cures and medical treatments that are based in religious practices. All of these elements, and others as well, are looked askance at, if not denounced outright, by the more formal or official institutions of each community (for more details, see Customs and Traditions).

Although the folk versions of Muslim and Christian stories may not be fully approved of officially, they offer important insights into Arab culture, for, as Abdel-Malek writes in *Muhammad in the Modern Egyptian Popular Ballad* (1995): "Our search for the meaning of Muhammad for present-day Muslims will remain partial and fragmented if no serious attempt is made to understand the kind of popular material produced and propagated by ordinary Muslim folk" (51). The following are scenes from the life of the Prophet Muhammad as portrayed in the folk ballads of Egypt.

One of the primary images in the folk version of Muhammad's life is the mystical concept of a primeval "Muhammadan light" or the "light of Muhammad" that was passed or transmitted through the Prophets and culminated in Muhammad himself:

> Adam is the father of all mankind but the Prophet existed before him
> In the garden of eternity, Adam saw the light of the Prophet
> He lived in the House of Bliss; living gratified him
> He obeyed Satan once, and became full of remorse
> When he sought the Prophet's help, the Lord then forgave him

(Abdel-Malek, 52)

When Muhammad was born his mother felt no labor pains, he was born fully circumcised, and his eyes were so beautiful it was as if they were painted with kohl (a type of dark eyeliner worn in the Middle East). When he was passed to his wet nurse, he would only suckle from one breast so that his "milk brother" would always have an equal share. Muhammad grows up a blameless youth and eventually begins to preach the new revelation of Islam. When the Meccans plot against him and he is forced to flee with his companion (later the first caliph) Abū Bakr, the two of them spend a night in a cave. While the Prophet sleeps exhausted with his head on Abū Bakr's lap, a serpent emerges from a hole. Abū Bakr blocks the hole with his heel so as not to disturb the Prophet, and is bitten by the snake. He remains silent and does not move, but the Prophet is awoken by his tears which fall on the Prophet's face. He immediately tends to his companion:

> [The Prophet] said: "O Abū Bakr, may no harm afflict you
> My heart and my Lord are satisfied with you
> I have a remedy—may our Lord cure you
> Do not fear, no harm shall afflict you."
> The Prophet applied his saliva [as a balm] to the wound
> The pain subsided because of his aromatic saliva
> Exalted is the One who bestowed (this power) on the chosen Prophet! (63)

The Prophet then turned angrily to the serpent, but the serpent explains that he meant no harm and was only coming out of his hole to discover the source of the powerful light that had suddenly appeared in the cave, and begs the Prophet's forgiveness. The Prophet forgives the serpent and promises it a place in paradise.

Another tale that is commonly sung in ballad form is "The Prophet and the Gazelle." A mother gazelle leaves her young and goes out to forage for food for them, but she is snared by a Jew or, in some versions, a Bedouin. She begs to be released long enough to go feed her young and then return, but the hunter will not relent. The Prophet happens to be passing by, hears her pleas, and offers himself as a hostage in her place:

> The Prophet said: "O Jew
> Release her from her fetters
> Let her go and come back,
> Take me hostage in her place" (70)

When she reaches her young and explains the situation, however, they refuse her milk, saying they cannot feed from her while the Prophet is prisoner in her stead. They tell her that God will provide for them and that she must return immediately to free the Prophet.

> The young gazelles said: "Why did you, mother,
> Leave our Prophet a hostage?
> Go back! Our sustenance is in God's hands,
> He provides even for the worms inside the rocks" (70)

When the gazelle returns as promised to the hunter, he is awed by her act of sacrifice, releases both the Prophet and the gazelle, and immediately converts to Islam. In some versions the gazelle converts to Islam as well and departs intoning that there is no god but God and that Muhammad is His messenger.

Another ballad tells of the construction of the first pulpit *(minbar)* in the first mosque. Previously Muhammad had preached his sermons simply leaning against a palm trunk, but as the number of the converts to Islam grew, his followers construct a pulpit from which he can preach. The first time he climbs up the pulpit and begins to speak, however, there is heard a grievous weeping and wailing:

> For the first sermon, the Beautiful One [Muhammad] climbed
> The pulpit to deliver the sermon to the congregation
> They heard loud crying and sobbing
> People looked toward the source of the noise
> Astounded were they when they saw what it was
> It was the tree trunk which was crying, "O people, [I weep]
> Because of being separated from the Prophet Muhammad!"
> The tree trunk was crying and sobbing
> Like a person who was grief-shaken,
> If a stone should happen to hear it, it would melt (with grief)! (85)

The Prophet goes to the palm tree trunk and comforts it. He then asks the trunk if it would rather be replanted and live again as a tree or be buried and then be resurrected on the Day of Judgment as a palm tree in heaven. It chooses the latter and is buried with full funeral rites.

Many of these miracle tales from the life of Muhammad appear very early in the written record, but their performance as narrative ballads is a more recent phenomenon. Again, as with most of the Arabic ballad traditions, there has almost certainly been an interaction between literate poets and illiterate folk performers. Images and verses move easily back and forth from the oral to popular written versions and back again, so that the boundary between the folk and the popular becomes almost impossible to define.

Among Coptic Christians are similar ballads about saints and about the Virgin Mary. Following is the beginning of a lengthy poem in rhymed quatrains that tells of Mary's pregnancy, her conversation with Joseph, the dance of Salome, the birth of Jesus, and the arrival of the Magi:

I start by invoking God	in light enwrapped
I praise the Virgin	in words embellished
I beg of her	to calm my fears
The day we stand	Before the Judge.
My verse sets out	to praise the Virgin
When the angel came	with his good tidings,

He spoke his greeting / and gave her the succour
Of the High One's immanence / in her illumined womb

The Virgin asked him / "Which is your tribe?
Tell me your race, / your stem and give me proof;
For my mother Eve / was overcome by ruse
And so was marked / by Satan's words."

Said he, "My greeting first, / O perfect in wisdom!
My Lord has sent me / to give a blessing
Listen and accept / the Word's Light
My words are true / and have no flaw."

Then spoke the Virgin / that unsoiled one,
"I have known no man / in any way at all.
How can I conceive / when I am a virgin,
And in all my life / have seen no human?"

He replied at once / in flowing words:
"Nothing do I know / of this predicament
My Master sent me / to you, O pure one.
Lady, I come, / and I rejoice."

(Cachia 1989, 171)

Less familiar to some Western audiences is the legend of St. George who battles a monster (or dragon) that lives in the Nile or, as in the version that follows, in a river in Beirut. This version is also composed in rhymed quatrains:

Every year, at the start of the month,
The devil occupied the river;
And people were sad and dejected
To have the water dammed up, brothers.

Each year he was given a virgin
Bedecked in green raiment.
This year the casting of lots determined
That the Sultan's daughter be sent down.

The King was sad, as was his household,
That his heart's delight should be sent down.
How anguished he felt within the palace
At the evil of the Serpent's tyranny.

He said, "O great ones in my city
Take my wealth and take my kingdom,

But spare me and my daughter,
Of dear ones I possess no other."

The King said, "Ah, but word has reached me
Of a hero quick to answer calls,
A man of resolution and of succour.
His name is George the Roman."

[…]

The girl went out beyond the walls,
Her spirit, good people, broken.
Her tears were falling from her eyes;
With tears of sorrow she was wailing.

The young girl let her eyes take in
The vastness of that land.
She saw a grey [horse] with burnished trappings—
Gold, of great value, in [the rider's] hands.

And on the grey there was a knight
Like a full moon, but of grave mien,
Deep-wrapped, as if submerged, in silks,
And heading straight inland.

He galloped zealously towards her,
The grey beneath him eager;
He kept his eye upon the girl,
The sword in evidence in his hand.

His lance was in his left hand,
His sword was in the other,
She saw him and was in distress;
It was for him she feared the Serpent.

[…]

At that time the dragon came
To take the girl, dear listeners,
All of you here, he opened his maw,
And grass dried up in the valleys.

Big as a town, his head looked cruel,
With fangs that stood out seven spans.

The hero said, "Open your mouth,
Heed my words, and let me tell you:
Take this gift, it will assuage you,
And in the valleys you'll have your fill."

The accursed bellowed, his blood coursing;
He stepped into the river, so it flowed over.
The hero came at him at a full gallop,
And tumbled him into the valleys.

To the girl he said, "Where is your foe?
I was the one to kill him before your eyes.
Off now to your father and mother—
Long may you live in this homeland.

Your peace is fully ensured, O bride,
And now I head for my affable Lady,
The saintly mother of the Messiah,
A succour to every Christian."

He faded from her sight, O listeners,
And ascended to the Lord of the Worlds.
In truth she looked to left and right,
But could not see him, brothers.

Straightaway she went into the valley,
Looking intently here and there;
She could not see him in that region,
And wondered, "Where is he, that Roman?"

(Adapted from Cachia 1989, 240–46)

The straightforward form of the rhymed quatrain offers ballad poets and singers a flexible vehicle for narrating in verse the core tales, legends, and stories of their religious communities. Many of these tales of miracles and wonders are not officially sanctioned (the Coptic Orthodox Church, for example, does not officially recognize the legend of the dragon), but they are for a great many believers part and parcel of their faith as they understand it. Not only are the tales an integral part of the tradition, but the versified versions that are recited or sung at different sorts of gatherings are equally part of the folk heritage of these different communities.

Although there are dozens, if not hundreds, of additional genres of Arabic folk poetry that could be cited here, they could scarcely be enumerated in a single volume, so let us instead turn from folk poetry to forms of prose folk narrative, an equally rich domain of folk culture in the Arab world.

Arabic Folk Narrative

The *Thousand and One Nights*

No other genre of Arab folklore has received as much attention from Western scholars as the folktale. Not only has the folktale been one of the foundational genres of all folklore research internationally, but prose narratives are far easier to translate than poetry. They thus offer themselves to both scholars and readers as an easier entrée into foreign folk cultures, even when they may not be viewed as the most important or most characteristic form of folklore within those cultures. The Arabic folktale in particular, however, has had a very visible presence in, and a broad impact on, Western literature and culture through the *Thousand and One Nights* (also known as the *Arabian Nights*). Ali Baba, Aladdin, Sinbad, Scheherazade, flying carpets, magic lanterns, genies in bottles…a whole vocabulary of the marvelous and the fantastic in Western culture is derived from the *Nights;* but, astonishingly enough, much of this is of European, rather than Arab, creation. To distinguish between the "fakelore" created by Europeans about Arabs on the one hand and authentically Arabic folktales and narratives on the other, we first need to understand how the *Thousand and One Nights* came to have the form and fame it has today.

The oldest historical references to the *Nights* appear in Arabic texts of the tenth century. A Baghdadi bookseller named Ibn Nadīm, for example, wrote a massive catalogue *(fihrist)* of all of the books known to him, and in this catalogue he mentions the *Nights,* telling us that it had been translated into Arabic from an earlier Persian work known as the "Thousand Stories." He also gives a short version of the famous "frame tale" of the collection, the story of Scheherazade (see the example following this section). Many scholars, however, think that the collection may actually have originated in India and been translated into Persian because several of the stories have parallels in Sanskrit texts. Sanskrit literature also had a tradition of writing tales in which animals spoke and acted as humans similar to a number of tales in the *Nights,* and the technique of the frame tale itself (creating stories within stories), for which the *Nights* is perhaps most famous, was well known in India long before it appeared in either Persian or Arabic.

Whatever the origins of the *Nights* might have been, over time Arab authors replaced most of that material with new stories of their own devising, many of which were probably drawn from oral tradition. This change in material is clear because many of the tales are set in ninth-century Baghdad and twelfth- to fourteenth-century Cairo and mention rulers, places, buildings, and other items specific to those times and places. Throughout the Middle Ages, the *Nights* circulated in Arabic as one of a number of collections of popular tales. It was not particularly famous, nor was it thought of as being notably superior to other collections of this type. In fact, the *Nights* might well have remained in partial or total obscurity had it not been for the intervention of one man, a Frenchman named Antoine Galland (1646–1715). He had been sent to work in Istanbul and eventually, over three separate visits, he lived there for a total of 15 years. For part of that time, he was employed as book dealer and antiquarian to the king of France, so he had intimate firsthand knowledge of the books available in Istanbul, Aleppo, Cairo, and elsewhere. But during those 15 years, he never saw a copy, or even heard a mention, of the *Thousand and One Nights.* He did, however, buy a copy of the *Seven Voyages of Sinbad the Sailor.*

When he finally returned to France, he applied himself assiduously to scholarly pursuits and aspired to becoming a professor of Arabic at one of the colleges in Paris, a dream that was finally fulfilled in 1709 when he was 63 years old. In the meantime, however, he produced a number of scholarly works and translations. Then one day he decided to translate *Sinbad* and, as a gift, to dedicate it to the Marquise d'O, the daughter of the former French ambassador to the Ottoman Empire, both of whom he had known in Istanbul. His reason for translating these fictional tales rather than something more serious is clear—fairy tales had suddenly become all the rage in France. While Galland was at home working on his translations, the very first fairy tales *(contes des fées)* and literary folktales, such as *Tales of My Mother Goose* by Charles Perrault, were being published with great success (Seifert 1996, Hahn 2002, Reynolds 2006a). Indeed, if fairy tales had not been *à la mode* in Paris, the *Nights* might never have been translated at all.

Galland wrote to the Marquise d'O explaining that he had translated the tales of Sinbad for her but had recently become aware that these tales were part of a much larger collection, of which he hoped to attain a copy. And here begins the mystery! How did Galland become aware of the *Nights* while living in France after never having heard of it during his 15 years living in Turkey and traveling through the Arab countries? And why did he come to think that the Sinbad tales were part of the *Nights* because, in fact, the Sinbad tales had never circulated as part of the *Nights* in Arabic? In any case, with much difficulty, he eventually was able to have an Arabic manuscript of the *Nights* sent to him from the Middle East. He translated the manuscript and published the tales, along with the Sinbad cycle, in seven volumes from 1704 to 1706. So the first change that was made to the Arabic *Nights* was that Galland added the Sinbad stories to the collection. The newly translated *Nights* was an instant and tremendous success with the French public. It was so popular that Galland's publisher wrote him many times asking for translations of more stories, but Galland had exhausted his materials. Western readers expected more because they thought that the remaining stories would bring the collection to a total of 1,001 nights; no Arabic texts, however, have ever been found with more than 282 nights, and the term *one thousand and one* was probably never anything more than a way of expressing the idea of *innumerable.*

The tales were simply too popular to be abandoned, however, and the market forces—the lure of profit—too strong, so the collection began to "grow" in various ways. Galland's publisher released a new volume of tales in 1709 from other sources claiming they were part of the *Thousand and One Nights.* Despite the fact that Galland protested vehemently that they were fake, those tales have been included in almost all subsequent Western editions of the *Nights.* Eventually Galland himself caved in to the pressure to produce more tales and began to add stories that he collected from a variety of sources (some of which have never been identified), including stories he had heard a visiting Syrian monk tell at dinner parties in Paris a few years earlier. Galland had made brief notes about these tales in his diary with no intention of including them in the *Nights,* but several years later, when he was looking for new materials, he set about reworking his short sketches into tales of hundreds of pages in length, drawing upon his own artistic sense of how to expand and embellish them. These tales, in fact, are now among the most famous tales from the collection and include "Aladdin and the Magic Lamp" and "Ali Baba and the Forty Thieves." Part of the popularity of these tales is clearly due to the fact that they were almost entirely, (re)created by a European writer with a very good sense of what sold well to a Western audience. In these tales, for example, first appear the "magic lantern," the "flying carpet," and those immortal words "Open sesame!"—all of which have become stereotypical images of Arab culture among Westerners, even though none of them are documented in Arab culture before their publication in Paris. Galland might be excused for including these fabricated tales if he had informed his readers of their motley origins, but he did not. Until the very end, he publicly maintained the pretense that these tales were translations from an Arabic manuscript, and that was utterly false.

Thus the *Nights* doubled, tripled, and quadrupled in size, with materials added from a wide variety of sources. A Frenchman named Pétis de la Croix then authored a collection of "Persian tales" and dubbed them the *Thousand and One Days* to great success. Thereafter followed dozens of works with titles such as the *Supplemental Nights,* the *Thousand and One Hours,* the *Thousand and One Quarter Hours,* and so forth, none of which were translations from authentic collections of Arab folktales. Parallel to those collections that claimed to present authentic tales from the Middle East, Europeans began to produce dozens of collections of tales and novels that were entirely of their own creation and that did not pretend to be from the Middle East but were often confused with translated Middle Eastern tales by the general public. These works, known as "Oriental Tales" (Conant 1908), were simply Western fantasies spawned from reading the *Nights* and its many imitations. The Middle East had become, as Edward Said in his work *Orientalism* (1978) so clearly demonstrated, a landscape of Western fantasy, and the fantasy version of the Middle East was for many far more real than reality itself

(Ali 1981). One might well argue that Western fantasy versions of the Middle East are still, in fact, more real than the real thing to many Westerners.

To further complicate matters, the expanded European versions of the *Nights* were then translated into Arabic in the nineteenth century, and now every Arab schoolchild reads versions of these texts presented as authentic Arab folktales! Only a handful of scholars are aware of the *Nights'* amazing history, a history that is almost as fabulous as the tales it contains. In sum, the *Nights* is a fascinating case study of cultural contacts, translation, folklore and fakelore, ethnic stereotyping, European colonialism, Orientalism, and the influence of capitalism and marketing on the creation of culture. Perhaps no other literary work so truly deserves the title of being a work of "world literature," for it combines at one and the same time Indian, Persian, Arab, French, and various other European influences.

What then can we turn to as authentic in this extraordinarily complex history? One, and to date only one, English translation of the *Nights* is based solely on an Arabic manuscript and avoids the temptation of including other tales just because they have become famous: Haddawy's (1990) translation of the fourteenth-century Arabic manuscript edited by Mahdi (1984–94). All of the other hundreds of versions in English contain tales from sources other than the Arabic *Nights*. The most useful and reliable tool currently available for determining the origins of a specific tale, as well as how and when it got incorporated into the *Nights,* is the *Arabian Nights Encyclopedia* (Marzolph and Leeuwen 2004). By looking up tales individually in this reference work, the reader can find a brief history of each tale and its origins.

One tale that is known to have remained fairly fixed since the earliest translation of the *Nights* from Persian to Arabic in the ninth or tenth century to the present is the story of Scheherazade (or Shahrazād), that is, the frame tale of the collection. Following is a portion of that tale, the very beginning of the *Thousand and One Nights:*

[*Plot Summary:* There were once two kings who were brothers named Shahrayar and Shahzaman. Not having seen his younger brother in ten years, Shahrayar sent him a message asking him to come and visit. Shahzaman gladly accepted and prepared to travel, but at the last minute he decided to return to his palace to say goodbye to his wife. To his horror he found her in bed with one of his cooks. Furious at this act of infidelity he pulled out his sword and killed them both, and then departed to visit his brother. During his visit, Shahrayar noticed that his brother Shahzaman seemed sad and depressed, so he proposed that they go out hunting. Shahzaman declined the invitation but insisted that his brother go ahead without him. While his brother was out hunting, Shahzaman happened to glance out of a window down into a garden and saw his brother's wife and her female servants making love to some of the slaves of the palace. It cheered him to see that his brother was being deceived by his wife exactly as he had been deceived by his own, and after that he began to eat, put on weight, and his mood changed for the better. Eventually his brother Shahrayar forced him to explain why he had been so pale and depressed when he first arrived and why he now had regained his health and good humor. When he heard his brother's tale, Shahrayar at first did not want to believe that his wife could betray him, but the two brothers set a trap and caught her in the act. He and his brother left the palace, traveled to far off places, and had several adventures. When they returned, he ordered that his unfaithful wife be put to death. After that he pledged that he would never trust another woman again, and vowed to wed a girl every evening, spend one night with her, and have her killed the following morning.]

Shahrayar sat on his throne and ordered his vizier, the father of [two daughters named Shahrazad and Dinarzad], to find him a wife from among the princes' daughters. The vizier found him one, and he slept with her and was done with her, and the next morning he ordered the vizier to put her to death. That very night he took one of the army officers' daughters, slept with her, and the next morning ordered the vizier to put her death. The vizier, who could not disobey him, put her to death. The third night he took one of the merchants' daughters, slept with her till the morning, then ordered his vizier to put her to death, and the vizier did so. It became King Shahrayar's custom to take every night the daughter of a merchant or a commoner, spend the night with her, then have her put to death the next morning. He continued to do this until all the girls perished, their mothers mourned, and there arose a clamor among the fathers and mothers, who called the plague upon his head, complained to the Creator of the heavens, and called for help on Him who hears and answers prayers.

Now, as mentioned earlier, the vizier, who put the girls to death, had an older daughter named Shahrazad and a younger one called Dinarzad. The older daughter, Shahrazad, had read the books of literature, philosophy, and medicine. She knew poetry by heart, had studied historical reports, and was acquainted with the sayings of men and the maxims of sages and kings. She was intelligent, knowledgeable, wise, and refined. She had read and learned. One day she said to her father, "Father, I will tell you what is in my mind." He asked, "What is it?" She answered, "I would like you to marry me to King Shahrayar, so that I may either succeed in saving the people or perish and die like the rest." When the vizier heard what his daughter Shahrazad said, he got angry and said to her, "Foolish one, don't you know that King Shahrayar has sworn to spend but one night with a girl and have her put to death the next morning? If I give you to him, he will sleep with you for one night and will ask me to put you to death the next morning, and I shall have to do it, since I cannot disobey him." She said, "Father, you must give me to him, even if he kills me." He asked, "What has possessed you that you wish to imperil yourself?" She replied, "Father you must give me to him. This is absolute and final." Her father the vizier became furious and said to her, "Daughter, 'He who misbehaves, ends up in trouble,' and 'He who considers not the end, the world is not his friend.' As the popular saying goes, 'I would be sitting pretty, but for my curiosity.' I am afraid that what happened to the donkey and the ox with the merchant will happen to you." She asked "Father, what happened to the donkey, the ox, and the merchant?" He said:

There was a prosperous and wealthy merchant who lived in the countryside and labored on a farm. He owned many camels and herds of cattle and employed many men, and he had a wife and many grown-up as well as little children. This merchant was taught the language of the beasts, on condition that if he revealed his secret to anyone he would die; therefore, even though he knew the language of every kind of animal, he did not let anyone know, for fear of death. One day, as he sat, with his wife beside him and his children playing before him, he glanced at an ox and a donkey he kept at the farmhouse, tied to adjacent troughs, and heard the ox say to the donkey, "Watchful one, I hope that you are enjoying the comfort, and the service you are getting. Your ground is swept and watered, and they serve you, feed you sifted barley, and offer you clear, cool water to drink. I, on the contrary, am taken out to plow in the middle of the night. They clamp on my neck something they call yoke and plow, push me all day under the whip to plow the field, and drive me beyond my endurance until my sides are lacerated, and my neck is flayed. They work me from nighttime to nighttime, take me back in the dark, offer me beans soiled with mud and hay mixed with chaff, and let me spend the night lying in urine and dung. Meanwhile you rest on well-swept, watered and smoothed ground, with a clean trough full of hay. You stand in comfort, save for the rare occasion when our master the merchant rides you to do a brief errand and returns. You are comfortable, while I am weary; you sleep, while I keep awake."

When the ox finished, the donkey turned to him and said, "Greenhorn, they were right in calling you ox, for you ox harbour no deceit, malice or meanness. Being sincere, you exert and exhaust yourself to comfort others. Have you not heard the saying, 'Out of bad luck, they hastened on the road'? You go into the field from early morning to endure your torture at the plow to the point of exhaustion. When the plowman takes you back and ties you to the trough, you go on butting and beating with your horns, kicking with your hoofs, and bellowing for the beans, until they toss them to you; then you begin to eat. Next time, when they bring them to you, don't eat or even touch them, but smell them, then draw back and lie down on the hay and straw. If you do this, life will be better and kinder to you, and you will find relief."

As the ox listened, he was sure that the donkey had given him good advice. He thanked him, commended him to God, and invoked His blessing on him, and said, "May you stay safe from harm, watchful one." All of this conversation took place, daughter, while the merchant listened and understood. On the following day, the plowman came to the merchant's house and, taking the ox, placed the yoke on his neck and worked him at the plow, but the ox lagged behind. The plowman hit him, but following the donkey's advice, the ox, dissembling, fell on his belly, and the plowman hit again. Thus the ox kept getting up and falling until nightfall, when the plowman took him home and tied him to the trough. But this time the ox did not bellow or kick the ground with his hoofs. Instead, he withdrew, away from the trough. Astonished, the plowman brought him his beans and fodder, but the ox only smelled the fodder and pulled back and lay down at a distance with the hay and straw, complaining until morning. When the plowman arrived, he found the trough as he had left it, full of beans and fodder, and saw the ox lying on his back, hardly breathing, his belly puffed, and his legs raised in the air. The plowman felt sorry for him and said to himself, "By God, he did seem weak and unable to work." Then he went to the merchant and said, "Master, last night the ox refused to eat or touch his fodder."

The merchant, who knew what was going on, said to the plowman, "Go to the wily donkey, put him to the plow, and work him hard until he finishes the ox's task." The plowman left, took the donkey, and placed the yoke upon his neck. Then he took him out to the field and drove him with blows until he finished the ox's work, all the while driving him with blows and beating him until his sides were lacerated and his neck was flayed. At nightfall he took him home, barely able to drag his legs under his tired body and his drooping ears. Meanwhile the ox spent his day resting. He ate all his food, drank his water, and lay quietly, chewing his cud in comfort. All day long he kept praising the donkey's advice and invoking God's blessing on him. When the donkey came back at night, the ox stood up to greet him, saying, "Good evening, watchful one!" You have done me a favor beyond description, for I have been sitting in comfort, God bless you for my sake!" Seething with anger, the donkey did not reply, but said to himself, "All this happened to me because of my miscalculation. 'I would be sitting pretty, but for my curiosity.' If I don't find a way to return this ox to his former situation, I will perish." Then he went to his trough and lay down, while the ox continued to chew his cud and invoke God's blessing on him.

"You, my daughter, will likewise perish because of our miscalculation. Desist, sit quietly, and don't expose yourself to peril. I advise you out of compassion for you." She replied, "Father, I must go to the king, and you must give me to him." He said, "Don't do it." She insisted, "I must." He replied, "If you don't desist, I will do to you what the merchant did to his wife." She asked, "Father, what did the merchant do to his wife?" He said:

After what happened to the donkey and the ox, the merchant and his wife went out in the moonlight to the stable, and he heard the donkey ask the ox in his own language, "Listen, ox, what are you going to do tomorrow morning, and what will you do when the plowman brings you your fodder?" The ox replied, "What shall I do but follow your advice and stick to it?" If he brings me my fodder, I will pretend to be ill, lie down, and puff my belly." The donkey shook his head, and said, "Don't do it. Do you know what I heard our master the merchant say to the plowman?" The ox asked, "What?" The donkey replied, "He said that if the ox failed to get up and eat his fodder, he would call the butcher to slaughter him and skin him and would distribute the meat for alms and use the skin for a mat. I am afraid for you, but good advice is a matter of faith; therefore, if he brings you your fodder, eat it and look alert lest they cut your throat and skin you." The ox farted and bellowed.

The merchant got up and laughed loudly at the conversation between the donkey and the ox, and his wife asked him, "What are you laughing at? Are you making fun of me?" He said, "No." She said, "Tell me what made you laugh." He replied, "I cannot tell you. I am afraid to disclose the secret conversation of the animals." She said, "And what prevents you from telling me?" He answered, "The fear of death." His wife said, "By God, you are lying. This is nothing but an excuse. I swear by God, the Lord of heaven, that if you don't tell me and explain the cause of your laughter, I will leave you. You must tell me." Then she went back to the house crying, and she continued to cry until morning. The merchant said, "Damn it! Tell me why you are crying. Ask for God's forgiveness, and stop questioning and leave me in peace." She said, "I insist and will not desist." Amazed at her, he replied. "You insist! If I tell you what the donkey said to the ox, which made me laugh, I shall die." She said, "Yes, I insist, even if you have to die." He replied, "Then call your family," and she called their two daughters, her parents, and relatives, and some neighbors. The merchant told them that he was about to die, and everyone, young and old, his children, the farmhands, and the servants began to cry until the house became a place of mourning. Then he summoned legal witnesses, wrote a will, leaving his wife and children their due portion, freed his slave-girls, and bid his family good-bye, while everyone, even the witnesses, wept. Then the wife's parents approached her and said, "Desist, for if your husband had not known for certain that he would die if he revealed his secret, he wouldn't have gone through all this." She replied, "I will not change my mind," and everybody cried and prepared to mourn his death.

Well, my daughter Shahrazad, it happened that the farmer kept fifty hens and a rooster at home, and while he felt sad to depart this world and leave his children and relatives behind, pondering and about to reveal and utter his secret, he overheard a dog of his say something in dog language to the rooster, who, beating and clapping his wings, had jumped on a hen and, finishing with her, jumped down and jumped on another. The merchant heard and understood what the dog had said to the rooster, "Shameless, no-good rooster. Aren't you ashamed to do such a thing on a day like this?" The rooster asked, "What is special about this day?" The dog replied, "Don't you know that our master and friend is in mourning today?" His wife is demanding that he disclose his secret, and when he discloses it, he will surely die. He is in this predicament, about to interpret to her the language of the animals, and all of us are in mourning for him, while you clap your wings and get off one hen and jump on another. Aren't you ashamed?" The merchant heard the rooster reply, "You fool, you lunatic! Our master and friend claims to be wise, but he is foolish, for he has only one wife, yet he does not know how to manage her." The dog asked, "What should he do with her?"

The rooster replied, "He should take an oak branch, push her into a room, lock the door and fall upon her with the stick, beating her mercilessly until he breaks her arms and legs and she cries out, 'I no longer want you to tell me or explain anything.' He should go on beating her until he cures her for life, and she will never oppose him in anything. If he does this, he will live, and live in peace, and there will be no more grief, but he does not know how to manage." Well, my daughter Shahrazad, when the merchant heard the conversation between the dog and the rooster, he jumped up and, taking an oak branch, pushed his wife into a room, got in with her, and locked the door. Then he began to beat her mercilessly on her chest and shoulders and kept beating her till she cried for mercy, screaming, "No, no. I don't want to know anything. Leave me alone, leave me alone. I don't want to know anything," until he got tired of hitting her and opened the door. The wife emerged penitent, the husband learned good management, and everybody was happy, and the mourning turned into a celebration.

"If you don't relent, I shall do to you what the merchant did to his wife." She said, "Such tales don't deter me from my request. If you wish, I can tell you many such tales. In the end, if you don't take me to King Shahrayar, I shall go to him by myself behind your back and tell him that you have refused to give me to one like him and that you have begrudged your master one like me." The vizier asked, "Must you really do this?" She replied, "Yes, I must."

Tired and exhausted, the vizier went to King Shahrayar and, kissing the ground before him, told him about his daughter, adding that he would give her to him that very night.

The king was astonished and said to him, "Vizier, how is it that you have found it possible to give me your daughter, knowing that I will, by God, the Creator of heaven, ask you to put her to death the next morning and that if you refuse, I will have you put to death too?" He replied, "My King and Lord, I have told her everything and explained all this to her, but she refuses and insists on being with you tonight." The king was delighted and said, "Go to her, prepare her, and bring her to me early in the evening."

The vizier went down, repeated the king's message to his daughter, and said, "May God not deprive me of you." She was very happy and, after preparing herself and packing what she needed, went to her younger sister, Dinarzad, and said, "Sister, listen well to what I am telling you. When I go to the king, I will send for you, and when you come and see that the king has finished with me, say, 'Sister, if you are not sleepy, tell us a story.' Then I will begin to tell a story, and it will cause the king to stop his practice, save myself, and deliver the people." Dinarzad said, "Very well."

At nightfall the vizier took Shahrazad and went with her to the great King Shahrayar. But when Shahrayar took her to bed and began to fondle her, she wept, and when he asked her, "Why are you crying?" she replied, "I have a sister, and I wish to bid her good-bye before daybreak." Then the king sent for the sister, who came and went to sleep under the bed. When the night wore on, she woke up and waited until the king had satisfied himself with her sister Shahrazad and they were by now all fully awake. Then Dinarzad cleared her throat and said, "Sister, if you are not sleepy, tell us one of your lovely little tales to while away the night, before I bid you good-bye at daybreak, for I don't know what will happen to you tomorrow." Shahrazad turned to King Shahrayar and said, "May I have your permission to tell a story?" He replied, "Yes" and Shahrazad was very happy and said, "Listen":

[Shahrazad tells the first part of the *Tale of the Merchant and the Demon*]

But morning overtook Shahrazad, and she lapsed into silence, leaving King Shahrayar burning with curiosity to hear the rest of the story. Then Dinarzad said to her sister Shahrazad, "What a strange and lovely story!" Shahrazad replied, "What is this compared with what I shall tell you tomorrow night if the king spares me and lets me live? It will be even better and more entertaining." The king thought to himself, "I will spare her until I hear the rest of the story; then I will have her put to death the next day."

(Haddawy 1990, 10–16)

Thus begins the endless chain of stories, each broken off in the middle at dawn so that the king wishes to hear its conclusion the following night, sparing Shahrazad's life one day after another. Scholars have interpreted the meaning of the frame tale in many different ways. One can read it as an allegory of the relations between men and women, or as a tale of how the brutish passions can be tamed by education and thought, or simply as a demonstration of the power of narrative to enthrall, entertain, and ultimately educate us. In this short opening we can also see several of the techniques that continue throughout the work, such as the role of talking animal tales and the famous technique of inserting one tale within another within another, all of which reverberate and echo among themselves.

This technique reaches one of its apogees in a sequence of tales told from nights 102 to 170 and is usually known in English as "The Tale of the Hunchback." The tale is set in China and the body of a dead hunchback is passed from a tailor to a Jewish physician, then to a Muslim steward, and then to a Christian broker. Eventually the whole series of events is narrated in front of the king of China, who at the end of these strange tales asked what at first appears to be a rhetorical question: "Has anyone every heard of a stranger event than this!?" However, this is the world of the *Thousand and One Nights,* so all of the main characters immediately step forward to say that indeed they have heard of stranger events, and each proceeds to tell a tale. In the last of these four tales, "The Tale of the Lame Young Man from Baghdad," which is told by the tailor, the young man who is the story's protagonist tells the tale of a strange encounter with a barber to the assembled guests at a large dinner party. As it turns out, unknown to the young man, the barber is also present at the party, so he then stands up and tells a tale of his own, and within his tale he recounts to the Caliph of Baghdad not only the story of his own misadventures but also the tales of each of his six brothers, one after the other.

Thus the anonymous narrator of the *Nights* is speaking to us, Shahrazād is speaking to King Shahriyār, the tailor is telling his tale to the King of China, and the barber is speaking to the dinner guests about the tales that he earlier recounted to the Caliph in Baghdad—five levels of story-telling embedded one inside the other. A prodigious feat indeed! Even more impressive, however, is that the themes and motifs of the tales interact in complex ways—the entire sequence of 12 tales begins and ends with the hunchback, and each tale tells of the acquisition of a physical defect and what cruel fate or compensation befell the characters afterward. The four tales told by the tailor, the physician, the steward, and the broker, for example, all involve young men who fall in love with beautiful women and then suffer some form of amputation or maiming as a result of their love. Three of the four eventually have their love fulfilled and live happily ever after, while the fourth does not: four different fates for four similar loves. The intertwined themes of love, physical defects, and compensation constantly reappear until the final moment when it turns out that the hunchback is not in fact dead at all and is revived by the Jewish physician, to everyone's delight.

The *Thousand and One Nights* is without doubt one of the great works of world literature, and all the stories, regardless of their origin, merit examination and study. Great caution must be exercised, however, if it is approached as a work of Arab culture or folklore, for much of the material that commonly circulates under the rubric of the *Nights* is neither.

Folk Narratives from Oral Traditions

Folklore scholars divide folk narratives into a variety of different general categories. *Fairy tales* (also called simply *folktales*) usually involve magical or supernatural characters or powers, are typically set in a nonhistorical time, and often announced by some sort of disclaimer or marker that the tale is fictional. English speakers are most familiar with the formula "Once upon a time...". In Arabic dozens of such formulas are used in different regions, but one particularly famous one is *Kān wa-mā kān* ("There was and there was not"). Another technique is to open the telling of a fictional tale with a religious formula such as "Assert the Unity of God!" to which audience members reply, "There is no god but God!" Following are three other formulae for the telling of folktales collected from a Chaldean Christian Arab of Baghdad:

Chān wmā chān	There was and there was not,
'al Allāh wittiklān	And our reliance is on God.
Kān mā kān hatta kān	There was, there was not, until there was;
Kān fil-' adīm azzamān	There was in a time long ago...
Hādhī hchāya nisha chidhbaya	This is a story, half of it is a lie
Wlō bētna garīb chint ajībilkum	If our house were near I would go bring you
Tibag himmis wtibag izbīb	A platter of chickpeas and a platter of raisins

(Adapted from Ferguson 1960, 335–38)

Another major category of folk narrative is the *legend*, and the primary distinction between the folktale and the legend for folklorists is that legends are usually told as if they were historically true, and often some members of the audience or the teller in fact accepts them as true. Legends are usually told as having taken place in a known physical location, sometimes even in a specific time period, and are often linked to some element of modern reality—a simple example might be a story that tells how a particular local cliff or rock came be known as "Lover's Leap."

Another very important category of narrative but one that is much less well studied includes the various forms of oral history found in personal narratives (sometimes called *memorates*) that older persons typically tell younger persons. In predominantly oral communities, these narratives are sometimes the main method through which knowledge of the community's past is transmitted to younger generations, and they are sometimes crucial to constructing and maintaining a group's identity. There are, of course, many other categories and subcategories of folk narratives (for instance, *animal fables,* two examples of which we have seen in the frame tale of the *Thousand and One Nights*), but the folktale, legend, and personal narrative are three of the most widespread.

Folktale, legend, personal narrative, animal fable, and so forth, are all, however, categories created by scholars and outsiders. Over the past few decades, scholars have begun to pay more and more attention to the system of genres, and the names of genres, as they exist within a given culture (see Chapter Two). The sequence of folk narratives presented in the following subsections go by various different names in Arabic in their respective communities but correspond primarily to the genres of folktale, personal narrative (memorate), and saint's legend. First are presented two Palestinian folktales told by Muslim women; next, two folktales told by Moroccan Jewish women; then Muslim and Christian tales told by men in Syria; and finally two personal narratives, one a saint's legend from Tunisia and the other embedded in an epic poem from Egypt.

Palestine: Female Heroines in Women's Folktales. In Palestine, as in every corner of the Arab world, there are many terms for different types of folk narratives including fairy tales, folktales, proverb tales, accounts of unusual events, historical incidents, legends, animal fables, saints' legends, myths, and personal narratives. The Palestinian genres that most closely resemble the common folktale are referred to as *hikāye* (story) or *khurrafiyye* (fiction) and are primarily a women's art form, in contrast to narrative forms usually associated with men such as epic poetry *(sīra)* and tales of raiding, heroism, and adventures *(qissa)*. While men listen to their genres in public spaces such as in cafés, Palestinian folktales have traditionally been narrated by women in domestic spaces, ostensibly with children as the primary audience, though adults often listen to and enjoy the performances as well. Young boys thus hear and learn the tales as well as girls while children, but after puberty they usually stop narrating such tales as part of their transition to manhood. Muhawi and Kanaana, in their remarkable collection of Palestinian folktales *Speak, Bird, Speak Again* (1989) offer a detailed introduction to the rich repertory of Palestinian folktales. The 45 tales in their collection were collected from 1978 to 1980 in the West Bank, Gaza, and the Galilee (since 1948 incorporated into the state of Israel), and were selected from a much larger corpus gathered almost entirely from female narrators, most of them unlettered housewives, who were asked to perform the best tales they could remember from storytelling events of the past. The tales were all recorded in the narrators' own homes in front of small, local audiences.

In this repertory of women's tales nearly all the main protagonists are female. Far from being passive, helpless creatures, most of the heroines in these tales take decisive action and usually, against all odds, succeed. Family relations, marriage, sexuality, the bearing of children, religion, and the supernatural are some of the most common themes, and they are often recounted with a frankness and openness that outsiders might find surprising:

Western readers will be struck as much by the tone of the tales—the narrative voice that speaks through them—as by their style, for the tales empower the women who narrate them to traverse, in their speech, the bounds of social convention. This speech is direct, earthy, even scatological, but without awkwardness or self-consciousness. The narrators are keen observers of the society around them, particularly those features of the social structure that touch directly on their lives. Because the tale-tellers are older women who have gone through the cycle of life, they are free of blame and at the same time endowed with the experience and wisdom necessary to see through hypocrisy and contradiction.

(Muhawi and Kanaana 1989, 12–13)

"Sackcloth" will be recognizable to most readers as a version of the Cinderella tale, but with several interesting features. To begin with, the tale opens with the threat of unbridled male sexuality, in this case father-daughter incest, which the heroine must escape to survive. In addition, the heroine herself plays a notably active role in the story, in contrast to the more helpless Cinderella of many Western versions who instead relies almost entirely on her "fairy godmother" for salvation.[7] This Palestinian Cinderella survives and eventually lives "happily ever after" by dint of her own intelligence and courage.

Sackcloth

TELLER: Testify that God is One!
AUDIENCE: There is no god but God!

Once upon a time there was a king who had no children except an only daughter. One day his wife laid her head down and died, and he went searching for a new wife. They spoke of this woman and that, but none pleased him. No one seemed more beautiful in his eyes, so the story goes, than his own daughter and he had no wish to marry another. When he came into the house, she would call him "father," but he would answer, "Don't call me 'father,' call me 'cousin.' "[8]

"But father, O man of legitimate birth! I'm your daughter!"

"It's no use," he insisted, "I've made up my mind."

One day he sent for the religious judge and asked him, "A tree that I've cared for, feeding and watering it—is it legally mine, or can someone else claim it?" "No one else can claim it," replied the religious judge. "It's rightfully yours." No sooner had the religious judge left than the father went out and brought his daughter jewelry and a wedding dress. He was preparing to take her for his wife.

---

7. For a detailed study of versions of Cinderella from many different societies, see Dundes (1988), *Cinderella: A Casebook.*

8. Since the preferred marriage in the Arab world is traditionally among first cousins (though such marriages constitute only a portion of all marriages), the term *cousin* is one commonly used between husband and wife, whether or not they are really cousins. Similarly, other family terms, such as *uncle, aunt,* and *grandfather* are often used for addressing elders whether or not there is any blood relation.

The girl put on the new clothes and the gold, and sat in the house. Her father came home in the evening. When she realized that he was absolutely intent on taking her, she went to a sackcloth maker and said, "Take as much money as you want, but make me a tight-fitting sackcloth that will cover my whole body, except my nostrils, mouth, and eyes. And I want it ready by tomorrow evening."

"Fine," he said, "I'll do it."

[When it was finished] the girl went and brought it home. She put it in a shed in front of the house and locked the door. She then put on the bridal clothes and jewelry [again] and lounged about the house. Her father came home in the evening.

"Father!" she called to him.

"Don't call me 'father'!" he replied, "Call me 'cousin.' "

"Alright, cousin!" she replied, "But wait until I come back from the outhouse (All respect to the audience!)."

"But you might run away."

"No, I won't," she answered. "But just to make sure, tie a rope to my wrist and every once in a while pull your end of it and you'll discover that I'm still there."

There was a big stone in the lower part of the house, and on her way out she tied her end of the rope to it, together with the bracelets. She then went out to the shed, put on her tight sack, and, invoking the help of Allah, ventured into the night.

Meanwhile, the father tugged at the rope every few moments, and, hearing the tinkle of the bracelets, would say to himself, "She's still here." [He waited and waited] till the middle of the night, then he said, "By Allah, I've got no choice but to go check on her." When he found the rope tied to the stone, with the bracelets dangling from it, he prepared his horse, disguised himself, mounted and went out to look for her.

She had already been gone awhile, and by the time he left the house, she was well outside the city. He followed after her, searching. When he caught up with her, she saw and recognized him, and clung to the trunk of a tree. Not recognizing her, but thinking she was a man, he asked, "Didn't you see a girl with such and such features pass this way?"

"O uncle, Allah save you!" answered the maiden. "Please leave me to my misery, I can barely see in front of me."

He left her and went away. Seeing him take one path, she took another. [She kept on traveling,] sleeping here and waking up there, till she came to a city. Hunger driving her, she took shelter by the wall of a king's palace.

The king's slavegirl came out with a platter to dump leftover food. Sackcloth fell on the scraps and set to eating. When the slave saw her, she rushed back inside.

"O mistress!" she called out, "There's a weird sight outside—the strangest looking man, and he's eating the leftovers."

"Go call him in, and let him come here!" commanded the mistress.

"Come in and see my mistress," said the slave. "They want to have a look at you."

"What's the situation with you, uncle?" they asked, when she came inside. "Are you human or jinn?"

"By Allah, uncle," she replied, "I'm human, and the choicest of the race. But Allah has created me the way I am."

"What skill do you have?" they asked. "What can you do?"

"By Allah, I don't have any skills in particular," she answered. "I can stay in the kitchen, peeling onions and passing things over when needed."

They put her to work in the kitchen, and soon everyone was saying, "Here's comes Sackcloth! There goes Sackcloth!" How happy they were to have Sackcloth around, and she stayed in the kitchen under the protection of the cook.

One day there was a wedding in the city, and the king's household was invited. In the evening they were preparing to go have a look at the spectacle.

"Hey, Sackcloth!" they called out, "Do you want to come with us and have a look at the wedding?"

"No, Allah help me!" she exclaimed. "I can't go look at weddings or anything else like that. You go, and I wish you Godspeed, but I can't go."

The king's household and the slaves went to the wedding, and no one was left at home except Sackcloth. Waiting till they were well on their way, she took off her sackcloth and set out for the festivities, all made up and wearing the wedding dress she had brought with her. All the women were dancing in turn, and when her turn came she took the handkerchiefs and danced and danced till she had had her fill of dancing. She then dropped the handkerchiefs and left, and no one knew where she came from or where she went.[9] Returning home, she put on her sackcloth, squatted alongside the walls of the palace, and went to sleep. When the slaves got back from the celebration, they started badgering her.

"What! Are you sleeping here?" they taunted. "May you never rise! If only you'd come to the wedding, you would've seen this girl who danced and danced, and then left without anybody knowing where she went."

That happened the first night, and the second night the same thing happened again. When the king's wife came home, she went to see her son.

"Dear son," she said, "if only we could get that girl, I'd ask for her hand—the one who comes to the wedding and leaves without anybody knowing where she comes from or where she goes."

"Let me wear women's clothes, mother," he suggested, "and take me with you [to the women's side]. If anyone should ask, say to them, 'This is my sister's daughter. She's here visiting with us, and I brought her with me to see the celebrations.'"

"Fine," she agreed.

Putting women's clothes on him, she took him with them. Sackcloth, meanwhile, gave them enough time to get there, then took off her coat of sackcloth and followed. She went in, danced till she had had her fill, then slipped away. No one recognized her, or knew where she came from or where she went. Returning home, she put on her sackcloth and went to sleep.

The following day the king's son said to the others. "You go to the wedding," and he hid outside the door of the house where the celebration was taking place. Sackcloth came again, went inside and danced, then pulled herself together and slipped away. No sooner had she left than he followed her, keeping a safe distance until she reached home. No

---

9. The celebration of Palestinian weddings is a very rich tradition (see Customs and Traditions); men and women traditionally do not dance with each other. Instead, the women form a circle and take turns dancing in the center of the circle holding a brightly colored kerchief in each hand.

sooner did she get there than she went in, put on her coat of sackcloth, and squatted by the palace wall and went to sleep.

"What!" he said to himself, "She dwells in my own house and pretends to be some kind of freak!" He did not say anything to anyone.

The next morning he said to the slaves who bring his meals, "I don't want any of you to bring my food up today. I want Sackcloth to serve my dinner, and I want him to share it with me."

"O master for the sake of Allah!" she protested, "I can't do it. I'm so disgusting, how could you want to have dinner with me?"

"You must bring up my dinner so we can eat together," he replied.

The servants prepared dinner, served it onto a platter, and gave it to Sackcloth. She carried it, pretending to limp, until she was halfway up the stairs, then she made as if her foot had slipped and dropped the whole platter.

"Please, master!" she pleaded, "Didn't I tell you that I can't carry anything?"

"You must keep bringing platters and dropping them," the son of the king insisted, "until you manage to come up here on your own."

With the second platter she came up to the landing at the top of the stairs, slipped and dropped it.

"This isn't going to get you anywhere," said the son of the king. "Do not for one moment hope to be excused."

With the third platter she limped and limped, leaning here and there, until she reached the top and served him his dinner.

"Come sit here with me," said the prince, closing the door. "Let's eat this dinner together."

"Please, master!" she protested, "Just look at my condition. Surely it will disgust you."

"No. Do sit down! I would like to have dinner with you."

They sat down to eat together, and the prince pulled out a knife and reached for the coat of sackcloth.

"You must take this thing off!" he said. "How long have we been searching, wondering who the girl was that came to the wedding. And all this time you've been living under my own roof!"

He made her remove the sackcloth coat, and called his mother. They called for the religious judge, and wrote up their wedding contract.

"For forty days," the public crier announced, "no one is to eat or drink except at the house of the king."

They held wedding celebrations, and gave her to him for a wife.

And this is my tale, I've told it; and in your hands I leave it!

(Adapted from Muhawi and Kanaana 1989, 125–30)

Various supernatural beings fill Arab fairy and folktales, among them the *jinnī* (origin of the English word *genie*); the *naddāha*—a water spirit that lures men to their deaths in ponds, wells, and rivers; the *'afrīt*—a type of demon or imp; and the *ghūla* (from which the English word *ghoul* derives)—a female creature mostly found in the desert or other open spaces, who can transform herself into any form and feeds upon human flesh. Following are two tales of a *ghūla:* The first (in which *ghūla* is spelled *ghouleh*) is told by a Muslim Palestinian woman, and the second is narrated by a Jewish Moroccan woman.

The Ghouleh of Trans-Jordan

Once there was a poor man. One day he said to his family, "Let's cross over to Trans-Jordan [i.e., to the east side of the Jordan river]. Maybe we can find a better life there than we have here." They had (May Allah honor you!) a beast of burden.[10]

Crossing eastward, they came upon some deserted ruins. When they found an empty house in the ruins, they wanted to move into it. A woman came upon them. "Welcome!" she said to the man. "Welcome to my nephew! Since my brother died, you haven't dropped in on me, nor have you visited me."

"By Allah," he answered, "my father never mentioned you to me. And in any case, we came here only by chance."

"Welcome!" she replied. "Welcome! Go ahead and stay in this house."

Now, the house was well stocked with food, and they settled in. The man had only his wife and a daughter. They would cook meals, and in the evening the daughter took the woman her dinner. She lived in the southern part of the ruined town, and they lived in the north, with some distance between them.

One evening the girl went to bring the woman her dinner. She came up to the door, and lo! The woman had thrown to the ground a young man with braids like those of a girl gone astray, and she was devouring him.[11] Stepping back, the girl moved some distance away and called out, "Hey, Aunty, Aunty!" The ghouleh shook herself, took the shape of a woman again, and came to the terrified girl.

"The name of Allah protect you, niece!" exclaimed the ghouleh.

"A black shape crossed my path," the girl explained, "and I became frightened."

Taking the dinner from the girl, the ghouleh said, "Don't worry! I'll wait here until you get inside the house." But she followed her to the door of the house to find out what the girl was going to say to her mother.

"How's your aunt?" asked the mother.

Now the girl was a clever one, and she answered, "When I got there, I found her sitting quietly with her head in her lap, like this."

After the ghouleh had gone back to her house to finish what she was eating, the girl said to her mother, "Mother, it turns out our aunt is a ghouleh."

"How do you know she's a ghouleh?" asked the mother.

"I saw her eating a lad with locks of those of a seductive girl," said the girl.

Her husband was sleeping. "Get up, get up!" she said. "It turns out your aunt is a ghouleh."

---

10. Whenever something distasteful or something that could be construed as an insult is mentioned, it is customary to insert a politeness phrase, for example, "Put it over there by—excuse me!—the donkey."

11. This description of the handsome young man being eaten is an indication of the tale's age—long ago young men used to grow their hair long and braid it, which was seen as a mark of handsomeness; in modern Palestine this would be seen as a mark of effeminacy.

"What! My aunt is a ghouleh!? You're a ghouleh!"

"All right," the wife replied. "Sleep, sleep! We were only joking with you."

When he had gone back to sleep, they went and filled a sack with flour. They brought a tin can full of olive oil and (May it be far from the listeners!) the beast of burden. Loading the provisions on it, they called upon the Everlasting to watch over their journey.

Meanwhile, the man slept till morning, and when he woke, he found neither wife nor daughter. "So," he thought, "it seems what they said is true." He mounted to the top of the flour bin and lowered himself in.

After sunrise the ghouleh showed up, but when she went into the house, there was no one there. Turning herself back into a ghouleh, she started dancing and singing:

My oil and flour, O what a loss!
Gone are the masters of the house!

When he heard her singing and prancing about, the man was so scared he farted, scattering flour dust into the air. She saw him.

"Ah!" she cried out. "You're still here!"

"Well, come down here," she said. "Where shall I start eating you?"

"Eat my little hand," he answered, "that did not listen to my wife and daughter."

After eating his hand, she asked again, "Where shall I eat you now?"

"Eat my beard," he answered, "that did not listen to my wife."

And so on, until she had devoured him all.

Now we go back to the girl and her mother. When they had reached home, the mother said to her daughter, "She's bound to follow us and turn herself (God save your honors!) into a bitch. She'll scratch against the door. I'll boil a pot full of olive oil, and you open for her. When she comes in, I'll pour the oil over her head."

In a while the ghouleh came, scratched at the door, and the girl opened for her. No sooner had she gone in the door than the woman poured the oil onto her head. She exploded, and behold! she was dead. There was no moisture in her eye.

In the morning the woman filled the town with her shouts, and people rushed to her rescue.

"What's the matter?" they asked.

I've killed the ghouleh. Any one who has strength can go load up on wheat, flour, and oil. As for me, I'll be satisfied with the food in the house where we stayed."

(Adapted from Muhawi and Kanaana 1989, 234–37)

Morocco: Jewish Arab Tales

My Sister Mas'uda and My Brother Mas'ud

A certain man had seven daughters and a wife. The luckless man, whatever he brought home in the daytime he would eat at night. One day he did not find anything to eat and he did not find anything to bring his daughters.

He said, "Bless God, I will go into the wilderness. If I don't die, I will live."

Good. He walked and walked into the wilderness till he came to a certain place, and there he sat down at night.

There came Mother Ghula and her seven children. She ra, da-da, da-da; she was happy that God had provided a supper for her. He fell upon her, embraced her: "Mas'uda, my sister."

"Mas'ud, my brother."

"Mas'uda, my sister, welcome!"

"Welcome, Mas'ud, my brother, welcome! Do you have any sons? Do you have any daughters?"

He said to her: "I have seven daughters and a wife. And I did not find anything to eat for them."

Good.

She said to him: "Close your eyes and open them."

He opened his eyes and found himself beneath the ground. There he found many things, God may bless you and us, without a story and without a tale, may God give you just that, everything is full of gold and silver, unlike any other place.

There he stays, eats, drinks; each day she slaughters a sheep for him; she slaughters each day. She fattens him up in order to eat him.

He said to her, "Oh my daughter, do not eat me. I have seven daughters."

She said to him, "Good, if you have seven daughters, take these seven horses laden with money, take them and bring your daughters and your wife and come."

He said to her, "Good."

An undated photo of an elderly Jewish Arab woman, Morocco. © Ted Spiegel/Corbis.

[Storyteller's aside: Woe be you, you unfortunate man, you took seven horses laden with money, go and stay at home!]

He said to his wife: "Rise, rise and come on now. I found a certain woman, Mas'uda, my sister, who will gladden your heart."

"A certain Mas'uda, my sister?! You unfortunate man, Mas'uda, your sister, from what place did she come to you?" He said to her, "Come on, rise, come on now, may your father's house be laid waste. Come on now, God has given us a place to live." She said to him, "Woe be to you."

Good. He took the money and hid it in the backyard. The fool, he took his daughters and his wife and walked, walked, walked up to the entrance of the pit. It was night.

One of the daughters said, "Mother, oh mother, where is she, where is Mas'uda? Where is Aunt Mas'uda about whom our father told me?"

She said to her, "Be quiet, oh my daughter, for your father brought you here to die. And now I am going to pull a trick on him, don't you be afraid."

Well, they sit there, and they sit there, and suddenly he jumps to his feet, "Mas'uda, my sister."

"Mas'ud, my brother, Mas'ud, my brother."

The mother said to her daughters, "Woe to us."

"Oh, mother, is this the aunt to whom father took us?"

They went beneath the ground. They sit; they eat and drink.

She said to the mother, "Now give me one of your daughters, I want her to sleep in my room."

She took her first daughter, the wretched creature, she took her and said to her, "Take her."

She gave her needles.

She said to her, "Clean my teeth. If you don't, I'll eat you."

She started cleaning her teeth. She cleans, and she cleans, and she cleans, and she cleans, and she trembles with fear, the poor girl.

The next morning, the girl said, "Mother, oh mother, this aunt bared her enormous teeth; she told me to clean them, and if I didn't she would eat me."

This is how the first night passed.

The second night she said to the mother, "Give me your second daughter."

She gave her her second daughter.

She brought her combs. She said to her, "Take them. Comb my hair, and if you don't, I'll kill you."

The girl said [to herself], "Woe unto me."

The second daughter too got through the night.

The third night she said to the third daughter, "Take my clothes and delouse them, and if you don't, I'll eat you."

The third daughter stayed with her and deloused her clothes.

In this way, she made all seven girls do some work for her. One cleaned her feet, another cleaned her head, another cleaned her teeth, and so on. Till she had forced all of them to spend the night in her room. And that is how, for a month, the poor girls lay in bed trembling in fear.

One [of the girls] said to the mother, "Is that what father brought us here for?"

She said to her, "Be quiet, oh my daughter."

The Ghula said to the mother, "And now you listen to what I am going to tell you: give your daughters to my sons in marriage. You have seven daughters, and I have seven sons; let them get married!"

She said to her, "Good."

They did so.

She [the mother] said to her, "Tell me, oh my sister-in-law, how do you sleep?"

She said to her, "When I have eaten my fill, I close my eyes and I open my mouth when I am asleep; and when I am hungry I open my eyes, and I close my mouth when I am asleep."

She said to her, "Good, thank you for telling me."

What did Mas'ud's wife do? She took the kerchiefs, gave them to the boys, and made her seven daughters put on the hats.

What did she do? She waited till Ghula had eaten her fill and opened her mouth and closed her eyes. Mas'ud's wife took her daughters and removed them one by one, one by one.

She put money on the backs of the seven horses, led them out into the open and left, slowly but surely. And 'Mas'ud, my brother'—she left him there, asleep in a corner.

[Storyteller's aside: Serves him right!]

The foolish Mother Ghula rose, found the kerchiefs. What did she do? She got hold of those who were wearing those kerchiefs. She ate her seven children, she ate, and she ate, and she ate, and she ate, and she ate, and she ate, and she ate till she had eaten all of them, and there was nothing left; then she left the room in order to look for the wife of 'Mas'ud, my brother.'

The woman said to her, "Oh Mother Ghula, you meant to pull a trick on me, but I pulled a trick on you. You see, you ate your sons, and my daughters are right here next to me."

Good. Mother Ghula left, she ran and she ran, and she ran, and she ran, and she ran, and she ran, and she ran and found her brother, Mas'ud.

"Mas'ud, my brother, my brother Mas'ud, where do I start eating you?"

He said to her, "Start with my ears because I didn't listen to my wife's advice."

She fell upon him, she eats, eats, eats until she has eaten him. She left, ran, ran, ran, until she left nothing but bones, and she threw herself into the river. And these Ghulas, when there is a river they cannot cross it. She fell into the river and died.

Mas'ud's wife said, "Go, and may you not be brought back to life."

Mas'ud's wife went to the king, she said to him, "Rise, and I will make you and your soldiers rich."

She took the king's soldiers and went to that place. She gathered God's good things, may you and we [do the same] without any story or tale. She took the money and took, forgive me for saying so, 'Mas'ud my brother' and put him into a sack.

She took all the money and left nothing beneath the ground.

Mother Ghula was dead, and her seven sons were dead, my God spare you, and Mas'ud's wife took her daughters and the money and made the king rich.

So may God give you and us [riches] without a story and without a tale.

(Adapted from Bar-Itzhak and Shenhar 1993, 93–97)

These two tales of the *ghūla,* one from an Muslim Palestinian-Arab house-wife and the other from a Jewish Moroccan-Arab woman from a village in the Atlas mountains who was 90 years old when this tale was recorded, are clearly variations of the same tale—all of the key elements are present in both: The husband who is easily convinced that the *ghūla* is a relative of his (perhaps due to his desire for the food and wealth she offers him), his willingness to place his wife and daughter(s) at risk against the advice of his wife, the intelligent wife who sees through the *ghūla*'s ruses and manages to outwit her, the rescue of the daughter(s), the death of the husband who did not listen to his wife, followed by the death of the *ghūla,* and, finally, the wife's lack of greed which leads to the sharing of the food and wealth with others. All of the various implications of greed versus generosity; intelligence versus foolishness, cleverness versus gullibil-ity, male-female relations, desire, sexuality, and so forth, leave the figure of the *ghūla* open to innumerable psychological and social interpretations.

The next tale, narrated by a woman from Marrakesh in southern Morocco who had been blind since the age of six, tells us of another wise and clever woman; in fact, her name *Alfahima* in Arabic means "she who understands." The tale opens with a version of the Solomon test of wisdom, but it is a test that this king fails. His wife's attempt at setting the situation aright leads to a confrontation between the king and his queen, which is finally resolved by a declaration of love.

Queen Alfahima

God was everywhere, and there was a certain king. His wife was called Alfahima because she understood many things.

One day two traders appeared with a pregnant she-ass and a pregnant mare. The she-ass gave birth, and the mare gave birth. The two of them gave birth. The owner of the she-ass stealthily placed the newborn ass with the mare, and the foal with the she-ass.[12]

The next morning the owner of the mare started shouting. He said to the owner of the she-ass, "This is not the newborn foal."

The other man said, "That is what she brought forth. Finished." He came and had a look. They found the newborn ass suckling from the mare because she had started suck-ling the newborn ass with her eyes closed and had got used to him.

At this point they went to the king for a decision. They were tried by the king.

He said to the king, "Sir, may God bless you. We brought these animals here while they were still pregnant, and they gave birth at night, and now the newborn ass is nursed by the mare, and the newborn foal is being nursed by the she-ass."

The king said to them, "Good, match them, and we shall see. If he suckles, the young ass was born to the mare, and if he doesn't, he is not her foal."

Good, they brought the animals, and the young ass suckled from the mare.

---

12. A young horse is of considerably more value than a young donkey.

The owner of the mare, the poor man, he started crying bitterly, and his cries rise to the sky, and he says, "No mare will ever give birth to an ass."

And he leaves, crying all the time.

As he was crying and screaming, the owner of the mare said to the owner of the she-ass, "A foal born to a mare cannot be a young ass."

When the king's wife heard how they were arguing, she said to them, "What is the matter with you, you two guys? Why are you fighting?"

They said, "May God bless you. Last night we brought the mare and the she-ass, and both were pregnant. During the night, they gave birth."

The owner of the mare addressed the king's wife, saying, "This man says that the mare gave birth to an ass and that the she-ass gave birth to a foal."

She said, "Listen! Go and get a fish. Let it be a big fish, and get a stick and hit the fish. Keep on beating the fish right in front of the king till he says, 'Oh, oh, what do you want with this fish? What are you beating it for?' Then tell him, 'This fish ate my field of cucumbers.' When he tells you, 'Can there be such a thing as a fish eating cucumbers?' you tell him, 'Can there be such a thing as a mare giving birth to an ass?' "

They left, as has been related, they left. He stood next to the king, and he started beating the fish with the stick, beating it again and again.

Then the king spoke to him. He said, "What do you want with this fish, you wicked man? What are you beating this fish for?"

He said to him, "Sir, may God bless you. The fish ate my field of cucumbers."

And the king said, "Can there ever be such a thing as a fish eating cucumbers?"

And the man said, "Can there ever be such a thing as a mare giving birth to an ass?"

The king said, "O dear me, it is my wife Alfahima, she is the one who told you to do this."

He kept silent.

Then he went back and took the ass. He returned the newborn ass to its mother, and he returned the newborn foal to its mother. The king left, and they left, the owner of the she-ass and the owner of the mare.

At night the king came and he said to his wife, "I am the judge in this country, and you are the judge at home? You ate at home, you ate the food God granted you. Take whatever you want, take what is dearest to you, and go back to your father's house."

She said to him, "I will leave because a mare will never bear an ass."

Good, she waited for him to finish his supper, and then both he and she had some tea, and he went to sleep. The wife put a sleeping draught in the king's tea, and he drank it. He lost consciousness, fell to the floor, and slept. Alfahima sent for a carpenter. The carpenter arrived. She said to him, "Make a crate that has room for a mattress." He did so. He made the crate and put in the mattress and a pillow, and she put the king in the crate. She nailed the lid down and called four people, telling them to carry the crate to her father's house.

They did so, and her father was working and her mother was busy. They were surprised and asked, "What about this crate, what about this crate she has sent us?" The crate was closed, they did not know what was inside.

The king's wife arrived along with the crate. She came to the house with the crate. They said to her, "What happened to this crate?" She said to them, "Something. Leave the crate here."

She stayed for the night. During the night, this king woke. He wanted to turn over, and he called his wife, "Alfahima!"

She said to him, "Yes."

He said to her, "What have you been doing to me?"

She said to him, "What do you mean? You told me, 'Take what is dearest to you.' Is there anything in your house dearer to me than you? Nobody is dearer to me than you and you said, 'Take what is most dear to you,' and that is what I did: I took you."

When he heard this, he was pleased. They sat down, they laughed, and his parents-in-law invited him to stay and were happy to have them. The next morning she returned with her husband. When they came to his house, she said, "What should be dearer to me in this house than you? You said to me, 'Take what is dearest to you,' and I took what is dearest to me."

(Adapted from Bar-Itzhak and Shenhar 1993, 129–31)

Syria: Christian and Muslim Tales from Aleppo

In many regions of the Arab world, fairy tales and folktales are traditionally narrated primarily by women and, as we have seen, often feature female protagonists. All of the stories in *Folktales from Syria* (2004), however, were collected by Samir Tahhan from male storytellers and then translated into English by Andrea Rugh. There are basically four genres of folk narrative in this region: *qissa* (story), *hikāye* (tale), *hudūtha* (episode), and *sīra* (epic/romance). The *sīra* is a very lengthy genre performed only by a professional storyteller known as a *hakawātī* in public contexts such as in a café. The other genres are more informal and are narrated by men or women, but usually within a domestic setting. The *qissa* is a more serious tale with a clear message—one might translate the term into English as *moral tale*—that might be told to a younger person by an older person as a way of giving advice or commenting on a situation. The *hikāye* and the *hudūtha*, on the other hand, are told more for amusement and entertainment and more closely resemble the common folktale. They are told primarily to children, often include talking animals and magical occurrences, and may also convey a moral message, though usually in a less formal manner.

Aleppo is a city that has a mixed Christian and Muslim population. Many folktales are well known and circulate through both communities, with some tales (or versions of tales) being understood as Christian and others being understood as Muslim. Outsiders, however, might find it difficult to distinguish Christian from Muslim tales, for the markers that Syrians use to identify them tend to be background details:

Christian stories would not mention divorce, polygamy, or revenge conflicts. They would be more likely to mention priests and holy symbols such as crosses and churches. Muslim stories tend to be peopled with sheikhs and Bedouin, and fateful incidents may occur that are not a direct consequence of the actions of the characters [. . .] Muslim stories are more apt to divide the world of men and women clearly, as, for example, when a character enters the women's quarters or joins the men in their reception rooms. A character's occupation is one important way of identifying religious origin, since the different religious communities in the past tended to monopolize certain of the trades. Christians generally pursued craft and manual occupations that were frowned upon by Muslims. Thus stonecutters, peddlers, goldsmiths, gardeners, and weavers appearing in the stories are probably Christian, while Muslims tend to be occupied in government and commercial professions. Many of these distinctions have broken down now, but at the time these stories emerged, significant differences still existed. (Tahhan 2004, 4–5)

The following two examples are from the genre of *qissa* or moral tale.

The Story of the Five Cakes

Once upon a time there was a poor widow with five children. She loved them as the earth loves the seeds, and they loved her as the seeds love the rains. One night when there was no food left to give her children except five cakes, she went and she prepared some tea. She brought the tea and distributed the five cakes so that each child could have one cake. Then she sat quietly drinking her tea with no food left for herself.

The oldest of the children looked at his mother and thought, "My poor mother! She divided all the cakes she had among us and left none for herself to fill her empty stomach. God knows how much she has worked for our sakes, washing clothing, cleaning, ironing, shopping, cooking, washing dishes, sewing, and all the other tiresome chores. I must share my part with her." Immediately, he divided his cake into two, giving one to his mother and keeping one for himself. When the next son saw what his brother had done, he presented his mother with his second half, and so did the third and the fourth and the fifth sons, so that their mother found two and one-half cakes placed in front of her. The mother looked at her children with a smile and said, "Look what has happened, when one makes little sacrifices, one is compensated with a lot. You see what has happened to me. I had nothing to begin with and now I have more than any one of you." She put out her hand and took one-half a cake like her children and put the remaining two cakes in the middle of the table, so if anyone felt the desire to have more he could help himself a second time.

So all of them were satisfied and slept happily, enjoying love and affection, which are more valuable than any wealth and sufficient compensation for any need or lack. Keep yourselves from calamity and evil. Learn that in selfishness there is dishonor, and that the road to greatness is through giving.

Thus ends the story, with its share of grief and glory!

(Tahhan 2004, 23–24)

The Story of the Merchant of Khan al-Wazir

Once upon a time, one of the honorable merchants of the Khan al-Wazir [lit. the Vizier's Market] faced a financial crisis which obliged him to seek a loan to solve his problems and start afresh. After a great deal of effort searching far and near, he came upon a petty moneylender. The man agreed to lend him what he needed on condition that he return the money on a certain day at a certain hour. If the merchant was late by even one minute of the fixed time, the moneylender would have the right to chop off his hand. There would be no going back on the agreement, nor would it be subject to repeal or higher appeal. Since the merchant had no other alternative, being as he was so badly in need of money, he agreed to the proposal under duress, even though the conditions were exceedingly harsh. He signed a legal note to that effect in front of a notary.

The poor merchant worked very hard, trying his best to gather the amount of money he owed. But the agreed-upon day and hour were soon upon him before he had the chance to accumulate enough money to pay back the loan. He ran swiftly from door to door, knocking at the homes of relatives, friends, friends of friends, companions, and acquaintances, but everywhere his requests were rejected. They all made excuses and evaded his pleas. In the end, he gave up, accepting his fate, and in the final moment sat surrounded by his crying children and his shrieking wife.

People gathered around him: the condolers, the gloaters, the rejoicers at misfortune, and the sympathizers. After a few minutes passed, the moneylender came to claim his debt, demanding that the articles of the contract be carried out minutely, one by one. The merchant, his family, and the bystanders tried hard to soften the heart of the moneylender and postpone for a few days or even half a day the execution of the contract in hopes that after an hour or two something might happen to avoid the calamity. But the moneylender refused all their pleas, insisting stubbornly that the articles be carried out to the letter. The merchant and the people were powerless to change the moneylender's mind or curb his cruelty in carrying out the agreement. As everyone stood at a loss, the moneylender brought out his dagger and held it close to the hand of the merchant, who was trembling from head to foot with fear and dread.

Just as the blade was about to touch the merchant's skin, a stranger sprang from the crowd shouting, "Stop, put away your dagger, I am ready to pay this man's debts for him." He walked over to the petty moneylender and paid the sum to the last penny. Then he walked slowly to the merchant, who was faint from utter amazement, and said, "Keep this in mind, if it weren't for me you would be without a hand now." The merchant fell upon the stranger, kissing his hand and saying, "I will be indebted to you for this good deed all my life. I will always remember you and will be grateful for your kindness. I will beg God to let me repay you, O noble and courageous man, O good and generous one. You are an angel come down from the sky...," and so on and so forth in words appropriate from someone who had experienced a great fright and then been delivered from it.

In this way the merchant was saved and the crowd dispersed. Everyone went home, telling about what they had seen. But the matter did not stop there. Rather it began. The next morning the stranger bought a shop next to that of the merchant in Khan al-Wazir. Every time he passed the merchant's shop he would enter and say, "You must remember that if it were not for me, you would have no hand now." The merchant would answer with heartfelt words of gratitude and warm words of thanks for this deed. And so it went, day after day, week after week, month after month until it became intolerable.

Because his affairs were improving somewhat, the merchant thought to himself, "Maybe if I give him back the sum I owe, he will stop exaggerating my debt to him." So he set to work energetically day and night, night and day, until he gathered the whole amount and returned it to the stranger with his deepest thanks. But the stranger continued to increase his pattern of visiting the merchant to remind him of his good deed.

So the merchant said to himself, "Maybe if I buy him an appropriate gift he will stop reminding me of my debt to him." He went out and bought an expensive gift and presented it to the stranger as a token of his gratitude. But every time the stranger met him, he continued to tell him, "If it weren't for me, you would be without a hand."

One day when the stranger came into the shop, as was his habit every time he passed in front of the door, he barely had time to open his mouth to repeat the words, when the merchant drew out a knife and cut off his own hand. He presented the hand to the stranger saying, "Please take this hand and leave me alone. By God, it is much better to live without a hand than to live without self-respect." Some customers were gathered around the shop and when they saw what happened they were shocked. But when they understood the reason, they said, "The merchant is right; even death is preferable to living always in debt. It is much better for a person who does a good deed to throw it in the sea, rather than to exact its price by demanding gratitude."

Thus ends the story with its share of grief and glory!

(Tahhan 2004, 25–27)

Tunisia: Oral History, Personal Narrative, and Legend

Folktales such as those that have been presented are usually performed within clearly marked discursive boundaries. They often begin and end with formulaic expressions that serve to delineate the narration of fanciful and fantastic events and set the world of talking animals, supernatural creatures, and magical transformations apart from the reality of daily life. Much of the narration that takes place in any group or community, however, is about the real past: oral history. Oral historical narratives take many different forms ranging from formally recited accounts of past events, to conversational retellings of personal experiences, to legendary tales about the origins of the world as we know it. Many of these types of performances are difficult to study because they are "porous," that is, listeners comment on the narrative as it unfolds, they interrupt and ask for clarifications, and they may even contradict the teller if they disagree with the account. When history is at stake, discussion and debate are much more likely than with a tale told primarily for entertainment or for the purpose of communicating a moral lesson.

Sabra Webber's study of oral historical narratives in Kelibia (Tunisia), *Romancing the Real* (1991), is a fascinating exploration of the many different types of stories and storytelling events that recount the community's past and help maintain and define its identity. Unlike many of the tales examined in her work that involve multiple voices and a very loose conversational structure, the following story is a rather coherent tale. It is a glimpse into the narrator's childhood, as well as a glimpse into the colonial past when the French ruled Tunisia, but eventually turns out to be a saint's legend, a tale of the mystical powers of one of the local saints, Sidi 'Ali Qsibi. The older narrator, Uncle Hmida, announces that the tale is about the saint in his opening line, but the saint does not then reappear until the final section of the tale. Uncle Hmida directs his tale to a younger man, Malek, who is his primary audience.

The Story of Sidi 'Ali Qsibi

Now we are going to talk about the story of Sidi 'Ali Qsibi. My father was crazy about falconry and I would be his lookout for the gendarmes. (Because falconry was forbidden. The gendarmes would arrest falconers.) I'd ride on the donkey and he'd hunt.

Well, he had a wonderful falcon, I mean, any quail that flew up, it would catch. Honestly, not one would get away. And I got caught in the same mire. I became more obsessed with it than he was. I was young. So when I saw such a good falcon... [My father] would sit with the falconers, sit on the ground, roll cigarettes, and feed the falcon a little. Well, I would beg him—tell him, "Give me the falcon to throw on a little quail." I knew the falcon was so good that anybody could catch something with it.

Malek: How old were you?

Hmida: I was twelve.

Malek: Still young.

Yeah, young, trailing along after him. He'd tell me, "Not now. Wait 'til the falcon can hunt even better and I'll let you." (He was just keeping me hoping. He wasn't going to give me the falcon because father would say, "The falcon is something apart from my family." Anyway, a great obsession. He was keeping me hoping.)

I asked him three or four times on different occasions when the falconers would be gossiping together and the falcon was next to him on his perch. I'd say, "Give it to me, let me take a turn [hunting with it]." He'd say, "Let the falcon molt a little and learn to hunt better." I thought to myself, "Anyway, I'll wait 'til a night when he isn't home and take it out secretly early in the morning. (Just like I'd seen him get up at dawn.) I'll take it and go hunt with it."

Things went as planned. One night, on the eve of the souk [market]... (He was going to the souk to bring back that twine used [for making] the warp for the mats from Menzel Temime so we could line up the warp on the loom. We were weavers together, he and I.) I thought, "I won't find a night better than this. In the morning, he's going to the souk on the donkey. He's going and I will take the falcon and go hunt with and after..." (It didn't occur to me that the falcon might get away. I just counted on my getting a quail with it or two, watch it, and go home with it.)

Yeah, well, [my father] on the eve before he was going to leave for the souk said, "Hmida!" I said, "Eh?" (Now he loved me a lot but he was strict, tough.) He said, "Well anyway, I'm going to the souk in Menzel Temime. You aren't to touch the falcon." (Now if he hadn't told me, I could have pretended I didn't know and done the deed and he would have forgiven me. But after he'd instructed me, there was no way out.) He told me, "Leave the falcon alone while I'm at the market. When I get home if we hear there are quail, I'll take you and we'll go hunting." I said O.K., but I was still determined to go.

Well, Sidi ["sir"—addressing Malek], he got up early and I saddled the donkey with him. The little moon was still shining, thus [points to the moon]. It was early morning. He started out to Menzel Temime, but the wind wasn't right for hunting and not right for quail. It was Corsican [blowing in from the north] and so very strong that the grain crops were being bent to the ground. Not for hunting. No one would go out in it.

Well, he left and I took the little hawk and the beating stick. (Mother still hadn't awakened. Because Mother wouldn't have let me go.) I went out toward Sidi 'Ali Qsibi and kept going until the Jdud farm and came to the Sharif's farm and headed down [towards home]. I didn't flush out one quail and I wanted to raise even one to throw [the falcon] at so I could watch and then go home. Nothing doing! When I got near the door of the house—the house wasn't far away anymore, about four or five plow widths is all, not very far—the caraway was in front of me and I saw in the middle of the crop a little bird—a tiny bird. Under similar circumstances my father, if he was hunting and there weren't quail and he didn't have any feed would on his way home cast [the falcon] on two or three birds [to feed it].

I thought, "By God, now here's a bird that has flown into the caraway and I'm about to go in..." And I hadn't seen, flushed out any quail, "I'll just toss it on the bird. Let me catch even this. I'll see how [the falcon] catches it and go home with him." I never took into consideration that he might fly away from me at that time. (And the falcon was really strong and I had listened when the experienced falconers had said that if the falcon flew off from the owner that person must immediately follow it, track it with his eyes as it keeps on rising into the air, rising and rising until the instant when the sky swallows it. When it looks like a gnat, and then disappears, when it disappears, fix his position. We might say, he disappeared by an olive tree or near a certain farm. Watch where it disappears from your [sight], he'll come down there or to the right or the left somewhat, but in that general area. In that spot there, he'll come down.)

Well, I went planning to shake the bird out. It had ducked into the middle of the caraway bush. I remembered where and started over, went like this with my stick [disturbed the plants] and it came out, saw the falcon on my hand, and returned! As soon as she popped up she returned because of the falcon on my hand. By that time I'd already thrown the falcon.

The falcon, when it left my hand... (he'd been used to finding a quail, but he didn't find anything). Like a shot he took off into the sky and the wind was Corsican so he'd drift to the back [i.e., inland]. He would go out of the town. Well, the falcon started to spiral and rise, to spiral and rise... "God damn what had I done?! After I had almost gotten home! O God, what a deed!! What am I going to say to my father? If only he hadn't warned me!"

Anyway, at least I remembered listening to the falconers talk about how when they had lost a falcon, how they followed it with their eyes. Well, I'm watching it with the light in my eyes and the falcon is circling and rising and [with] every turn he moves away five or six kilometers. Yes! So every turn he took he went higher and higher and I follow him, follow him, follow him... until he was like a gnat, until the sky swallowed him.

When he went into the sky and I had been tracking him thus when the sky ate him up I fixed the position (as I had heard from the elders—people obsessed with falcons). I calculated it [to be] from the Hamura neighborhood, for example, from the Hamura neighborhood near the Zmirli farm. There was a kind of jujube tree there in the Zmirli farm and the Limam gully next to it belonged to the Samouds. It would come down in the Limam gully or in Zmirli's farm. He was maybe five or six kilometers behind the town.

I took up the stick and started running after him. But my idea was to go to the Zmirli farm to look there for signs of him. I ran directly to the Zmirli farm (and it was far, the Zmirli farm lies about six or seven kilometers [away]). I got to the Zmirli farm. (The point where I felt the falcon might have landed was there.) I went around the bushes and around the Ben Majlif orchard, but those I asked had not seen a falcon. I couldn't hear jingling. [Falcons had little bells on their tails.] I went to the Kordoghlis' land looking everywhere. Nothing.

I ran to all the landmarks like that. When I got tired and the important places I was counting on for finding the falcon were exhausted, I no longer knew where [it could be]. I was out of control and thinking about my father, who was about to come home. It was mid-afternoon and the sun had gotten hot. I ran this way and that way. I asked people. I asked workers. No one said he'd seen it. Not a one. It was getting hotter. My legs were scratched. My clothes were torn... "I'd better go home. [But] what would I tell my father? If only he hadn't ordered me. Damn that act [of mine]." (And my father was a little strict and he really loved the falcon so.)

I was heading home and desolate. Going home I passed Sidi 'Abdallah Taherti there— started going down and came to those olive trees of Qsibi until I came to the shrine of Sidi 'Ali Qsibi and Sidi 'Ali Qsibi faced east and the door on the east side was open. It crossed my mind to go into [the shrine of] Sidi 'Ali Qsibi. I just went in to take a look. Now, I knew Sidi 'Ali Qsibi was a holy man.

I went into Sidi 'Ali Qsibi and came up behind the tomb like this facing the grave marker. [Gestures] Here [to Malek], I'll show you. [Gets up and shows him how he stood.] There now, the marker was in front of me. I said to him, "O Sidi 'Ali Qsibi, I've come to you and if you're sleeping, get up," and I pounded the marker once. "Get up, Sidi 'Ali Qsibi, and listen to me. I want to tell you something." (Well, I was young. See what I had in mind?) "If you're asleep, wake up, and if you're awake, listen to what I'm going to say. I, in any case, can't do anything for you [but] I'll weave you two rush mats and bring them and lay them out in your midst and here is al-fatiha for you [he recites al-fatiha, the opening verses of the Qur'an]. If you really think you are Sidi 'Ali Qsibi and you claim, 'I am Sidi 'Ali Qsibi, a holy righteous man,' well [when] I go from here and go into the orchard of Mohamed Kalash that has date palms in it, I'll get into the olive trees and I'll find my falcon perched there. I'll take the falcon and go home without having to search at all. I promise I'll make you two floor mats and bring them and spread them in your midst, and here is al-fatiha ("Praise to God on high...").

I went out of the domed shrine and cutting across the country I went along and came to that orchard of Mohamed Kalash that I had told you about. There were olive trees there. I went in and followed the little path by the cactus fence and the planted area. I was going along the path thus. (Now, I was out of my mind, "What will I tell my father, and father is going to come any time now.") I arrived and went into the middle of the olive trees. I ran into the leash. It hit me here [gestures to his face], thus. The leash of the falcon!!! I raised my eyes and found the falcon perched rubbing his head on his shoulders, ruffling his wing feathers, opening his wings and going like this [demonstrates]... puffing himself up. He didn't run away from me, didn't run from me. He wasn't stuck, wasn't tied up. Just perched and the leash was swinging down and that's it. I went like this to the leash [pulled on it] and grabbed him and started home, as happy as if I'd found the Prophet, and I hugged it with happiness—safe from the wrath of my father.

What can I say? I got to the house, went in and found my mother at the door. "My son, my son, why did you take the falcon?" I said, "O mother, please don't tell father. See, I took it and wanted to watch it with a bird, throw it on a little one, but there weren't any. Well, I came home with it, is all." (I didn't tell her anything except, "Please don't tell father.")

"Come on, get in here—don't do that any more. Your father would have a fit."

Well, I perched the falcon and paced back and forth in the entrance hall. Mother got down [from the stove] couscous made with *droa'* [a grain] and put out the dinner. She put my father's dinner to one side and put mine out. "Come on and eat." I said, "No, I am not eating. I'm waiting for father." Father arrived, he arrived and I went out to meet him, helped him unload the donkey baskets, tied up the donkey, and he went into the house. Mother set out the low table, she put out a pottery dish of couscous made from *droa'* (it's like I'm seeing it all now) and pumpkin and fava beans . . .

He sat down there and she put the low table before him. And I went there [gestures] a little distance from him in the middle of the room and sat. I decided not to tell him until he had eaten. Maybe he'd get mad and not eat. Well, he sat down and ate. After he had finished (I was peeking over at him) . . . After he had finished dinner he pulled out the tobacco pouch and started to roll a cigarette. I said, "O Father!" He said, "Eh?" I said, "I'm going to tell you a little something. Don't get mad at me." [He tells him the story and they make the mats for Sidi 'Ali Qsibi.]

(Adapted from Webber 1991, 102–8)

At one level this is a straightforward narrative of personal experience, a childhood misadventure of the type that nearly everyone has encountered in one way or another. But in the context of oral history, we can also see that it is densely packed with the details of how life was when the narrator was a child. The listener, who might well be an urban, educated young man unfamiliar with the details of everyday life in the countryside, is given a glimpse of life as it was several decades ago: Falconry, now disappearing, was still a craft practiced in the Tunisian countryside; the French ruled Tunisia and had prohibited falconry, so that the boy had to act as a lookout to avoid getting caught by the gendarmes; the narrative is filled with geographical landmarks and references to who owned which farm and orchard and also includes a number of details of the art of falconry; the narrator presents himself as a young person who had no clear idea how to address a saint and ask for his intercession, but in the end his sincerity seems to have earned the saint's intervention. At yet another level, the story may be seen as a didactic tale about the results of disobeying one's father, and at the same time it concludes as a saint's legend promulgating belief in the efficacy of the saints and their sacred powers.

Egypt: Personal Narratives in Context. When folklorists study personal narratives, they often find that the relationship between a given narrative and the rest of the performance event is as interesting and as meaningful as the narrative itself. We have already examined extracts from the Epic of the Banī Hilāl—because these performances often last from four to eight hours, the epic singer needs to take a break from time to time at which point tea and cigarettes are often offered to everyone present. During these breaks the conversation frequently turns to various aspects of the story of the epic; the behavior of the heroes, customs, and traditions of days gone by; or other topics. Following is an example of how a personal narrative emerged during a pause in an epic performance in the village of al-Bakātūsh in Northern Egypt and then affected the rest of the performance.

Mustafa's Tale of the Wolf

One evening when Shaykh Tāhā was performing a segment from "The Wars of Tunis" (6/24/87), audience members began to comment on the name of the hero Diyāb (lit. wolves). The topic shifted to how times had changed, and people began listing the technological changes that they had personally lived through. The example of the shift from the *nōrāj* ("threshing floor"), which used horses or water buffalo driven round and round in a circle, to the modern gasoline-driven threshing machines was brought up. Then the discussion shifted to the subject of the hand-powered *tambūr* ("Archimedean water-screw") to the proliferation of livestock-driven waterwheels to modern gasoline-powered pumps. Suddenly a young man named Mustafa launched into a narrative that linked the two topics of wolves and technological change, a story of how his grandfather had spent an entire night turning a *tambūr* while fending off a wolf by tossing it scraps of his own food. Mustafa added that he himself had only seen a wolf once, but that he would never forget it though it occurred when he was quite young and working as a camel driver (as he still does).

Mustafa recounted: One night during cotton harvest, the landowner I was working for insisted I take one last load of cotton into [the town of] Qallīn, though it was near 2:00 A.M. I said no at first, that it was too late, and besides I couldn't go alone. But the overseer insisted. He said he would ride with me. Once we'd loaded and I was setting out, the man said he would go back and get the donkey, and then catch up with me on the way. I walked and walked and kept saying to myself, "Any moment he'll catch up with me, any moment now." I shouted and shouted but there was no answer—the man had lied and gone home.

I arrived in Qallīn and the people there said, "Boy, are you crazy? It's 2:00 A.M., couldn't it wait till morning?" I told them the overseer would be along soon, so they weighed in the cotton and all. I waited and waited, but the man didn't come. So I said to myself, "I'll go home." So I was riding the camel—perhaps 3:30 at night—to where the bridge is now—and there was the wolf. I scarcely knew it was a wolf—dog, wolf, I was young and had never seen one. But when I tried to pass, it would growl [Mustafa growls], and if I tried to pass it on the side, the wolf would herd the camel back to the path. I didn't know what to do. I was afraid to get down, I couldn't get by, I thought to myself, "I could take off the camel's *kimām* [muzzle] and let it fight off the wolf—but it might turn around and bite me."

Shaykh Tāhā the poet interrupted: "A fasting camel [*jamal sāyim,* i.e., 'hadn't been fed']?"

Yes. And he could well turn around and bite me rather than the wolf. I thought and thought and thought and decided: Better to be bit by the camel than eaten by the wolf! So I decided to unfasten the *kimām,* saying to myself, "Don't worry about the wolf, just watch out for the camel and be ready with the stick!" So I unfastened the *kimām.* The wolf growled and the camel seized it in its mouth and threw it in the air higher than me. I screamed. I thought the wolf was going to land on me. When it hit the ground the camel held it, excuse me, with its feet and began to eat it [*bada yinissir fīh* (lit. "eat and tear at it as a hawk eats its prey") Mustafa imitates the camel tossing its head from side to side]. It chewed on one piece all the way back to the village.

I arrived at the house, but I was afraid to get down in case the camel bit me—its mind was "changed" [*kān dimāghuh mitghayyar*]—it might do anything. So I knocked on the door and finally my father (May he rest in peace!) answered, saying, "Where have you been?" So I told him that this and that had happened. He said that son of a bitch [the landowner] had come home long ago. He said, "Stay where you are—don't get down." And he left me on the camel. It was time for dawn prayers and every time I saw someone enter our alley I'd shout at him to go back [*rudd! rudd!*] and tell him that the camel would bite him. I thought, "Am I going to spend the night on this camel?" But my father appeared on the roof with a wooden ladder and a rope. He lowered the ladder on the rope and said, "Jump and climb as fast as you can." So I did, and he also pulled up on the rope at the same time. The camel turned to bite me but it missed. Can you imagine? That camel was tired out [*ta'bān*] for two months."

Listeners: "Of course! Of course!"

And I was too—I kept seeing the wolf flying through the air. I'd point up in the air and shout, "There's the wolf! [*id-dīb ahō*]. They even had a doctor examine me—I told him too—"There's the wolf!" [cringing and pointing up into the corner of the room].

My father said, "I'll have my rights from that landowner." He complained to the village headman [*'umda*], and the headman said the man must be punished and informed the district police. My father said, "I don't want 20 Egyptian pounds or 50 or 100, I want my rights from that man." And didn't he get a year in jail?

The listeners nodded.

One listener: "That was during the days when 'Abd al-Salām was village headman."

Mustafa: "Yes, now that was when a headman was a headman!"

The listeners nodded.

(Reynolds 1995, 186–88)

Mustafa's tale sparked a number of comments. More notably for our purposes here, however, it refocused the evening's performance on the hero Diyāb. Later discussions all dealt with Diyāb's character and his role in the epic, and when Diyāb was mentioned during the performance, Shaykh Tāhā lingered over the name and nodded to Mustafa as did other listeners. Several times when Diyāb made an appearance in battle, audience members called out, "There's the wolf!" Conversation during each of the tea breaks that evening drifted back to the wolf story; a few similar incidents were recounted, but none was as dramatic as Mustafa's tale.

In this example, a personal narrative not only gave voice to part of the community's history, a glimpse of the way things were years ago, but also, like a prism, refocused the larger epic performance in which the personal narrative was told. Personal narratives are meaningful in and of themselves, but they can be even more powerful when they build connections between traditional tales and everyday life. Both the epic and Mustafa's wolf tale captured dramatically a sense of real life dangers and the ever-tenuous struggle for survival.

Conversational Genres: Proverbs, Riddles, Jokes, and Curses

Many of the most-widespread, best-known, and commonly performed genres of folklore are types of verbal art that are so brief that they almost always occur embedded in larger conversations: proverbs, adages, riddles, jokes, classic comparisons, and clever turns of phrase. As the Arabic saying goes, "Proverbs from the common people are like salt for the food" *(amthāl al-ʿawāmm milh al-taʿām)*, and it is certainly true that the "flavor" of a culture is sometimes best perceived through these everyday forms of folklore. Some of these conversational genres, like the Arabic adage just quoted, are easy to understand and can be presented in translation without additional commentary, but many other proverbs and images from folk speech genres are distilled from whole complexes of attitudes, customs, and practices such that even when all of the words are explained, the larger meaning of a proverb and how it might be used socially are still obscure. Some early collections of these genres did little more than provide a series of isolated texts, but folklorists in recent decades have become more and more interested in observing and studying how and when these genres are deployed in conversational situations.

Proverbs from the Bedouin of the Negev and Sinai Deserts. Proverbs might well be the most ancient form of folklore to be preserved in writing—they appear on cuneiform clay tablets, in Ancient Egyptian hieroglyphics, and, of course, in the Hebrew Bible. In the Middle Ages, Arab linguists and litterateurs compiled many collections of Arab proverbs, and these collections constitute one of the earliest uses of colloquial Arabic in writing. Translating the dialect proverbs into Classical Arabic was simply not possible without losing a great deal of the rhythm and rhyme that make most proverbs so memorable, so these early compilers used the characters of the Arabic alphabet in a variety of innovative ways to transcribe proverbs from the spoken vernaculars.

Scholars have found that nearly every culture has proverbs that contradict each other, some urging caution ("Look before you leap," "Caution is the better part of valor"), for example, whereas others urge decisive action ("He who hesitates is lost," "Strike while the iron is hot"). So it is not an easy matter to study a community's worldview or attitudes from proverbs; for any one selection of examples, there could well be others that offer a completely different picture. Yet there is something compelling about the terse wisdom that these phrases embody that does seem to provide a window into the beliefs and values of societies and cultures that makes *paremiology*—the study of proverbs—a fascinating field.

Clinton Bailey's *A Culture of Desert Survival* (2004) is a rich collection of 1,350 proverbs collected over three-and-a-half decades of fieldwork among the Bedouin of the Sinai and Negev deserts. The collection is organized thematically, which makes it possible to see how at times many different proverbs are used to express a similar idea, and at other times, equally well-known proverbs convey conflicting messages. Following are clusters of proverbs dealing with two different themes—maternal uncles and hospitality.

MATERNAL RELATIVES. One widely held belief in many regions of the Arab world, among Bedouin and non-Bedouin alike, is that there is a special relationship between a boy and his maternal uncle, to the extent that a boy's personality and character are thought to be inherited from his maternal uncle, rather than from his father. In many traditional families, the paternal uncle *('amm)* is seen as an extension of the father and his paternal authority, whereas the maternal uncle *(khāl)* is seen as an extension of the mother and her more compassionate and nurturing role. If a boy is in trouble, he might therefore be more likely to go seek help from a maternal uncle than from a paternal uncle. Arabic has completely different terms for maternal and paternal relatives; the paternal terms have stronger connotations of authority and respect, whereas the maternal terms give a sense of friendliness and empathy. If a younger man stops an older male on the street to ask directions or any type of favor, he might address the stranger as "my paternal uncle"; if a friendship springs up between them, however, a certain sense of closeness can be expressed if the younger man shifts to calling him "my maternal uncle."

A Bedouin considers only his relatives on his father's side (his *'amūm*) to be his kinsmen and vital connection, owing to their role as the providers of his security. Still, his maternal relatives, or *khwāl,* are among the closest ties that he maintains with persons outside his *khamsa* (clan). They too play a role, however minor, in his life. First, they are believed to be the fount of many of his qualities and thus worthy of respect as his prototype. Second, they are often there to help solve problems that do not require the use of force. Hence, maternal kin are deemed deserving of special regard.

410. Thilthayn al-walad li-khālih

Two-thirds of a son come from his maternal uncle.

This is the standard assertion that many of a child's qualities come from his mother's family. Thus as a compliment to his wife's family, a Bedouin who has married outside his *khamsa* (clan) may declare that he chose his wife because "I was searching for a maternal uncle for my son" *(dawwart l-ibni khāl)*.

411. Is'al 'al al-khāl ū-khāl al-khāl

Ask about the maternal uncle and the maternal uncle's maternal uncle!

To reaffirm the importance of choosing a bride from a good family so as to endow one's children with good qualities, this proverb urges a prospective groom to inquire about more than one generation of his bride's maternal lineage. It asserts that asking about only the brother of the girl, from whom her sons will inherit many of their qualities, is insufficient. One must also ask about the brother's own maternal uncles to reinsure that the desired qualities are deeply rooted in the bride's family.

413. Al-khāl 'irwa

One's maternal uncle is like a loop.

Because Bedouin believe that a child's qualities come from his maternal relatives, his personality is dependent on theirs. The "loop" simile refers to the loop of a saddlebag or sack with which it is hung up, just as a child's personality is metaphorically hung on or tied to his mother's menfolk.

414. Man jadd khālih jadd

He whose maternal uncle is serious will be serious, too.

415. Khālak mithil thōbak fōg mitnak – wi-n sibbaytih mint min ar-rjāl

Your maternal uncle is like the shirt on your back—if you belittle him, you're not a man.

As a child's qualities derive from his maternal uncle (hence "the shirt on your back"), belittling one's uncle is tantamount to belittling oneself.

416. Kalām illī fi khālak fik

Belittling your maternal relative belittles you [lit. "Talk about your maternal uncle is talk about you"].

417. In jāk al-jūa' i'mid khwālak w-in jāk al-jōr dowwir 'ā zlāmak

If hunger besets you, go to your maternal kin, but if oppression besets you, seek your paternal kin.

While the role of paternal kin is to assure security and the defense of one's rights, a main role of maternal relatives is to help one economically. The difference is that the obligations of the paternal kin are legally binding, whereas those of the maternal relatives are voluntary. For "oppression," some Bedouin use the word *daym* instead of *jōr*.

418. Kul khāl yinām ghayr khāl al-'amm

Every maternal relative sleeps but the mother's brother.

Owing to the voluntary and nonbinding nature of relations between a Bedouin and his maternal relatives, the latter, being absorbed in matters pertaining to their own *khamsa* (clan), generally show little regard for the welfare of the children of their womenfolk that are married to outsiders. The possible exception might be the brother of one's mother, to whom she can turn in matters that affect the welfare of her children. Thus one finds maternal uncles trying to mediate problems that involve their sister's son.

(Adapted from "Maternal Relatives," Bailey 2004, 161–64)

HOSPITALITY. A very important value shared by Arabs of all walks of life is hospitality *(diyāfa)*, a concept that includes both the act of offering hospitality and the proper behavior of a guest. The offering of hospitality is an obligation, no matter who the guest might be, and in return, the guest should accept what is offered without criticism and should not make additional requests. In return, however, the guest, after his departure, becomes the "poet" of his host, meaning that he either sings the praises of his host's generosity or instead spreads news of his stinginess. The hospitality concept in Arab culture is also deeply rooted in a sense of "What goes around, comes around," meaning that hospitality offered to a guest will come back to one later in unforeseeable ways from one's own future hosts or directly from God. In any case, the offering and accepting of hospitality in Arab culture is seen as a blessing for all parties concerned and is a behavior that almost achieves the level of sacredness.

521. Ar-rājil yudrub bi-s-seif ū-yigrī ad-deif

A true man strikes with a sword and feeds his guest meat.

Owing to the sacrifice that Bedouin must make in sharing their usually limited food with a passerby or other guest, they place hospitality on a level with bravery, in determining what constitutes manliness. This proverb is also used as the definition of a Bedouin, as opposed to a peasant or other sedentary person, and of an adult Bedouin as compared with a child.

522. Ila zarat at-tīb fi-r-rab' ribhān ila mashyū lāzim tijī lak irwāya

If you've sown bounty with guests, you'll gain; after they've left they give you a name.

This proverbial line from a poem spells out one reason for Bedouin hospitality: to gain a reputation for generosity. Being generous demonstrates a certain disdain for wealth, especially when slaughtering a head of one's livestock for a guest's meal. Such a reputation is important to a Bedouin's security, indicating that thoughts of material loss would never deter him from defending values and interests he holds dear.

524. Zād al-jawād 'end al-jawād gurda

Food offered by a worthy man to a worthy man is but a loan.

Aware that life in the desert requires frequent movement from place to place and the attendant need to find shelter and food in the tents of strangers, Bedouin view whatever they give to guests, or receive from hosts, as an essential element in social intercourse. Here, it is depicted as but the partial payment of a floating debt that Bedouin owe one another, a debt that people, to be deemed "worthy," should acknowledge.

525. Al-karam sidād

Hospitality is the payment of a debt.

As in this proverb, the general word for generosity (*karam*) is often synonymous with hospitality, owing to the natural largesse involved in sharing limited provisions.

526. Ad-deif deif Allāh biyātī bi-rizgih

A guest is the guest of God, who provides his provision.

One implication of this proverb is that a guest is to be received, respected, and protected as acts of submission to the will of God, who wants good hospitality. It is also an expression of a Bedouin's complete deference to a guest, considering him "a guest of God" in the sense of God giving a host the wherewithal to provide for him. Accordingly, instead of thanking a host in whose tent one has been fed, it is proper to say, "May God replenish you" *(Allāh yikhlif 'alayk)*. If one mistakenly should thank the host, his reply would be, "It is from God's purse"*(min kīs Allāh)*, that is, it is God that provided, not me.

527. Wājib ad-deif thilālit ayyām ū-thilth

A guest's due is three and a third days.

Any guest that arrives at a Bedouin tent is entitled to remain there for three and a third days. This entitlement is not only a show of basic respect for the guest as a person, but also a legal right. If a guest is asked to leave before this period has elapsed, he may press a claim before a judge and ask for compensation if the reason for his humiliation proves unfounded. The third of a day is added as a grace period, in the event that a guest's arrival was toward the end of a day.

563. Salāmit ad-deif min bakht al-mahillī

The welfare of a guest is the host's good luck.

In that every tent serves as a sanctuary, vigilance for a guest's safety and inviolability is ultimately the responsibility of the host. If any harm should befall the guest, the host has a problem. Conversely, it is his good luck whenever a guest leaves unharmed.

567. Ad-deif min al-muhsināt lō gōmānī

A guest is inviolable, even if he's a foe.

The proverb affirms that a guest, although an enemy, is to enjoy safety in the tent at which he has arrived.

575. Al-jūd min al-mowjūd

Generosity depends on what's available.

It is incumbent upon a guest to accept what is offered to him graciously without requesting more. The proper attitude of a Bedouin is that a host provides his guest with what is available and reasonable.

576. ʿEinin mā shāfat ū-kibdin mā ʿafat

The eye shouldn't notice and the liver not refuse.

It is considered bad etiquette for a guest to scrutinize what he is offered, lest it be little, or to refuse to eat it, even if the food is poorly prepared or consists of leftovers. To violate this convention might humiliate a host and contravenes the assumption that every host offers his best. Because Bedouin consider the liver to be the source of appetite, one's failure to eat is depicted as "the liver has refused," the verb *ʿayya* for "refused." Accordingly, the loss of one's appetite is a sign of being ill, which is termed "refusing" *(ʿayyān)*, that is, the liver's refusing food.

583. Ad-deif yōm jā amīr ū-yōm gaʿad asīr ū-yōm ʿaggad shāʿir

The guest—the day he arrives he's a prince, the day he sits he's a prisoner, the day he leaves he's a poet.

By way of explaining this proverb, the Bedouin relate that a guest once came to the tent of an old woman who met him with, "Greetings, O Prince!" When he had sat on the carpet and was served food, she said, "Welcome, O Prisoner!" And when he left, she said, "Farewell, O Poet!" Before departing the guest asked her the reason for the different titles she had given him. She replied, "When someone appears in our tents, he's like a prince, for we don't know his wants, but are ready to serve him. When he sits down, he's like a prisoner, for he's forbidden to say, 'Bring this! Bring that!' When he leaves he's a poet, for then he can tell everyone if we receive our guests properly or not." Bedouin concern about being recognized as hospitable creates the image of a guest as a poet, for poems are often composed about one's reception and may enjoy wide exposure.

(Adapted from "The Importance of Hospitality," Bailey 2004, 196–99, 211–17)

Proverbs from a Druze Village in Lebanon. Most collections of Arabic proverbs that include English translations and explanations are organized alphabetically (Burckhardt 1972; Frayha 1953; Jewett 1893, for example), which makes it more difficult to study specific ideas or themes but does make it easier to locate and research an individual Arabic proverb. Following are two series of proverbs selected from Frayha's *A Dictionary of Modern Lebanese Proverbs* that give a sense of proverbs from a nontribal setting in the modern Arab world. All of the 4,155 proverbs in this work were collected in the village of Rās al-Matn, a predominantly Druze village to the east of Beirut.

88. Ijr li-warā w-ijr li-qiddām

One foot forward, the other backward (said of a hesitant person).

89. Al-ijr mā bitdibb illā matrah mā bithibb

One's feet carry him only to places where he loves to be.

90. Al-ijr an-naqqāla mish shaghghāla

Feet which are always on the move are not the feet of a hard-working man.

91. Ijrat is-sillum himlānuh?

Is the reward for (lending) the ladder carrying it back?

Not every householder owns a ladder. So the ladder is one of the articles that are often lent. Sometimes people fail to return it, and the owner has to go and carry it back himself.

92. Ijrayn ʿawj wa-baddhun bābūj

Crooked feet (and yet) he asks for a fine pair of shoes!

93. Ijʻalnī bayn il-aqdām wa-lā tijʻalnī bay n il-afwāh

(Oh God) Throw me underfoot, but put me not in the mouths (of people).

It is better to be trodden over than to be slandered.

94. Ijū ybaytū khayl al-sultān maddat il-khanfasa ijrhā

(When) they came to shoe the horses of the sultan, the beetle stuck out her foot.

Said of an insignificant person who tries to thrust himself upon others or when someone tries to put himself in places where he does not belong.

(Adapted from Frayha 1953, 19–20)

2388. Al-ʻaql jawhara

Intelligence is a gem.

2389. Al-ʻaql zīna

Intelligence is a decoration (**for a man**).

2390. Al-ʻaql zīna li-kull razīna

Intelligence is a decoration for every serious woman.

2391. ʻAql al-kabīr kabīr

The intelligence of a great man is great.

2392. ʻAqlātuh bi-rās tarbūshuh (bi-rās shurrābtuh)

His brains hang at the top of his tarbush (fez hat, or the tassle of his fez)

2393. ʻAqlātuh bi-nuss kimm

His brains are half-sleeved (short-sleeved)

He is lacking in intelligence.

2394. ʻAqlātuh ʻalā sūs w-nuqtah

His brains hinge on a point.

2395. ʻAqlātuh mā byiqlū bayda

He has not brains enough to fry an egg.

2396. 'Aqlak b-rāsak itnayn bidīrūk

You may have your own brains, but two make you think differently.

(lit. "Your brain is in your head but two turn you around"). Cf. "two heads are better than one."

2397. 'Aqlak b-rāsak bta'rif khalāsak

(As long as) your brains are in your head, you (ought to) know what is good for you.

(Adapted from Frayha 1953, 434–35)

Arabic proverbs provide a fascinating window into social values and folk beliefs, and they provide a portrait of both extremely local cultural images as well as images and concepts that are widely shared throughout the Arab world.

Riddles from the United Arab Emirates. In some cultures around the world, riddles are associated primarily with childhood, or perhaps more accurately, with the interaction between adults and children. In many places, however, particularly in rural areas, riddling sessions, even competitions, are a favorite pastime for adults as well. Many riddles clearly have an educational purpose, and the posing and answering of riddles certainly sharpens both mind and wit. Beyond these didactic and ludic purposes, however, riddles can be seen as an introduction to the world of symbols and metaphors—things are described by their parts or their functions (metonymy, synecdoche), or they are referred to as being like something else (simile, metaphor). They force us to see things in very different ways (the moon as a plate, or a wheel of cheese, or something that grows old and then young, or something that is white against black in contrast to the sun which is yellow against blue, or something that is inconstant because it changes versus the sun's steady form, and so forth). And these ways of seeing things in images of similitude and contrasts is also crucial to the function of poetry, which as we have seen, plays a very important role in Arab culture. In Arab culture riddles have been couched in poems, and they frequently appear in folktales, saints' legends, epic poetry, and other genres.

In translation, of course, the rhythm and rhyme of riddles is often lost and instead we find only the imagery, stripped of its distinctive texture. Perhaps this is part of the reason that riddling in Arabic has attracted the attention of so few Western scholars despite the fact that it is a widespread form of verbal art. North Africa may be the best represented region in the Arab world for it has been the subject of several studies on riddling including: Giacobetti (1916), a collection of 619 Algerian Arabic riddles; Hamidou (1938), a collection of Algerian riddles that, unfortunately, appear only in French translation; al-Murtād (1982), a full-length study of Algerian riddles that includes 176 riddle texts; Quéméneur (1944), a collection from Tunisia; and Webber (1975) which includes 50 riddles from Tunisia. Chyet (1988) offers a structural analysis of these and examples from other parts of the Arab world and provides a useful overview of scholarly writing on Arabic riddles.

The following examples have been translated from al-Tābūr's (2001) study of riddles and riddling from the other end of the Arab world, the United Arab Emirates, on the Arabian Peninsula:

> A blue bowl in an empty river, at night it is filled
> [the sky] (67)
> A metal washbasin, a troop of dates, a wheel of cheese, and a loaf of bread
> [the sky, the stars, the moon, and the sun] (68)
> A thing, whenever it increases, it decreases
> [the moon] (71)
> God created a thing without a shape, it's found everywhere in the world.
> [air/wind] (73)
> What piece of land has the sun shone on only once?
> [the bottom of the Red Sea where Moses parted it] (76)
> What thing eats and is never sated, but when it drinks it dies?
> [fire] (80)
> What thing lengthens and shortens [at the same time]?
> [a lifetime—the longer you live, the less of your life remains] (91)
> A tree that has twelve branches, and every branch thirty leaves, and every leaf five fruits.
> [the year, the months, the days, and the five daily prayers] (93)
> It overpowers my father and yours, it overpowers the sultan and the king.
> [sleep] (100)
> It sticks like glue and to everything it sticks.
> [a name—everything is called by its name] (111)
> A traveler who has come from a journey, not over land, nor over sea, he drinks from two skins filled with neither water nor honey.
> [a newborn baby] (115)
> Doors which are open during the day, closed at night, and when you look into them you see yourself
> [the eyes] (119)
> Your paternal aunt is your father's sister; her son's maternal uncle, who is he to you?
> [your father] (125)
> Mother of your brother and sister to your maternal uncle, wife of your father, who is she to you?
> [your mother] (126)
> We watch it, but it doesn't watch us; we hear it, but it doesn't hear us; we see it, but it doesn't see us.
> [the television] (141)

(Translated and adapted from al-Tābūr 2001, 67–141)

Jokes: Pan–Middle Eastern versus Regional. It would be difficult to say that one was familiar with Arab culture and folklore if one knew nothing about the rich body of jokes and humorous tales that have been a prominent characteristic of Arabic culture for centuries. Medieval Arabic literature includes volume upon volume of jokes, humorous anecdotes, and comic tales. Some of these works are general anthologies of jokes *(nukat)* or amusing anecdotes *(nawādir)*, whereas others are organized around a particular theme (sexual humor, jokes about misers, etc.) or even around a particular character such as the ubiquitous "wise fool" Juhā or the medieval epitome of greed, Ashʿab ibn Jubayr. In modern times, it is Egyptians who are most famous, even notorious, among Arabs for their love of joke and humor—in Arabic one says, "Their blood is light" *(damahum khafif),* meaning they are lighthearted and witty—and it is no accident that the Egyptian film industry in the twentieth and twenty-first centuries has produced enormous numbers of comedies enjoyed across the Arab world.

Two sequences of jokes are offered as examples: The first are tales of Juhā, which are found throughout the Middle East; and the second are examples of Egyptian political humor about the three Egyptian presidents Gamāl ʿAbd al-Nāsir (Nasser), Anwar al-Sādāt, and Ḥusnī Mubārak.

JUHĀ, GOHĀ, AND NASRUDDĪN: A PAN–MIDDLE EASTERN JOKE TRADITION. Perhaps the single most widely distributed folk tradition in the modern Middle East is the figure of the "wise-fool" known in Arabic as Juhā or Gohā. In Arab texts of the 9th century he is already renowned for his foolish and humorous escapades. He is described by the famous Arab author al-Jāhiz (d. 869), and a collection of tales about him appears in the booklist of the 10th-century Baghdadi bookseller Ibn Nadīm (d. 990). From Arabic tradition, Juhā passed into Sephardic Jewish folklore in al-Andalus ("Moorish Spain") and he continues to survive in both Judaeo-Arabic and in Ladino (the Spanish-Hebrew hybrid language of the Sephardic Jewish community). A very similar character is found in Turkish, Persian, and as far East as Urdu, the national language of Pakistan, under the name Nasruddīn Khōja ["Nasrettin Hoca" in modern Turkish] or Mulla Nasruddīn. It may be that this character was originally separate from that of the Arabic Juhā, but by the 19th and 20th centuries the repertory of jokes and tales about these two figures had merged nearly completely and they are now often thought of as being one and the same character under two different names.

Some tales of Juhā focus simply on his stupidity, but others present more of a trickster character or that of a wise fool who, while saying or doing something that at first appears foolish, in fact manages to point out some deeper truth, resolve a difficult problem, or avoid getting into trouble. Juhā tales have even been converted into Sufi didactic tales through precisely this paradoxical interaction between the wise and the foolish to highlight the interplay between superficial appearances and deeper reality. Following is a series of tales of Juhā, drawn from a number of different collections from several different Middle Eastern languages:

Juhā passed by a group of people with plums concealed in his sleeve. He said, "Whosoever tells me what I have in my sleeve, I will give him the biggest plum." When they told him he had plums in his sleeve, he said angrily, "Whoever disclosed this to you, his mother is an adulteress!"

A certain healthy man used to beg alms, and cared little for the criticism to which he was subjected by the people. One day when he visited the house of Juhā the latter asked him what he wanted. When the beggar said that he was the guest of God, Juhā came out of his house and asked the former to follow him till they reached the mosque of that locality. Then Juhā said to him, "You went to my house by mistake. This is the house of God, O guest of God!"

One day Juhā went to a public bath. But the attendants of the bath did not pay him the attention which he deserved and gave him old, dirty towels. Nevertheless he put the large amount of 10 *qurūsh* near the mirror at the time of his departure from them. The attendants were naturally much pleased to receive the unexpectedly large amount.

Juhā visited the bath again after a week. Now the attendants paid him extraordinary respect and attention. But when at the time of his departure he put only one *qirsh* near the mirror, the attendants wondered, as well as became angry, at his payment of such a paltry amount. Then Juhā said, "There is nothing unusual in it. The payment which I have made today is meant for the previous visit, and the previous payment was for this visit."

(Adapted from Ali 1998, 14–15, 16–17)

"Laws as such do not make people better," said Nasrudin to the King; "they must practice certain things in order to become attuned to inner truth. This form of truth resembles apparent truth only slightly."

The King decided that he could, and would, make people observe the truth. He could make them practice truthfulness.

His city was entered by a bridge. On this he built a gallows. The following day, when the gates were opened at dawn, the Captain of the Guard was stationed with a squad of troops to examine all who entered.

An announcement was made: "Everyone will be questioned. If he tells the truth, he will be allowed to enter. If he lies, he will be hanged."

Nasrudin stepped forward.

"Where are you going?"

"I am on my way," said Nasrudin slowly, "to be hanged."

"We don't believe you!"

"Very well, if I have told a lie, hang me!"

"But if we hang you for lying, we will have made what you said come true!"

"That's right: now you know what truth is—*your* truth!"

(Adapted from Shah 1966, 12)

Hoca asks a friend, "How does one know when somebody is dead?"

His friend explains: "His hands and feet turn cold, ice-cold."

A few days later, Hoca goes up to the mountain to chop wood. It's a terribly cold day. His hands and feet turn cold, ice-cold. He remembers what his friend had told him. Thinking he's dead, he lies on the ground. He waits for some time for people to remove him and bury him. But no one shows up. So he rises to his feet. Trudging with great difficulty, he comes home. His wife opens the door. Hoca says to her:

"I was up there on the mountain—and I died. Let our friends and neighbors know and ask them to arrange my funeral." Then he goes back to the mountain.

His wife breaks into tears. She tears her hair out desperately. She goes from neighbor to neighbor crying: "My husband died up on the mountain!"

Some of the neighbors wonder: "If he died up on the mountain, who brought you the news?"

Hoca's wife explains: "Poor soul had nobody with him...he died all alone, so he had to come home himself to deliver the news."

(Adapted from Nesin 1994, 30)

A bunch of boys who see Hoca approaching decide to play a trick on him: they will wager that no one can climb a nearby tree and if Hoca falls for it and claims he can climb it, they will take his shoes when he goes up and they will run away.

When Hoca comes along, they say to him: "We were just saying that no one could climb this tree here. What do you think, Hoca?"

Hoca says, "I can climb it."

"Let's see you do it then."

Hoca takes his shoes off, sticks them into his shirt, and begins to climb.

The boys are alarmed: "Hoca, why are you taking your shoes with you?"

"You never can tell," says Hoca, "maybe there's a road at the top of the tree."

(Adapted from Nesin 1994, 74)

Nasrudin was walking past a well, when he had the impulse to look into it. It was night, and as he peered into the deep well, he saw the moon's reflection there.

"I must save the moon!" the Mulla thought. "Otherwise she will never wane, and the fasting month of Ramadan will never come to an end!"

He found a rope, threw it in, and called down: "Hold tight, keep bright, succour is at hand!"

The rope caught in a rock inside the well, and Nasrudin heaved as hard as he could. Straining back, he suddenly felt the rope give as it came loose, and he was thrown on his back. As he lay there, panting, he saw the moon rising in the sky above.

"Glad to be of service," said Nasrudin. "Just as well I came along, wasn't it?"

(Shah 1968, 42)

Many tales of Juhā are merely funny, such as the joke about the plums or the moon in the well presented previously. But in others he is clearly wise, such as when he demonstrates the foolishness of the King's search for truth or gives the bath attendants exactly what they deserve. In still others one can only wonder whether he is indeed a fool or instead has managed to outsmart those around him, such as when he thinks there may be a road at the top of the tree and therefore takes his shoes with him, which foils the young boys' plan to trick him, or when he delivers the Guest of God to the House of God, and thus avoids having to offer hospitality to a con man. It is the constant interplay between these diverse aspects of his character that make him, under many different names, one of the favorite humorous figures in several different languages and cultures in the Middle East, a position he has already held for over a thousand years!

POLITICAL JOKES IN MODERN EGYPT. Egyptians are infamous among their fellow Arabs as lovers of jokes and humorous tales. Much of that humor, however, has an acerbic bite to it and never more so than when they are telling jokes about the political situation in their own country. Nasser was a pan-Arab hero, but during his presidency all forms of criticism and opposition to his regime were ruthlessly suppressed. His handpicked successor, Anwar Sadat, reversed Nasser's isolationist economic policies by opening the Egyptian economy up to world markets, but this also opened the door to widespread corruption and Western-style opulence among the very rich. Mubarak was Sadat's handpicked successor, and many jokes portray him as being of limited intelligence and of having done nothing during his decades in office, leaving Egypt in economic and social stasis. Following is a selection of jokes taken from two articles that analyze political humor in Egypt by Samer Shehata and Afaf Marsot:

About the internal security police during Nasser's presidency: A fox in the western desert escaped to Libya and the Libyans asked, "Why do you come here?" The fox said, "Because in Egypt they arrest camels." The Libyans said, "But you are not a camel." The fox then said, "Of course not, but try telling that to the police!"

A little ancient Egyptian statue was found but no one could find out anything about it. They summoned experts from abroad, and they still couldn't find out a single thing about it. The secret police heard about the statue and they said, "Give it to us for twenty-four hours."
    "Twenty-four hours? What can you do in twenty-four hours?"
    "None of your business. Just give it to us."
    They took it and before the day was over they came back with it and said, "This is King So-and-so, son of So-and-so; he ruled at such and such a time and..., and..., and...!"
    "How did you find all that out? Did you locate his tomb?"
    "No, sir! He confessed."

Once someone saw a man with his nose bandaged and asked him, "Why is your nose bandaged?" The man said, "I had a tooth removed." The first man said, "Why didn't you have it removed from your mouth?" whereupon the reply was, "Can anyone in this country open his mouth?"

Once when Sadat was leaving Egypt to go to America, he became afraid of what could happen to [his wife] Jihan in his absence. He decided to put a chastity belt on her which was constructed in such a way that whatever would go into it would immediately be cut off. Sadat then left and went to America. When he returned to Egypt he called all of his ministers into a room and made them take their pants off. Everyone one of them had his dick cut off except Husni Mubarak. Sadat went to Mubarak and said to him, "You are a very good man, Husni, I knew I could count on you." Mubarak said, [speaking in a mumble], "Thank you very much, Mr. President." [The joke teller utters this in such a way as to indicate that Mubarak's tongue has been cut off.]

Anwar al-Sadat, [the Coptic] Pope Shenouda, and the [Muslim] Sheikh of the al-Azhar [mosque and university] are on a plane and it is about to crash yet there are only two parachutes. Sadat says, "I am Anwar al-Sadat, president of Egypt, and I must have one parachute." Sadat told the two men that he would give them a quiz and the one that passed the quiz would get the remaining parachute. He asked the Sheikh of al-Azhar which Arab country had "the revolution of a million martyrs." The Sheikh of al-Azhar responded correctly and said, "Algeria." Sadat then asked Pope Shenouda, "What were the names of the million martyrs?"

Whenever [President] Mubarak goes anywhere an ambulance and a donkey follow his car. Once a man asked Mubarak's doctor why the ambulance and the donkey follow Mubarak. The doctor said, "The ambulance is in case Mubarak gets into an accident and the donkey is in case the president needs a blood transfusion."

[Prime Minister] Atif Sidqi went in to talk with [President] Husni Mubarak, but Mubarak's assistant said that he was very busy and that Sidqi couldn't come in. Atif Sidqi said it very important and that he must see him. He went into Mubarak's office and found him playing chess with a donkey. He said, "You're playing chess with a donkey?" Mubarak immediately said, "Don't call him a donkey, he's beaten me four times already!"

(Adapted from Shehata 1992, 80, 81, 82, 84, 86)

When Nasser died, the question of where to bury him arose during a cabinet meeting. One minister said, "Let's bury him in the tomb of the Unknown Soldier." Another objected, saying, "You can't bury a colonel [Nasser's military rank] with a common soldier." A third suggested that he be buried in one of the tombs of the Mamluk sultans [medieval sultans of slave origins]. "No! No!" was the objection. "You can't bury the president with a slave!" Finally, running out of burial sites, someone suggested Jerusalem, whereupon the rest of the cabinet rose in horror and said, "Never! The last time they buried someone there he came back after three days!"

(Adapted from Marsot 1993, 263)

Marsot's essay "Humor: The Two-Edged Sword" (1993) ends with an eloquent call for the study of humor, particularly political humor, to better understand the views of the broader population, the folk, rather than trying to understand cultures only through the policies and statements of its political ruling class:

> What applies to Egyptian humor applies equally to that of other countries, and makes a study and analysis of humor a valid and necessary chapter in our study of the social histories of peoples. This study will tell us a great deal about the common folk, the ones who are mere statistics in the archives we [historians] all love to consult and quote; and who are seldom, if ever, viewed as living, dynamic entities who interact with that institution called the government and who exert pressure on it, even when it exerts pressure on them. For one can never claim to understand a people or its mental condition unless one has grasped the sense of humor and the hostilities it reveals. (Marsot 1993, 262)

Curses and Insults from Iraq. Although writers at times shy away from including curses and insults along with the other conversational genres, these expressions are equally as valid a subject of folkloristic research as proverbs, jokes, and other types of verbal art. The types and categories of curses and insults, whether one typically insults an individual directly or via their family or specific family members, whether one accuses them of religious laxity, sexual depravity, or just plain stupidity, whether one compares them to specific animals or parts of the body, are all deeply rooted and highly informative cultural behaviors in any society.

Sadok Masliyah's study "Curses and Insults in Iraqi Arabic" (2001) offers an analytical typology along with fascinating examples from both Muslim and Jewish dialects of Baghdadi Arabic. Following are some of the types of curses he studied with selected examples from each category:

1. *Curses and insults attacking one's honor:* Many traditional insults accuse female members of the family of prostitution, male members with practicing deviant sexuality, or—one of the most common and most powerful of insults—accuses the addressee of being of illegitimate birth *(ibn harām).* A variety of terms for prostitute or whore can be fit into stock phrases such as "Son of a—," "Brother of a—," "Sister of a—," and so forth. Men are also often insulted by saying that they are being cuckolded by their wives or by accusing them of being homosexual.

2. *Curses and insults pertaining to health:* A variety of curses call on God to afflict the addressee with a specific illness or physical disability:

   Ad'ilak bil-jirdām "I wish that you be afflicted with leprosy!"
   Inshallah tā'ūn ti'anhum "God willing, a plague will strike them."
   'asāchī shalal wadhak 'alēch[13] "May you become paralyzed and I laugh at you."
   Ittubbak sittin alf marad "May sixty thousand diseases enter you!"

---

13. In Iraqi and Kuwaiti dialects, the letter *k* is often pronounced <ch> as in *church.*

3. *Curses against property and religion:* A very common target of curses is the house *(bēt)*, both in its physical reality and in its metaphorical reality as an image of the family. Many of these phrases, however, have become so familiar that they are used as often in jest or congeniality as they are in anger, as in the phrase "May God destroy his house but he's smart one, isn't he?" roughly equivalent to English, "Damn, but he's smart!"

Inhajam bētu 'alā rāsu "May his house be destroyed on his head."
Inshallah yinhadd bētak 'alā rāsak "God willing, your house will collapse on your head."

4. *Bodily defects and professions as insults:* A wide variety of physical characteristics are turned into insults or are the target of specific insults—tall people, short people, skinny people, and so forth:

Rāh 'aqlah ibtūlah "His brain disappeared into his stature" [of a tall person].
Il-tūl tūl il-nakhlah wil-'aqil 'aql il-sakhlah "His height is that of a palm tree and his brain is that of a lamb."
Sīkh māl tinnūgh "[Like] a skewer from the oven" [of a skinny person].
Ibtūl il-zebb "[He is] as long as a penis" [of a short person].

A number of professions have traditionally been held in low regard and are used in insults such as the terms for brothel-owner, pimp, public bath worker, vendor of second-hand goods, and so forth, as well as certain social categories such as gypsies, effeminate men, and Bedouin.

5. *Animals employed in curses and insults:* The cultural associations of different animals differ from society to society; some Arabic images are shared with English, whereas others are quite different; they also vary quite a bit from region to region and country to country within the Arab world. In Iraq, sheep are used as an image of stupidity, water buffalo for obesity, parrots as an image of someone who repeats things without understanding; owls and ravens are signs of bad luck or even omens of death; and people with particularly strong sexual drive are associated with sparrows, perhaps from the belief that eating sparrows' brains acts as an aphrodisiac. But the most common insulting image from the animal world is the dog *(kalb)*—phrases such as "son of a dog," "son of a hundred dogs," and so forth reflect the very low status of the dog in Arab culture in general. Dogs are also impure in the religious sense. In Islamic practice, people do ablutions (ritual washing) before praying—if, having completed one's ablutions, one touches a dog, the dog's impurity negates the ablutions and one must rewash before doing prayers. In addition, because mating dogs are a common sight when a female is in heat, they are also considered the epitome of unbridled, shameless behavior.

Il-chalib [kalb] mā yithar "The dog never becomes pure."
Mā yistihī mithl il-kalb "He is unashamed like a dog."

6. *Insults pertaining to bad character:* Any number of personal behaviors are the fodder for insults in Iraqi Arabic, such as lying, hypocrisy, boastfulness, and ungratefulness, but perhaps no single bad characteristic is more cited than miserliness:

> *Il-khasīs yimūt futis* "The miser dies [like] a dead animal" [without burial, because people hate such a person and don't care to bury him].
> *Rizq il-khasīs li-iblīs* "The earnings of the miser [go] to the Devil" [because the inheritance is spent on forbidden deeds, thus his inheritance ends up with the Devil].

In addition to these given categories, many Iraqi Arabic insults are of types that occur in a variety of cultures, such as insults directed at either the mother or the father of the addressee ("May your father be cursed," "Son of a filthy woman," "May the grave of your mother be dug up and her body burned") and insults that feature parts of the human body such as the genitals and the buttocks.

Curses and insults offer a glimpse into a culture's sense of the taboo, the obscene, social stereotypes, unacceptable sexual practices, as well as the reverse, that is, what a culture holds to be most sacred, most inviolable, and most deserving of respect. Curses and insults often derive their potency precisely in juxtaposing the latter (mother, sister, religion, personal integrity, etc.) with the former (prostitution, homosexuality, private body parts, shameless behavior, impure animals, etc.). Some patterns are found in many different societies, whereas others are extremely local. They delineate, perhaps more clearly than any other form of folklore, what a community's public values are, and where the limits of acceptable behavior lie. The sensitive nature of many of the words and images deployed in curses and insults and their capacity to provoke anger, shame, and ridicule are powerful clues to a community's worldview.

Forms of Address in Egyptian Colloquial Arabic. We have noted previously that one of the stereotypes that other Arabs have about Egyptians is that they are lighthearted and love to tell jokes. Another aspect of Egyptian society that is striking for many Arab visitors from other countries is the number and variety of terms that Egyptians use to address one another in conversation. Some of these terms are ones that are common throughout the Arab world, whereas others are distinctive to Egypt or are known elsewhere but not used with the same frequency. Dilworth Parkinson's detailed study of forms of address in Cairo, *Constructing the Social Context of Communication* (1985), offers a rich introduction to the various social factors that can come into play when these terms are used. As was previously noted in the section on proverbs, it is common in many areas of the Arab world for a younger man to address an older man as "my paternal uncle" *('ammī)* as a form of respect, whereas the use of "maternal uncle" *(khāl)* usually indicates a closer emotional attachment. Following are a number of other terms that a younger man addressing an older man in Cairene Arabic might use, with various implications of class and status.

Siyādtak	your dominance	very formal, addressee of much higher rank
Hadritak	your presence	formal, addressee of notably higher rank
Fadīltak	your excellency	very formal, reserved for addressing Muslim clerics
'Udsak	your holiness	very formal, for addressing Christian clerics
Bāshā	pasha	formerly a title of nobility in the Ottoman Empire, but now used loosely for upper class males by lower ranking persons, also frequently used in jest
Bey	bey	similar in meaning to the term *Bāshā*
Afandī	sir/efendi	also an Ottoman Turkish term, but more widely used than *Bāshā* and *Bey,* often with the sense of "a man of means"
Shēkh	elder/sheikh	common address for elderly men or for leaders; also common in a variety of familiar and convivial contexts
Hāgg	pilgrim	common respectful address for elder Muslim men, in particular those who have made the pilgrimage to Mecca
Sīdī	my sir/master	common respectful address for elder males
Doktōr	doctor	respectful address to any highly educated male, not at all restricted to medical doctors or those holding the doctor of philosophy degree
Ustāz	teacher/professor	respectful address to any educated male; also any middle- or upper-class male when addressed by someone of a lower class
Muhandis	engineer	respectful address to any educated male, not restricted to engineers; also *bashmuhandis,* which means "head engineer"
Usta	craftsman	used in addressing workers who have a particular trade such as taxi drivers, mechanics, plumbers, and so forth; but not used for educated, or for middle- and upper-class males
Rayyis	headman/boss	used to address someone in charge of a team or group of some sort, such as the head musician in a band, the head of a boat's crew, and so forth
Mi'allim	teacher	literally "teacher/master" but sometimes with underworld or even criminal connotations, sometimes used in addressing the owner of a bar or workshop, or the head of a gang; also used frequently in jest

Kabtin	captain	borrowed from English, the term is used in addressing a young man of some social status, particularly by those of lower rank
Akhī/akhūya	my brother	normally used by men of the same social rank, but can be used in addressing an older man in an appeal or other contexts
Bābā	dad/papa	very familiar, even teasing, when used to address males who are not related by blood

(Adapted from Parkinson 1985, 77–186)

These terms are but a few of those that might be used by a younger male addressing an older male. To this list must be added all of the variations for older males addressing younger males, men of equal age and rank addressing each other, and then all of the female equivalents. The permutations number in the hundreds. Beyond simply listing the possible forms of address, however, lies their dimension to communicate respect, familiarity, good humor, flattery, or disdain. Use of too formal a form of address may well signal sarcasm rather than respect: A working-class male might be offended or angered, for example, at being addressed by an upper-class Egyptian with a title that is too formal for his station in life (imagine addressing the local mechanic as "your excellency"), which may cause him to feel that he is being made fun of rather than being treated with respect. On the other hand, these terms are equally capable of erasing class boundaries and age differences, as when two speakers carefully negotiate the use of familiar, friendly terms in a situation that might otherwise call for more formal titles. (This process is similar in some ways to the manner in which speakers of European languages that have a formal and informal *you* signal each other that they wish to switch to the informal pronoun or the way in which English speakers shift to interacting on a "first-name basis.")

These many different forms of address add a rich social dimension not only to daily life but also to Egyptian folklore. Whether within a folktale, a historical narrative, a personal experience tale, a proverb, or other genre, folklore performed in Egyptian colloquial Arabic has a capacity to express through these terms of address the attitudes of speakers toward their addressees. They are a remarkable resource for storytellers to communicate to the audience the relationship between characters, and even, for example, to transform otherwise serious scenes into comedy by deploying completely inappropriate terms of address. Arabs most clearly identify this highly articulated system of terms of address with Egypt, and it is thus an excellent example of regional cultural variation within the larger Arab world.

Greetings and Salutations: The Fine Art of Saying Hello. Elaborate forms of address may be most highly developed in Egypt, but the exchange of greetings and salutations *(salāmāt wa-tahayyāt)* is an integral part of Arab culture throughout the Arabic-speaking countries even though the specific patterns and choice of words may differ from region to region. At issue are not only the greetings themselves, but who should initiate the exchange of greetings and whether one's response is less, equally, or more eloquent than the greeting one has just received. The Qur'ān includes a number of passages that deal directly with greetings:

> When you are greeted with a greeting, return it or respond with one better than it. (Q 4: 86)

> When those who believe in Our revelation come unto you, say: "Peace be upon you!" (Q 6: 54)

> When you enter houses, salute one another with a greeting from God, blessed and sweet. (Q 24: 61)

> It is not proper for you to approach houses from the rear. It is proper rather to be pious; therefore, approach houses by their [front] doors and fear God so that you may prosper. (Q 2: 189)

> O Believers! Do not enter houses other than your own until you have asked permission and greeted the family within; it is better for you that you remember this. If you do not find anyone inside, do not enter until given permission. And if you are told "Leave," then leave. (Q 24: 27–28)

Greetings are a religious obligation in Islam, and the failure to exchange greetings is often seen as an act of deliberate coldness or rudeness. The question of who should initiate the exchange of greetings is subject to a clear set of cultural rules. Following, for example, are the rules taught to children (and occasionally to visiting foreign folklorists) in villages of the Nile Delta region of Egypt:

> *Ir-rākib yisallim 'a l-māshī*
> *Il-māshī yisallim 'a l-gā'id*
> *Il-dākhil yisallim 'a l-mawgūdīn*
> *Ig-gamā'a is-saghīra tisallim 'a l-kabīra*
> *Wi-l-gharīb yisallim 'alā ibn il-balad*

> He who is riding greets he who is walking;
> He who is walking greets he who is sitting;
> He who enters greets those who are present;
> The smaller group greets the larger group;
> And the stranger greets the "local son."

The logic of this set of rules is tied to the previously described Qur'ānic injunction to return a greeting with its equal or one more beautiful. In local terms, the idea of a more beautiful response is a response that includes an offer of hospitality—to have a seat, a cup of tea, a cigarette, or a meal, for example. This custom is expressed in the simple exchange of greetings that follows:

as-salāmu 'aleykum
wa-'aleykum as-salām, **itfaddal!**

"Peace be upon you."
"And upon you be peace, **please** [sit down, have some tea, have some food, etc.]."

The term *itfaddal* is used when offering something to someone, when handing them something, when gesturing that they should go first (through a doorway, for example), when inviting them to enter a room, when inviting someone to share your meal, and other similar contexts. It is a common experience in the Arab world to sit down near a complete stranger who is eating a sandwich or any other type of food, no matter how humble, and immediately have the stranger offer to share it *(itfaddal)*; normally, of course, the polite response is to refuse, but a social engagement has already been set in motion with that simple offer of hospitality. So the rules of who should greet whom first are based upon a logical calculation about which party is more likely to be close to home or have the wherewithal to offer hospitality to the other. Someone riding a mount is likely to be further from home than someone walking; someone who is sitting is more likely to have tea or food at hand than someone walking by; and the same applies to people who are already in a room or house as opposed to someone entering; if two groups pass each other, the larger group is likely to have more resources than the smaller; and finally, the local person is more likely to be able to offer hospitality than a traveler ("a stranger").

During my first few days living in the village of al-Bakātūsh in the mid-1980s, I was struck by two very different reactions from my neighbors. Whenever I went out accompanied by friends from the village, we were surrounded by a flurry of greetings and salutations everywhere we went. But whenever I wandered out alone, I was met with stony silence and people who followed my every movement with their eyes but said nothing to me. I began to worry that I might not be able to interact socially with people in the village unless accompanied by intermediaries. Finally, however, an acquaintance explained that it was *my* duty to greet others first, because I was the stranger and I was the one walking past them while they were seated. On my first foray outside after these instructions, I embarrassedly mumbled a greeting to a cluster of men seated on a mud-brick bench in front of a neighboring house. They virtually exploded with greetings, salutations, inquiries about my health, and queries about how I was enjoying their village; they drew me immediately into their conversation, forced me to take seat, offered me a cigarette, and called to the women inside to bring out some tea.

I had been convinced, through what I thought was careful observation, that when I went out walking alone I was being met with hostility or at least cold reserve, whereas the problem was in fact that I had never been taught one of the simplest rules of social interaction—how and when to initiate the exchange of greetings. I later observed that the cloud of greetings that surrounded us when I went out with friends was generated not because of their presence as locals but rather because they initiated the greetings wherever we went, and a similar, indeed, even more enthusiastic barrage of greetings and offers of hospitality were showered upon me when I was alone—once I began the exchange.

Another fascinating aspect of greetings in Arabic is the degree to which greetings may be chained together to form lengthy social interactions. Any foreign student of Arabic is taught a few simple greetings, for example, to express the idea of "Good Morning!" and learns that in some cases there are traditional responses. An opening "Morning of goodness" *(sabāh al-khēr)*, for example, almost always generates the response, "Morning of light" *(sabāh al-nūr)*. When the mood strikes, however, these basic greetings can be elaborated upon until they become a spontaneous and masterful performance of verbal art. Following is a series of morning greetings collected from a group of young men standing in front of a Cairene shop in 1982. A friend was passing by on the other side of a crowded street in a hurry and did not have time to cross through the heavy traffic and greet us in person, so he called out "Good morning" over the din of the cars, to which each of the young men on our side of the street shouted out fancier and fancier greetings, which lasted for several minutes until the friend finally turned the corner and disappeared from sight:

Sabāh al-khēr	Morning of goodness!
Sabāh al-nūr	Morning of light!
Sabāh al-ward	Morning of roses!
Sabāh al-yasmīn	Morning of jasmine!
Sabāh al-full	Morning of Arabian jasmine!
Sabāh al-sabāh	Morning of the morning!
Sabāh al-'asal	Morning of honey!
Sabāh al-'ishta	Morning of cream!
Sabāh al-kunāfa	Morning of kunāfa [a type of pastry]!
Sabāh al-kunāfa bi-l-'ishta	Morning of kunāfa with cream filling!
Sabāh al-qamar	Morning of the moon!
Sabāh al-nūr bi-l-lēl	Morning of light in the middle of the night!

This exchange took place in a particular context and would be totally out of place, for example, at a meeting of businessmen, but the imagery of the greetings and the very idea of making the moment of greeting someone into an act of verbal artistry is part and parcel of Arab daily culture.

Folklore is not just a body of tales and proverbs that can be collected, translated, and analyzed; it is also the rich ways of speaking, the rules for daily behavior, the hand gestures, and the bodily positions we use (see Customs and Traditions) that make up the day-to-day and lived experience of a culture. No amount of grammar or book learning can make up for a lack of knowledge of these deeply embedded cultural traits and behaviors.

MUSICAL ARTS

If poetry is the art form that Arabs have historically most valued and prized, the second most prominent art form in the Arab world is undoubtedly music. Nearly everywhere in the Arab world, one finds music of many different varieties being performed, patronized, listened to, recorded, purchased, and played. Although music may rival poetry as the most popular art form of Arab culture, it is important to note a distinction between them: There has been a religious polemic about the admissibility of music (particularly secular or profane music) within the Islamic religious tradition since the beginning of Islam, whereas poetry is accepted and valued by nearly all Arabs with little or no debate. The historical discussion about the religious permissibility of music, which is referred to by scholars as the *samā'* debate (from the Arabic word for *listening,* i.e., to music), is complex, but religious authorities have several different common understandings about what is religiously acceptable and what is not.

Singing to the accompaniment of percussion instruments (such as tambourines and drums) is accepted by almost all groups, as long as the lyrics are not immoral, because there are accounts of the Prophet Muhammad listening to just such performances at weddings and other joyous occasions. When it comes to the use of melody instruments, however, there are major differences of opinion. Some religious authorities do not accept the use of melody instruments in either religious or secular music, whereas others accept the use of melody instruments in the performance of religious music and rituals but reject all forms of secular music. Other legal opinions over the centuries, however, have allowed the performance of secular music as long as the lyrics are not objectionable but have, on the other hand, prohibited dance. Still others have held more tolerant views toward both of these arts, and these authorities have supported their rulings by arguing that music and dance are not in themselves forbidden, but only the licentious behaviors that sometimes are found in their proximity (such as illicit sexual activity or the consumption of alcohol or drugs). If one were to read only these religious writings about music, and they are indeed voluminous, one might expect to find little to no music in the modern Arab world. The reverse is true, however, for other than in a few very strict religious communities, music is found throughout Arab culture in almost every context imaginable: at weddings and other private celebrations, on the radio and television, at saints' festivals, in taxi cabs and buses, in private homes, in schools, clubs, villages, towns, cities, and elsewhere. Although the religious debate is constantly present, in the end it prevents only a small percentage of the population from enjoying music as part of their daily lives.

In the preceding section on the verbal arts, we saw that many types of Arabic poetry are sometimes performed musically—epic singing, for example, as well as the genres of *bālah* wedding poetry in Yemen, women's *ghinnāwa* poetry among the Egyptian Bedouin, the *hawfī* poetry of women and girls in Tlemcen, and the Egyptian *mawwāl* with its intricate punning. It is not an easy matter to separate *poetry* from *song* in Arab culture, for they are very closely intertwined. In this volume those genres that focus primarily on the individual improvisation of poetry, even when done to a simple musical background, have been dealt with as poetry in the preceding section, whereas traditions that involve more complex musical performances or are truly *song* traditions (e.g., where many people know the words and can sing along) are dealt with in this section as musical traditions. This distinction, however, is made only for the purposes of this volume and is not drawn from Arab culture itself (that is, it is an *etic* distinction; see Chapter Two).

Introduction to Arab Music: Four Basic Concepts

In discussing Western music, we usually begin with three key concepts: melody, harmony, and rhythm. Arab music is conceptualized around two rather different ideas: melodic modes *(maqāmāt)* and rhythmic cycles *(īqāʿāt)*. In Western music there was once a variety of modes (i.e., the medieval church modes), but in modern times only two remain: major and minor (or four if one counts the natural, melodic, and harmonic minors separately). Every major scale, no matter what note it starts on, has the same intervals and the same basic structure—the lowest note (the *tonic*) is the most important note, and melodies in a major key typically end (or *resolve*) on that note; the second most important note in the major scale is the *fifth,* and so forth. The same may be said for the versions of the minor scale.

In Arab music, however, each mode comes with its own unique set of rules about how to play that particular set of notes correctly. These rules are often not consciously conceived but rather are learned through listening and imitation, similar to the way we learn the grammar of our native language. For example, in some modes the melody should start low and climb higher and finally return to the lower notes; but in others, the melody should start in the higher register and develop through a *cascading* pattern working its way downward toward the lowest notes. In some modes the lowest note is the most important, and the melody should begin and end there, but in other modes one should start playing in the middle, work one's way down to the lowest notes, then climb back to the middle, move on to the higher notes, and finally return to the lowest note at the very end. In one mode the first and fifth notes might be the most important ones, whereas in another mode that uses exactly the same notes the most important notes might be the first and fourth. In some modes certain notes receive less emphasis than others, and some notes may be used going one direction and not the other—for example, playing a higher note when going up but a lower note when going down. In short, to perform an Arab melodic mode correctly, therefore, one must not only know what the notes are, but also a complex set of rules about the "path" of that mode and the relationships among the notes.

One way to understand all these rules is to think of the notes of an Arab musical mode as the list of characters in a play, and the rules explain their relationship to each other. Each one has its own personality and level of importance: The "king" will be more important than the servants, the "queen" will have a close relation to the king, and so forth. To compose a melody or improvise correctly in that mode, one has to have an understanding of all these relationships. In addition, each of the modes has historically been associated with a particular set of emotions—certain modes are meant to sound sad and mournful, others happy and lighthearted, and still others dignified and stately.

As a result, the melodic modes of Arab music are each understood to have a different "feel," the way the major and minor keys "feel" different to Western listeners. Art music traditions in the Arab world have cultivated many different melodic modes *(maqāmāt)*—well over 50 modes—but folk music traditions typically use a much smaller number of modes, often only a half dozen to a dozen or so. The melodic modes are an element of Arab music that is not easily grasped by Western listeners without some study.

The second major element of Arab music is rhythm, which is in contrast readily apparent to most Western listeners. Although there are some genres of Arab music that are performed nonrhythmically, the vast majority of song and dance traditions, particularly in Arab folk music, are performed to distinctive rhythms. Much as Arabic poetry is composed in meters of various combinations of long and short syllables, Arab music is composed in rhythmic cycles made up of low-pitched strokes made by striking toward the center of the drum skin (known as *dumm*) and high-pitched strokes played on the rim of the drum (known as *takk*). Every rhythm in Arab music can be conceived of as a particular sequence of *dumm* strokes and *takk* strokes with rests (silences) in between. One of the most common Arab rhythms in the eastern Arab countries is called *maqsūm* [divided] or *duyak*:

1	and	2	and	3	and	4	and
dumm	takk	—	takk	dumm	—	takk	—

This rhythm is sometimes played in contrast to a second "sister rhythm" in the same song or song sequence that is called *masmūdī saghīr* [short *masmūdī*] or *baladī* [local or folk]. *Baladī* has only one drum stroke that is different (the second—in boldface type in the following example), but this gives it a heavier feel than *maqsūm,* so the transition from one to the other is usually easy to hear—the lighter *maqsūm* suddenly changes to the heavier *baladī:*

1	and	2	and	3	and	4	and
dumm	**dumm**	—	takk	dumm	—	takk	—

Another characteristic of many Arab rhythms is that they do not have the "square" two- or four-beat pattern of many Western compositions. Rather they have an affinity for syncopated structures and often have accents on what would be considered the "up beat" by Western musicians.

A third major element of some, but not all, Arab music traditions is that they possess notes that are not found in Western music, notes which scholars refer to as *microtones* or *quarter-tones.* If one plays notes on a Western piano, there is a half step between each of the keys when one plays both the white and black keys (c, c#, d, d#, etc.). Arab music, in addition to having all of the notes of the piano keys, also has notes that fall "between the keys" as it were, that is, intervals of less or more than a half-step, which are referred to in English as *half flats* and *half sharps.* These different notes can at first give some types of Arab music an "out of tune" sound to a Western-trained ear, but to other listeners, particularly those who are used to hearing *bent* notes in jazz and blues, the microtones will sound perfectly agreeable.

Finally, a fourth characteristic of Arab music is that, to a Western ear, the musicians often do not seem to be playing "together," at least not the way a symphonic orchestra does with every violinist, for example, playing exactly the same note at the same time or a church choir does where every singer in each section is singing and even breathing in exact unison. When music has only one melody and everyone is playing or singing exactly the same melody, scholars of music call this *monophony* (medieval Gregorian chant is monophonic music, for example). If music has more than one melody at the same time, such as in a choir when the soprano, alto, tenor, and bass sections are each singing a different line of music, this is called *polyphony.* Arab music, however, is based on a different idea, which is known as *heterophony,* meaning that the individual musicians each embellish in different ways the one main melody being played, creating a rich texture of changing ornamentation. In theory, no two repetitions of the melody would ever sound exactly alike. This, too, is a practice that is akin to jazz and blues, where a great deal of improvisation is often part of the performance. Heterophony means that the musicians are not playing exactly the same thing at the same time and also that there is a continuous sense of change that can be summed up with the phrase "repetition with variation." In general, when Western listeners hear a repeated musical phrase, they cognitively search for the elements that remain the same, but Arab music invites us instead to listen to a repeated phrase or melody while picking out and enjoying the minute differences in ornamentation, accent, and timbre. A Western listener might hear a piece with a passage repeated four times over and say, "They played the same phrase four times," whereas an Arab listener might hear the same piece and relish the small details that made each repetition different from the other and declare, "They played the phrase four different ways."

Thus, four basic concepts of Arab music are (1) melodies are structured into modes *(maqāmāt)* that have a complex cluster of characteristics involving directionality, emotional feel, and the distinct relationships between the individual notes; (2) most Arab music is performed to rhythm cycles *(īqāʿāt)* that are organized into sequences of low, deep drum strokes *(dumm)* and high, sharp strokes *(takk)*, and each has a typical tempo and feel to it; (3) many Arab music traditions possess intervals that are either smaller or larger than those of Western music; and finally (4) one of the basic principles of Arab music is *heterophony*, in which individual musicians ornament the music in different ways, which creates a constant sense of "repetition with variation."

Folk Musical Instruments of the Arab World

The scholarly study of musical instruments—how they are built, how they have changed over time, their geographical distribution, and so on—is known as *organology*. In general, scholars group musical instruments into four large families according to how their sound is produced: chordophones or "string instruments"; aerophones or "wind instruments"; membranophones, instruments with a "skin" such as drums or tambourines; and, idiophones, instruments that are basically solid and are sounded by being struck, such as cymbals, castanets, or marimbas. There are many different instruments from each of these large families in Arab folk musical traditions, most of which are not very familiar to Westerners; only a handful of the most representative instruments are examined in the following section.

Chordophones (String Instruments)

Lutes. Perhaps the single most characteristic instrument in Arab art music traditions is *al-ʿūd* (the lute), but it is also found in a number of Arab folk music traditions, as well. Lutes are one of the most ancient of musical instruments in the Middle East. Representations of lutes in a variety of shapes and sizes are found in ancient Egypt and in ancient Mesopotamian cultures, though the instrument curiously achieved comparatively little popularity in the cultures of ancient Greece and Rome. In the early centuries of Islam, there were several different types of lutes in the Arabian Peninsula, some with long necks and some with short, some with skin covering over the front and others with a wooden front. The most common form of lute in the modern Arab world, however, is the short-necked, wood-faced lute—in fact, the term *al-'ūd* literally means "wood," a term that originally distinguished it from skin-covered lutes. It is this Arabic word from which the English name "lute" (and the terms used in most other European languages as well) derive because it was the Arab form of the instrument that was introduced to Europe via Muslim Spain (al-Andalus) and Muslim Sicily, which then spread throughout the West during the early Middle Ages. In Arab art music it was common to refer to the lute as the "king of instruments," in part because it was for centuries the primary accompaniment for solo singers. There are several different variations in the size, shape, and decoration of the standard lute in the Arab world There are also several separate but related instruments that are of the lute family but are more commonly associated with folk music than the standard lute. One of these is the Lebanese *buzuq,* a long-necked lute with wire strings, closely related to the Greek *bouzouki.* Another is the *guimbri,* found in North Africa, which is a lute with a skin front of ancient African origins. Yet another is the *kwitra,* found primarily in Algeria. Arab lutes are almost always played with a plectrum (or "pick") rather than being strummed or plucked with the fingertips, which gives them a sound and timbre distinct from the Spanish guitar or the European medieval lute, despite their close historical relationship to those instruments.

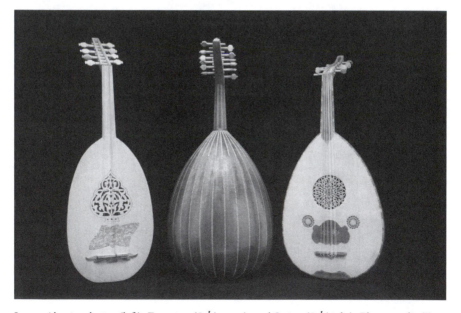

Lutes: Algerian *kwitra* (left), Egyptian *'ūd* (center), and Syrian *'ūd* (right). Photo credit: Tony Mastres.

Fiddles. The idea of producing musical sound by drawing a bow across a string is so widespread in modern times that it comes as a surprise to many that the technique is of relatively recent invention. The ancient Middle Eastern cultures did not know the technique of bowed string instruments, and stringed instruments were not found at all in the indigenous cultures of the Americas. The technique seems to have originated in Central Asia, perhaps in the region of modern Uzbekistan, and to have spread through the Islamic world in the eighth century C.E. The earliest bowed instrument in the Middle East was known in Arabic as the *rabāb,* a term that was adopted into Spanish *(rabel),* as well as in French and English *(rebec),* after the Arabs introduced it to Western Europe through al-Andalus. The violin, viola, cello, and bass all evolved from this single ancestor. The earliest known image of a bowed string instrument in Western Europe occurs in a tenth-century Mozarabic manuscript (a text produced by Arabic-speaking Christians) from medieval Iberia where angels in heaven are portrayed playing *rabāb.* In the modern Arab world there are several varieties of *rabāb* (fiddles). A rectangular, one-string, skin-faced *rabāb* is found among the Bedouin of Egypt, Jordan, Syria, and the Arabian Peninsula; as recently as the nineteenth-century this instrument was much more widely used, but nowadays it is found primarily among the Bedouin. The North African *rabāb,* on the other hand, is a small, boat-shaped fiddle with two strings, held on the knee and played with a short, curved bow, and is associated almost exclusively with the classical art music tradition of Andalusian music; it is nearly identical with the images found in the thirteenth-century Spanish songbook, the *Cantigas de Santa María* assembled by King Alfonso the Wise, demonstrating that it has changed very little over the last thousand years, still retaining its distinctive face, half-covered with skin and half with metal or wood. Yet another type of *rabāb* is fashioned out of a coconut shell, has two strings, and is used for many different types of folk music in Egypt, including the epic-singing tradition of *Sīrat Banī Hilāl* examined previously. A four-string version of the coconut-shell *rabāb* known as the *jawzeh* is found in Iraq and is associated with the art music traditions of Baghdad and other Iraqi cities.

Lyres. Another instrument type that was widely known in the ancient Middle East and was also very popular in ancient Greece and Rome was the family of harps and lyres. Although medieval Arab culture possessed a harp *(jank),* this instrument has since fallen out of use. Several forms of folk lyres, however, are found in the regions surrounding the Red Sea, the Indian Ocean, and the Persian Gulf (known to Arabs as the *Arab Gulf*) and are known as *simsimiyya* or *tanbūra.* These instruments are constructed of a resonance chamber such as a metal bowl covered with skin or a wooden box, two wooden "arms," and a crossbar to which the strings are attached. They are closely associated with sailors and fisherman on the one hand, and in some regions with the exorcism rituals known as the *zār* (see Customs and Traditions).

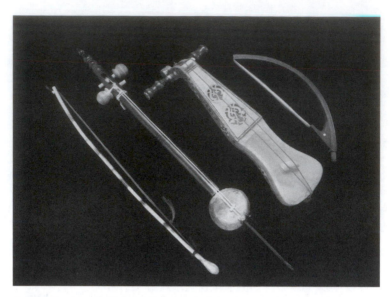

Rabābs: Egyptian (left) and Moroccan (right). Photo credit: Tony Mastres.

Medeival Spanish musicians playing the *rabāb* (left) and lute (right). Courtesy of Dover Pictoral Archives.

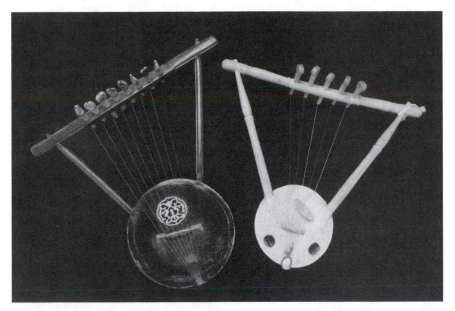

Egyptian *simsimiyyas*. Photo credit: Tony Mastres.

Aerophones (Wind Instruments)

Flutes. The end-blown reed flute, or *nāy,* and closely related folk versions such as the *salamiyya, qasaba, shabbāba, kawla,* and others, are known in virtually every region of the Arab world. The *nāy* is associated primarily with art music traditions and comes in many different sizes, so that a musician during a concert will switch instruments constantly according to the *maqām* (melodic mode) of the piece being played. The various folk versions of the reed flute, however, do not need to do this because folk music typically uses far fewer modes and musicians can therefore produce all of the required tones from a single instrument by using various fingering and breathing techniques. Reed flutes are closely associated with some Sufi musical traditions such as *dhikrs (zikrs)* but are also used in a variety of other folk music traditions such those performed at weddings and other celebrations (see Sufi Ritual and Religious Chant). The association with Sufism comes not only from the instrument's musical qualities but also from its role in Sufi allegoric teachings. The medieval poet Rumi, writing in Persian, began his masterwork, the *Masnavi,* with the line "Listen to the reed!" He goes on to explain that the reed grows up in a reed bed, tightly packed among its brothers and never alone, but it is then snatched from that happy state and fashioned into a flute, after which it must endure painful solitude, longing for its home back in the reed bed, which is why its song is so mournful and sad. This poetic image is then equated to the state of the human soul, which before being born exists

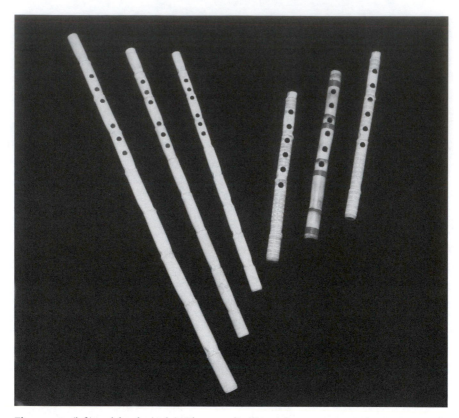

Flutes: *nāys* (left) and *kawlas* (right). Photo credit: Tony Mastres.

with God and all other souls but is then thrust into this material world to live life alone, trapped in corporeal form, and therefore suffers a constant longing and yearning to return to God and once again experience union with the Divine. Other poets and writers have also equated the reed flute with the human soul because the reed is an empty husk (i.e., a body) that can only come to life when it is filled with breath (i.e., the soul). The reed flutes are an excellent example of the cultural richness that an instrument can acquire, not just for its musical qualities but also through its association with literary and spiritual imagery.

Oboes. The folk oboes, or *mizmārs,* are also known in nearly every part of the Arab world, and often play a role in large, public celebrations. A single *mizmār* alone can produce a rather astonishing amount of sound, and an ensemble of several *mizmār*-players performing together can be heard for miles out in the countryside. One of the most fascinating techniques used with the *mizmār* is known as "circular breathing," which allows players to play indefinitely without stopping for a breath. When they need to take a breath, they fill their mouth and cheeks

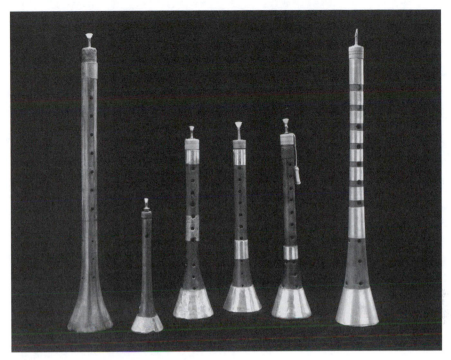

Egyptian *mizmār*s. Photo credit: Tony Mastres.

with air from their lungs; then they close the back of their throat and fill their lungs with air breathing through their nose, while using the air in their mouth to keep playing. They move back and forth so smoothly between these two sources of air (lungs and mouth), that there is never a break in the sound. Marcus (2007) provides an excellent examination of several different regional *mizmār* traditions in Egypt, demonstrating the remarkable variety that can be found within traditions of a single instrument.

Double Clarinets. A distinctive class of instruments that gives a real folk "feel" to any music in the Arab world is the double-clarinet family. The *mizwij* (or *mijwiz*) is a short instrument with two reed pipes of equal length with fingerholes in both pipes, whereas the *arghūl* (also *yarghūl*) is an instrument with two pipes, with fingerholes in only one pipe because the other acts as a drone. In a large *arghūl* one pipe may be only a foot long while the drone pipe reaches nearly to the ground when played standing up. On the *mizwij* the player lays his fingers flat across both sets of holes rather than stopping them with the pads of the fingertips, thus playing the melody on both pipes at the same time, which produces a distinctive pulsating sound. On the *arghūl,* on the other hand, the drone note produces a deep, almost bagpipe-like sound. Both of these instruments are found

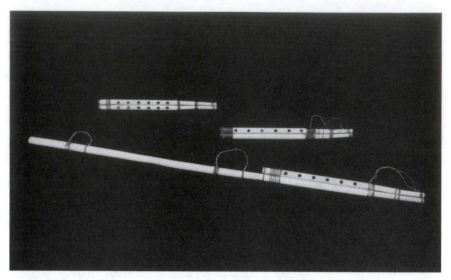

Large *arghūl* (bottom), Small *arghūl* (center) and *mizwij* (top). Photo credit: Tony Mastres.

only in folk music and almost never in performances of classical art music unless it has been included for the purpose of giving a folk flavor to a particular piece. Their distinctive timbre is as instantly recognizable to most Arabs as "folk" music as, say, the sound of a banjo might be for many Americans.

Membranophones and Idiophones (Percussion Instruments)

Although there are several varieties in the Arab world of each of the different string and wind instruments described, these are relatively few in number in comparison with the vast number of different drums, tambourines, and cymbals found everywhere in the Arab world. There are goblet-shaped drums, two-headed drums, ceramic drums, wooden drums, large and small kettledrums, attached pairs of bongo-like drums, narrow almost tubular drums, drums played with the hand, drums played with one stick, two-headed drums played with two matching sticks and others played with one light stick and one heavier mallet, and so forth. Tambourines come in round (and occasionally square) forms of nearly every size, of various depths, covered with fish or other animal skin, with or without side cymbals that can range from small and light to much larger and heavier sizes, and with or without snares under the skin. Finger cymbals too can range from smaller ones worn by dancers to much larger ones played at Sufi rituals, to large "double" cymbals or "clackers" such as the *qarāqib* played in Morocco. Not only are there a large number of forms and types, but the same shape of drum might be referred to by many different names in different areas of the Arab world. Following are a handful of the most common forms given with one or two of their best-known names.

Drums (clockwise from right): Goblet-shaped drum (*tabla* or *darbukka*), tambourine (*riqq*), medium-sized frame drum (*mazhar*), and large frame drum (*duff*). Photo credit: Tony Mastres.

Drums. The goblet-shaped, one-headed drum is probably the most widely known drum form in the Arab Middle East and is known as the *tabla* in Egypt, or the *darbukka* (also *dirbaki*) in the Mashriq region of Palestine, Lebanon, and Syria. These drums were traditionally made of fired clay, but more recently metal drums have eclipsed ceramic drums due to their durability. Traditional drum heads were made of various types of animal skins, but skin expands and contracts a great deal with changes in temperature and humidity that affect the sound of the drum and at times makes a drum unplayable because the skin has become too slack and loose. Until recently it was rather common to see percussion players warming their drum heads over an open flame, an electric light bulb, or whatever source of heat was available during live performances of all sorts. In the past two decades, however, plastic drum heads have replaced the traditional skin variety almost everywhere because the plastic heads not only are unaffected by temperature or humidity changes but also last much longer.

Tambourines. Another common form of Middle Eastern drum is the frame drum, which usually consists of a round wooden frame with a single skin head, the smallest form of which is the tambourine. These go by a number of different names, but one common Arabic name for the tambourine is the *riqq*, and one of the common names for a medium-sized frame drum is the *mazhar*. Every region has different associations for the various sizes and forms of drums; in Egypt, for example, large frame drums are often played in Sufi contexts and in wedding processions. The tambourine, on the other hand, is found not only in folk musical traditions but has a very respected place in urban art music traditions as well, particularly as the main percussion instrument in small classical ensembles. (For a much more detailed guide to musical instruments in the Arab World, see Hassan 2002.)

In what follows, four different examples of musical traditions from around the Arab world are presented in some detail. In the first, we follow the history of folk music from the city of Port Said, Egypt, at the Mediterranean entrance of the Suez Canal, and trace how it has been shaped by international political events from the founding of the city of Port Said to the present. The second example demonstrates the astonishing number of genres of song and dance found in the Arab world by examining the genre system of one location, the Sultanate of Oman, and noting the various cultural contacts and influences that have helped create such diversity. In contrast, the third case study, Sufi ritual and chant, involves a genre of singing that is found throughout most of the Arab world with some regional variation. Finally, one of the most common yet ignored genre of folk song, the lullaby, is examined with Jewish and Muslim examples from four different Arab countries.

Port Said, Egypt: The Birth of a Folk Music Tradition

[Note: Almost nothing has been written in Arabic or in Western languages about this remarkable tradition. The information in the following section is drawn primarily from interviews I was privileged to conduct in 1995 with Zakariyā Ibrāhīm and Muhammad al-Shināwī, musicians of Port Said, and members of the al-Tambūra folk ensemble, and from a variety of historical sources.]

Scholars do not often get to observe the emergence of a new regional folk tradition ex nihilo. The case of Port Said, Egypt, the northern entry to the Suez Canal, is therefore of considerable interest for it is a city that was created in the mid-nineteenth century and was populated by the Anglo-French Suez Canal Company with workers from Egypt, Palestine, Lebanon, Cyprus, Greece, and Europe. There is historical evidence that within two decades this artificially assembled population had developed a musical culture distinct from both those of the surrounding areas and those of the workers' regions of origin. In short, a new musical folk culture was born that came to play an important role in the formation of Port Saidi identity. In addition, this musical culture is a remarkable example of a local tradition that has been shaped to a great extent by larger international events that have transformed and influenced it over and over again.

On August 25, 1859, the first barracks and tents for housing workers were set up on the site of Port Said. The Anglo-French Suez Canal Company brought in Europeans to fill upper management positions; they imported Christian administrators from Greece, Cyprus, Lebanon, and Palestine as middle management; and they brought in Egyptian workers to provide the manual labor to dig the 98-mile canal. These workers were supplied, by agreement with the Egyptian government, through a *corvée* system: Every village had to supply two able-bodied men, and if one of them died, as thousands of them did, the village had to send a replacement. They worked, as one European visitor to the construction site remarked, "like oxen, lived on an onion a day, and ventilated their resentment only in song." Almost exactly 10 years later, on August 15, 1869, the waters of the Mediterranean and Red Seas met, and November 16 to 20 of that same year a lavish celebration was held to which hundreds of international guests were invited (including Empress Eugénie of France and Franz Josef of the Austro-Hungarian Empire), which itself had interesting musical aspects. The Italian composer Verdi was asked to compose the opera *Aida* for the event, but did not at first accept the commission, so the opera did not, in fact, debut until Christmas Eve 1871 at the Cairo Opera House, two years after the opening of the canal. The Western male visitors at the festivities were taken out into the desert one evening where they were regaled by "Bedouin" female dancers (the origins of whom are more than a little doubtful); female guests were not invited because the dancers' movements were considered too lascivious for respectable foreign women to see. These performances were covered extensively by the international press and the stereotype of the "belly-dance" was thus launched in the European imagination.

The Canal Company built the city of Port Said on a grid pattern, but the city was also divided into two halves by what is now Muhammad 'Ali Street: One side was for the Europeans (the *ifrangi* quarter), and the other for Arabs. To pass from one sector to the other, Arabs had to report to one of the guarded entry points, declare their business on the other side, and show identification. As might be expected, the city developed into two separate worlds. There was, however, occasional musical contact between them. The Europeans held public band concerts in the bandstand of the main park that could be heard on the Arab side, and Arab musicians and dancers were often hired to perform in the European quarter for the entertainment of partygoers and guests. Cafés and other venues on both sides of the city offered live musical entertainment of various sorts. In addition, the ships passing through the canal often had evening music and dancing on the decks that could be seen and heard by all.

By the turn of the century, a well-defined folk music tradition had established itself in the Arab quarter that was called the *damma* (gathering), a term that is not used anywhere else in this sense. In a unique adaptation to the unfamiliar landscape of multistoried apartment buildings and the grid pattern of the streets, these musical events took place in the center of street intersections. Women would pass down their low laundry stools and the singers would sit on them in a circle. The male public stood outside the circle in the streets and looked inward at the performance, while women and girls watched from the upper balconies and roofs of nearby buildings. Singers took turns as soloists and stood in the center of the circle when they sang, while the other singers remained seated and acted as a chorus. A variety of dance steps and styles were also performed. The vocal style of the *damma* was elegant and highly embellished, and it was accompanied only by a drum or rhythmic clapping. The singers were skilled, though not professionals; this was not a context where just anyone was welcome to stand up and sing. The *damma* was a respected and very public art form.

Like almost all port cities, Port Said also had a seedier side that included a number of taverns, or *makhānāt,* where less reputable music and other activities were to be found. In the late 1930s a black musician arrived in Port Said named 'Abdallah Kebarbar, who may have been Nubian (from southernmost Egypt) or from even further south. In any case he brought with him an instrument that was well known in the southern reaches of the Red Sea but which was not yet well known in Port Said—the *simsimiyya.* The *simsimiyya* was at that time a simple, five-string folk lyre composed of a metal dish or other type of resonance chamber, a skin covering, and three pieces of wood that stuck into the instrument and formed the frame for the strings. It could be assembled and disassembled easily, and it could be carried about in a small pouch or bag. The musical style associated with it was faster and snappier than the heavier *damma* style, and it soon began to acquire an audience, though it was at first a rather disreputable one. In 1952 the Egyptian Revolution freed Egypt from British control and ended the Egyptian monarchy. In the ensuing years *simsimiyya* musicians began to create a "cross-over" repertory by taking songs from the *damma* and recomposing them in the faster, lighter *simsimiyya* style.

Then the 1956 Suez War erupted. Egyptian President Nasser had asked the United States for financial support to build the Aswan Dam to provide Egypt with electricity and to help control the annual flooding of the Nile. When the United States rejected that request on July 19, Nasser turned to another means of financing Egypt's development—on July 26 he nationalized the Suez Canal. The original lease was due to expire in 1968, so he was in effect taking possession of the Canal 12 years early. In retaliation, England and France began preparing to invade Egypt. Israel, which had only been in existence for eight years at that point, had no claims to ownership of the canal but nevertheless decided to join the colonial powers in attacking the newly independent Egypt, thus deepening the enmities that had been created with the seizure of Palestinian lands in 1948 for the creation of the Jewish state against the will of the Palestinians and the other Arab nations. War broke out on October 29, and house-to-house fighting took place in Port Said. To the surprise of many, the lightly armed civilian population of Port Said was able to hold off the far superior forces of the Tripartite Alliance. President Eisenhower was furious that the United States' supposed allies had launched a colonial-style war behind his back without even consulting the United States (his famous television appearance is one of the most vehement speeches by an American president ever recorded), and eventually pressure from the United States and other nations forced Great Britain, France, and Israel to withdraw.

The population of Port Said celebrated their unexpected success at fending off three of the most advanced armies of the world in song, and the songs that were sung were performed on the *simsimiyya,* which thereafter became the symbol of both Port Said and the '56 War. Only 11 years later, in 1967, Israel invaded again. Egypt's defeat in the Six Day War was devastating for all Egyptians, but for none more so than the inhabitants of the Canal Zone. Because the Israeli army now occupied the other side of the Canal, the Egyptian government evacuated the civilian population to the Nile valley, where they lived in refugee camps for many years scattered up and down Egypt. Young people from the refugee camps formed *simsimiyya* ensembles and traveled from camp to camp keeping the memory of their homes and neighborhoods alive through wistful, sad songs that recounted their desire to return to Port Said and the other cities along the canal. After the October War of 1973, the civilian population was able to return to their natal cities along the Canal. Some *simsimiyya* groups were supported by the government at this point and performed primarily nationalistic songs recalling the victories of 1956 and 1973. Other less official groups sang those songs but also kept alive other parts of the older repertory, including a handful of songs from the early *damma* repertory and the sad songs of the Evacuation (1967–1974). The *damma* repertory, however, was rapidly disappearing.

Port Said music today and, in particular, its dance traditions bear traces of a variety of traditions, including Palestinian *dabke* dancing, Western dance steps ranging from the Charleston to "break dancing" learned from watching parties on the decks of cruise ships traveling through the Canal, Western military music from the colonial period, and others, yet it remains a rich, distinctive local tradition. It is a music culture where one historical layer after another has been created, absorbed into the repertory, and transformed: the old *damma* songs, the early *simsimiyya* cross-over versions of *damma* songs recomposed in the early 1950s, the victory songs of the 1956 Suez Canal War, the mournful songs of the Evacuation after 1967, and the nationalistic songs propagated on state radio and television after the return to the Canal Zone. Each of these stages of development are tied to external events that intruded into and reshaped both the community and culture of Port Said: the digging of the Canal, the Egyptian Revolution, the nationalization of the canal, the 1956 invasion by the Tripartite Alliance, the

1967 Israeli invasion followed by the Evacuation, and the 1973 October War followed by the return to the Canal Zone.

One of the most active groups in preserving these different styles is *al-Tambūra,* led by Zakariyā Ibrāhīm, who has done extensive historical research on this tradition, as well as forming and supervising the ensemble. The recording *La simsimiyya de Port-Saïd: Ensemble Al-Tanbūrah* (The Simsimiyya of Port Said), produced by the Institut du Monde Arabe in Paris in 1999, is the best available recording of this tradition. Following are the lyrics to one of the older songs in their repertory, sung in Classical Arabic and therefore probably from the *damma* tradition:

> O most gracious one of our quarter, when will my eye see thee?
>> And when shall I hear your voice from that house?
> I pass by your doors needlessly,
>> That perhaps I might see thee or see those who see thee.
> Love poured out a cup of pure yearning for me,
>> O how I wish when it poured for me it had poured also for thee.
> O how I wish the judge of passion would pass judgment on what is between us,
>> And that the summons of love when it summoned me had also summoned thee.
> Take me as a slave for your slaves, a servant for your servants,
>> A purchased man, yours for you to buy or sell.
> I am your slave as long as I live and endure
>> And if your wealth should decrease, then my soul shall be your ransom.
> Bury me not 'neath a vineyard that shades me,
>> But rather atop a mountain that my eye may see thee.
> Halt near my grave and sing me your name,
>> My very bones will feel affection at hearing your voice.
> And say, "May God preserve you, you who died of love,
>> And may He cause you to dwell in paradise for the passion you endured."

Oman: Crossroads of Cultures

The Sultanate of Oman, located in the easternmost regions of the Arabian Peninsula, represents a remarkable example of a musical culture that has preserved elements of early Arabian musical culture on the one hand and on the other has absorbed and transformed musical influences from several neighboring regions. Oman is bordered by Yemen to the west and by Saudi Arabia and the United Arab Emirates to the north. Equally important, however, have been its contacts by sea with East Africa, Iran, Pakistan, and across the Indian Ocean, for Omanis have been a seafaring people for millennia. In the early eighth century, for example, an Omani sea captain, Abū 'Ubayda 'Abdallāh ibn al-Qāsim, is said to have journeyed as far east as Canton, China. In the sixteenth century, Oman was conquered and ruled by the Portuguese and the remains of several Portuguese forts from this time period can still be seen there. Once the Omanis had expelled the Portuguese in 1649, however, they spread their influence across the seas in several directions and established a commercial empire that came to dominate much of the eastern African and Indian Ocean trade for several centuries. The Sultanate of Oman was historically the Sultanate of Oman and Zanzibar (the fabled clove-producing island off the coast of Africa), and that relationship was only fully severed in 1964. The musical culture of Oman still retains the traces of these many contacts: Yemeni and Bedouin influences have come from one direction; African rhythms, instruments, and dances from the other; and Iranian, Baluchi, Pakistani, and Indian influences from yet another. Taken as a whole, this fascinating mixture is distinctively and uniquely Omani.

The number of different genres of song and dance in Oman is remarkable: A listing of these genres in El-Mallah (1998, 180–91) enumerates 143 main genres, many of which possess several subgenres. Some of these songs and dances are performed in only one region or location; some are distinguished from each other by their social function rather than their geographic distribution (wedding songs, work songs, religious songs); some are performed only by specific social groups

Omani dancers leap high in the air as they perform traditional dances during the Muscat Festival 2000. Omanis and Muslims throughout the world celebrate the Eid al-Adha Feast at the end of the Haji pilgrimage. © Magdy Shazl/epa/Corbis.

(Bedouin herders, fishermen, sailors, women, children); many are associated with a particular type of dance, a specific rhythm, or a particular form of poetry; and some are characterized by a specific orchestration of one or more instruments. To get some sense of the richness and diversity of song and dance culture in the Sultanate of Oman, let us first review the larger categories that scholars have used to map these many genres and then examine a few examples in more detail. Two scholars have worked in detail on mapping the musical genres of Oman, Yūsif Shawqī (Youssef Shawki Moustafa) and ʿIsām al-Mallāh (Issam el-Mallah); their work has been published in English by the Oman Centre for Traditional Music. Following is a summary of their findings (see El-Mallah 1998, 167–221).

Musical Song and Dance Genres of Oman: An Overview

One of the most distinctive categories of Omani music, dance, and song is that of the saber or sword dances that are found in many regions of the Sultanate. These performances combine the singing of improvised poetry in groups, drumming, and stylized sword duels in which the competition is primarily based in the artistic manipulation of the swords and in gymnastic-like leaps into the air by the dancers who then land on their feet or on their knees while maintaining a defensive posture vis-à-vis their opponent. The most common of these, the *Razha*, will be described in detail in the following section.

Oman's historic tradition of seafaring has created a particularly rich collection of songs and dances that have to do with celebrating the departure and return of boats and with the various work activities aboard ship, many of which are conducted while singing work songs. There are special chants that accompany the raising of the anchor, the raising or lowering of the masts, the carrying of heavy goods when loading or unloading the ship, and so on, all of which help coordinate the collective force needed to accomplish these tasks. There are also song genres that are performed purely for entertainment, necessary on long voyages, which are performed almost exclusively by sailors, such as the *midīma*, a song-dance form where men stand in a circle, the leader singer sings in a high-pitched voice to the accompaniment of drums, and individuals take turns dancing in the center; each dancer then crosses the circle and selects a man from the other side to dance until everyone has had a turn or the song ends.

The interior desert regions are characterized by various Bedouin genres, almost all of which are sung *a capella* (without musical instruments). Some genres have texts which praise horses or camels, others are work songs for tasks such as gathering firewood, and one known as the *wanna* is used to describe one's travels in verse. The *mazīfina* is unusual in that it is performed by a man and a woman, or pairs of men and women, dancing together to the sung poetry (also performed without musical instruments).

Agricultural songs are for the most part sung to accompany collective tasks such as winnowing grain, raising water from wells, and so forth. Typically they are characterized by either a call-and-response structure in which a soloist gives the "call" that is then sung chorally by the others, or simply choral singing.

Religious genres are performed at a variety of religious festivals such as the *Mawlid* (birthday) of the Prophet Muhammad, the two feasts that mark the end of the fasting month of *Ramadān* and the pilgrimage to Mecca, as well as lesser feasts held on the 15th day of the months of *Sha'bān* and *Ramadān,* and local celebrations such as the celebration of a child having completed the memorization of the Qur'ān. The most prominent of these genres is the *mālid,* which contains several different sections but which is organized around the reading of a version of the life of the Prophet Muhammad and includes prose, poetry, and chanting, sometimes accompanied by tambourines and large drums. This genre is normally performed on the birthday of the Prophet Muhammad but can also be performed on other occasions, including as part of a curing ceremony for a sick person.

Several musical genres in Oman are associated with healing traditions (such as the *mālid* just mentioned). A number of them resemble the *zār* rituals of Northern Sudan that are discussed in detail under Customs and Traditions. They involve a belief in spirit possession and the practice of curing ceremonies in which the spirits are called out by the playing of particular musical rhythms or the singing of special chants. Some of these involve the playing of the *tanbūra,* a very large decorated folk lyre closely related to the *simsimiyya* previously described in the section about Port Said. Another remarkable instrument associated with some of these rituals is the *manjūr,* which is a girdle or skirt onto which have been sewn hundreds of dried goat hooves. The performer ties the *manjūr* around his waist and turns himself into a type of "human rattle"; his movements produce a deep, resonant, percussive sound.

Omanis, like nearly all societies, have many forms of music that are tied to the celebration of weddings as well as forms of singing and dancing that are simply performed as entertainment, some of which are all male, others all female, and some are mixed. (One of the male entertainment genres, the *lēwa,* is described in detail in the following section.) Omani musical culture also includes songs that are attached to the early life of children (birth songs, lullabies, circumcision songs, etc.), and, at the opposite end of the life cycle, lamentations for the dead. Certain songs are also associated with various sports such as horse racing, camel racing, and certain children's games.

The ethnic diversity of Oman is equally represented in its musical traditions. The "South Arabic-" (or Mehri- and Socotri-) speaking people of the southern mountains and the island of Socotra (referred to in Chapter One), possess not only their own language but their own musical genres and dances as well. The Baluchi-speaking immigrants from Baluchistan (southwestern Pakistan) perform special types of song and dance in a mixture of Arabic and Baluchi. And in the southern provinces, families who have their origins on the east coast of Africa perform the *raqs al-zinūj* (Dance of the Blacks) together—men, women, and children—in complex geometric patterns that symbolize the safe return of a ship from a voyage, portraying the sailors shouting to their families on shore and the women coming down to the harbor to welcome home their menfolk, all of which is sung in a mixture of Arabic and Swahili.

Two Genres in Detail: The Razha and the Lēwa. The *razha* is a genre that combines dance, poetry, singing, acrobatic feats, and music and is one of the most widely performed genres in Oman. Its origins probably derive from calling tribesmen together before battle and generating a spirit of bravery, but the performance of the *razha* has also traditionally been used as a means of presenting demands to leaders or for calling men together for some serious matter such as negotiating a truce or a contract. It can also be performed as entertainment at a variety of different occasions such as weddings and other celebrations. Typically the *razha* involves two groups of men competing in saber dancing that involves dramatic leaps by the dancers, moments when the swords are tossed high in the air and then caught by the hilt as they fall, as well as a stylized sword duel between the two main participants. At the same time, the poets representing each side are competing in the composition of poetry on a given theme such as love, praise, satire, or even the telling of riddles in verse.

The men form two rows facing each other. The poet from one side composes his verses, known as a *shalla,* which he then teaches to his row of singers. Each side brings with them two drummers, one with a larger *rahmānī* drum and the other with a smaller *kāsir* drum; both of these are two-headed drums typically played with two thin sticks, one in each hand. Once the *shalla* verses have been composed and taught to the singers, the rhythm is determined. Next there is a loud drum roll and the singers begin to intone the verses to the accompaniment of the drums. The drummers play moving back and forth between the two sides for the duration of the *shalla.* At the same time, one man from each side has moved toward the center, sword in hand, to engage in a duel. When the verses have ended, the drummers stop and move back to their own side, and the duelers do so as well. It is now time for the opposing side's poet to compose a response, teach it to his singers, and so forth. The *razha* is an indigenous Arab genre and shows virtually no traces from any neighboring cultures. The *rahmānī* drum in particular is often viewed as stereotypically Omani and sometimes serves as an icon of indigenous Omani culture. Omanis recognize more than a dozen different variants of *razha* performed in different regions and for different occasions, sometimes to quite different rhythms and to different styles of poetry, but the overall structure of the event is in most cases quite similar.

The *lēwa,* on the other hand, is recognized as having originated with Omanis in Eastern Africa and having been brought back to the Arabian Peninsula from that region by families and their slaves returning to Oman. The word itself

Omanis perform the *al razha* dance to celebrate the Eid al-Adha, Al-Hamma, Oman. The musicians are wearing traditional Omani dishdashas and wearing kummas (traditional embroidered Omani hats) or massars, the Omani turban. © Charles O. Cecil/Alamy.

apparently comes from Swahili and is associated with phrases used when offering someone something to drink: "*kī lewah*" and "*kō lewah*." Some, however, argue that it is derived from the Arabic word for banner *(liwā')* because the performance often takes place around a flag or banner. Unlike the *razha,* which uses only drums and voice, the *lēwa* is performed to the *mizmār* (folk oboe) as well as to a particular arrangement of percussion instruments:

Lēwa consists of playing, singing, and dancing, accompanied by the *mizmār* (oboe), a *musundū* drum played either standing or sitting, a *kāsir* drum, a *rahmānī* drum, and a *tanak* (metal container struck like a drum, from English "tank"). The poetry is in a mixture of Arabic and Swahili; it concerns the sea, the African coast, God and the Prophet, and the role of the Omanis in spreading Islam in Africa. *Lēwa* dance movements have two primary elements: the circular movement of the musicians as a group, and the movement of each individual musician. The circle moves counterclockwise around the group of drummers who sit under the flag (in this case, the Omani flag). The oboe player moves freely inside the circle, between the drummers and the other players. The *mizmār* player completes a melody to which all the other performers respond. *Mizmār* playing and singing alternate until the player changes the melody; the performance is punctuated by short repeated blows on the *jim* (conch shell trumpet). Individual movements are composed of two elements: a light bending of the shoulders, complemented by a sideways movement of the arms and the bamboo stick that the dancer holds in his right hand; and a turning movement using the whole body, in such a way that the feet trace a figure eight. (Shawqī 1994, 105)

The *lēwa* is a "sequence genre" that can include several different subgenres: In the opening *sabāta,* men dance a simple step that does not include the turning of the body; in the *būm* the melody and poetry are different, and women and children are allowed to participate; in the *katmīrī* the rhythm is faster and the poetic meter used is shorter, and so forth. The whole, of course, makes for a remarkable performance of dance, poetry, and music, invigorated with constant movement.

This brief overview touches upon only the most common genres of Omani song and dance, but it should serve to demonstrate the astonishing richness of poetry, music, and dance in a society that has, until very recently, been primarily an oral culture. Although Oman may be slightly unusual within the Arab world for the obvious influences from Africa, Arabia, Iran, India, and Pakistan, this amount of diversity could be equaled in any number of other settings in the Arab world. Morocco, Algeria, Tunisia, and Libya, for example, bear traces of African, Arab, Berber, and Mediterranean musical cultures; Egypt and the Sudan have received influences from Mediterranean cultures, the Nubians of Upper Egypt, as well as Africa up and down the Nile Valley; Lebanon and Syria share some musical features with Turkey to the north and have been influenced by the music of their Christian communities and immigrant Armenian communities; and Iraq shares a number of musical genres with neighboring Iran. Nations may be surrounded by boundaries, but cultures are not, and music is one aspect of human society that often proves to be a meeting ground for influences from every conceivable direction.

Sufi Ritual and Religious Chant (dhikr *and* inshād dīnī)

A particularly rich body of musical traditions in the Arab world is associated with the many diverse Sufi brotherhoods (Ar. sing. *tarīqa,* "path") and the various rituals referred to as *dhikr* (or *zikr*). Sufism, in general, is the mystical dimension of Islam, and although the term can be applied to many diverse beliefs and practices, most forms of Sufism share a few core beliefs: (1) The perceivable world around us is not the only reality—a deeper, spiritual reality is equally present that human beings can become aware of and make contact with through effort and proper spiritual training or guidance; (2) the ultimate goal in this life is to immerse oneself entirely in the love of God, which eventually involves "losing" one's own sense of self to experience an ecstatic oneness with the Divine; (3) certain spiritually developed humans (usually rendered into English as "saints," though the Islamic concept is quite different from the Christian one) are in constant contact with the Divine and possess a special spiritual power referred to as *baraka* (lit. blessing) that can be transmitted through touch or other forms of contact; and (4) the most easily accessible paths to these higher states of spiritual consciousness are found in the precepts of a Sufi brotherhood, usually including some form of the *dhikr* ritual.

The literal meaning of the term *dhikr* is "mention," "remembrance," or "mindfulness," but it is not a remembrance in the sense of recalling something from the temporal past. Rather it refers to both the technique of "mentioning" God (often literally through multiple repetitions of the name *Allāh* or one of the other Ninety-Nine Names of God, such as the Almighty, the All-Merciful, the All-Knowing, etc.) and to the mental or spiritual state of being completely and totally "mindful" of God, that is, thinking of nothing other than Him. The physical act of constantly mentioning God enables one to empty the mind of everything but God and thus fulfill the Qur'ānic injunction (Q 33: 41): "Be ever mindful of God" *(udhkurū Allāha dhikran kathīran)*. Each Sufi order or brotherhood has developed its own *dhikr* ritual, but most involve a handful of key elements: standing or sitting in a particular formation (often in rows or in a circle), reciting or chanting religious texts, and the performance of a series of prescribed body movements ranging from a gentle rocking back and forth to elaborately choreographed gestures and movements. In most, but not all, *dhikr* ceremonies, these actions are performed to a musical accompaniment and also feature a singer (Ar. *munshid*), who sings religious texts, particularly the genre of *madh an-nabī* or "praise to the Prophet Muhammad."

The most famous musical Sufi ritual known in the West is that of the so-called "Whirling Dervishes," or Mevlevi Dervishes, who are more closely associated with Turkey, though they have also had a historical presence in some regions of the Arab world, as well, such as Syria and Egypt. Theirs is a particularly dramatic and sophisticated ritual performed to the accompaniment of a very highly developed musical tradition that includes a large repertory of precomposed pieces of music that are meticulously transmitted from one generation to another. Many forms of *dhikr* in the Arab world are more popular in nature and rely more on a repertory of well-known folk melodies upon which singers and musicians are capable of improvising for lengthy periods of time.

Historically Sufism has taken many forms, some of which have reached tremendous complexity and beauty, such as in the philosophical poetry of Sufi masters such as Ibn 'Arabī, Ibn Fārid, Rumi, and others. But many popular or "folk" forms of Sufism that involved rituals such as eating glass, piercing one's body with swords or skewers, walking on hot coals, and so forth have often been condemned by Islamic religious authorities as being mere superstition, outright fakery, and even un-Islamic. For these reasons, many modern Islamist movements reject Sufism out of hand. Although these most recent attacks have had some effect in certain regions, in others, particularly in the countryside, Sufi brotherhoods and lodges still form a very strong force in the day-to-day religious practices of their communities in some regions of the Arab world.

The Friday *dhikr* of the Sammaniya Sufi sect led by Shaykh Hassan Qariballah in Omdurman, Sudan. Dhikr or zikr (literally "remembrance") is a Sufi practice in which the names of God or Quaranic phrases are chanted as a means of prayer and meditation accompanied by jumping in unison. © Michael Freeman/Corbis.

Dhikr ceremonies take place in a number of different contexts, but one of the most common is within the "lodge" *(zāwiya)* of a Sufi brotherhood. Here the participants gather at regular intervals to observe or perform the *dhikr* ritual, and sometimes even attain a state of trance. In the following two descriptions of the *dhikr* observed by Western scholars in Tetuan, Morocco, and Aleppo, Syria, we can see a number of similarities (the use of music, vocal chanting, coordinated body movements, the presence of an "overseer" in charge of setting the tempo and bringing the ritual to an end) as well as other elements that are found in one setting but not the other (the jumping movements and the running in circles in Morocco are not found in the Syrian ritual, and the chanting of the Ninety-Nine Names of God and the testimony of faith in Syria are not described in the Moroccan example). Some of these differences are regional, and others have to do with the precepts of different Sufi brotherhoods.

Tetuan, Morocco

After *maghrib* [sunset] prayers, we proceeded to the main *zāwiya* [Sufi lodge] on the second floor of the newly painted white complex, built into the hillside. Already adepts were milling around the door, removing shoes and placing them against the wall along the south side of the room. The room itself was large, approximately 15 meters by 30 meters, with a raised dais along the east wall enclosed by a guardrail. The sheikh, an entourage of officials, *munshidūn* [singers], and musicians entered and moved to the northern end of the hall, where they sat against the wall or, in the case of the musicians and *munshidūn,* cross-legged on the floor. The chanting began with the *Burda* [a famous thirteenth-century Sufi poem] and the slow recitation of the *wird* [prayer]. Then began the chanting of the *dhikr,* with the younger and training singers going first and contributing one song. A drummer wandered among the adepts who were now stretched out in a rough circle around the room, with arms linked. They began a slow rocking back and forth, but moved to a little jump when the rhythm increased and the cycle changed speed. All the while the *naqīb* [overseer] of the dance, a man of over sixty years, kept time by clapping his hands and directing the musicians. Throughout the evening, a cycle of *dhikr* would be followed by a cycle of rest and drinking of special nectar and tea. During the jumping *dhikr,* young men, dressed in very fine robes, moved into the centre of the circling adepts, and suddenly were seized by great excitement. They began moving rapidly back and forth within the circle, now jumping straight up in the air and waving their feet back and forth like wings before descending again to the floor. All this they accomplished with eyes tightly closed. They appeared to be in trance. Some broke off and began racing with great abandon around the inside of the ring. With several running with their eyes closed, it seemed only likely that they would collide; that they did not was a further sign, I was told, of the *baraka* of the saint. The *dhikr* lasted until about midnight, and all kept up the running or jumping for considerable amounts of time. Finally, at the climax of the evening, the whole group performed a small jumping pattern. The youths gradually ceased to run, the music ended, and the adepts slowly moved from the hall. The next evening, I had an opportunity to talk to the young men. They were euphoric, and reported tremendous joy and lightness from the trance state. Three of them indicated that they were training to be *munshidūn* [singers].

(Adapted from Waugh 2005, 27–28)

Aleppo, Syria

The *zāwiya* [lodge] measures about 30 feet square with a high, domed ceiling. Dark wooden bookcases filled with old manuscripts and copies of the Qur'ān line the walls, rich carpets cover the floors, and a number of ceiling fans circulate the air on this hot day. A group of older men file in and stand along the back wall; these are the descendants of the founding sheikh and each wears a beige turban, as does the main sheikh, who sits on the floor just in front of the back wall, which contains the prayer-niche (*mihrāb*). Others line the side walls, and the rest of us sit on the floor facing the main sheikh. As people enter, they approach the sheikh, kiss his right hand and then press their foreheads to his hand, repeating this two or three times in a rapid motion. Other, usually older men, attempt to do the same but the sheikh quickly removes his hand before it can be kissed, refusing this sign of deference, and instead kisses his own hand and then places it on his own forehead. He indicated to older members that they should sit closer to him, while others take spaces nearer the walls and door of the *zāwiya.* While my teacher goes to kiss the sheikh's hand, I take a seat, uncertain whether it would be appropriate for me to do so as well [. . .]

The recitation of the Qur'ān concludes and the ensemble begins chanting the [Ninety-Nine] Most Beautiful Names, slowly and in a low voice: *Yā Rahmān! Yā Rahīm! Yā 'Alīm! Yā 'Azīm!* [O All-Merciful! O All-Compassionate! O All-Knowing! O All-Powerful!] [. . .]

The Names having been recited, the participants begin chanting the first part of the proclamation of faith *(shahāda)*: There is no deity but God *(lā ilāha illā Allāh)*. The chanting follows a syncopated rhythm, the "*ha*" of "*ilāha*" aspirated to provide a rhythmic stress: ha! Over this chanting, the vocalists begin to sing a *muwashshah* [strophic song] and the rhythmic chanting of the *shahāda* provides a background tempo for the singing. Finishing this *muwashshah,* the vocalists *(munshid* –s) begin another one, then another, the pitch subtly rising, gradually, stepwise. The lead vocalist *(rayyis)* stands before the main sheikh and slaps out the tempo with his right hand on the back of his left until it turns red; I imagine it must get sore from all the vigorous slapping. As the pitch rises, the tempo accelerates and the chanting gets louder. The men along the walls, now numbering over seventy, begin to sway their upper bodies in coordination with the tempo, first to the right, then to the left, to the right, to the left, right left, right left. The effect is astonishing: a circle of motion and sound swirling around a stationary center from which rise the voices of the young vocalists. They finish proclaiming the unity of God. I look over to the back wall and find that one man's eyes have turned up into his head, his body moves spasmodically—right...left, right, left—and his mouth dangles open in a sort of grin. Another repeatedly knocks his head against the wall, seemingly oblivious to the tempo of the chanting. The main sheikh, ever composed, now rocks back and forth on the carpet and calls out *Allāh! Aywa! Allāh! Aywa!* (Allāh! Yes!). The tempo increases to a frenetic pace, the volume increases to a veritable roar, and the men are nearly screaming: *Lā ilāha illā Allāh! Lā ilāha illā Allāh!* The center begins to sway and I find myself moving along with my companions on the carpet, right, left, right, left, *lā ilāha illā Allāh! lā ilāha illā Allāh!*

Suddenly the main sheikh shouts *Allaaah!* and everything stops. The group falls silent and still. Only the sound of the ceiling fans can be heard swishing the hot air around. The sheikh then proclaims: "Wish God's blessings on the Prophet!" All relax and murmur the standard prayer: "May God bless the Prophet Muhammad and his family and companions, and grant him peace!" After a momentary pause, the *rayyis* takes up another *muwashshah* [strophic song], slapping out the slow, heavy rhythm on his bare hands. The participants begin to chant *Allāh hū! Allāh hū!* (He is God!) and the men along the walls slowly begin to move again, first to one side, then to the other, then the other...

(Adapted from Shannon 2006, 109–11)

Though the permissibility of using music in religious ceremonies, as we saw in the beginning of this section on Musical Arts, has been hotly debated over the centuries in Islamic contexts, is it clear that music—both instrumental and vocal—has played a very important role in Sufi rituals since the early Middle Ages. Sufi teachings can be found in both highly esoteric and erudite forms and more popular and accessible forms, but music, singing, and *dhikr* have been central to Sufi practices across the entire region of the Arab Middle East for centuries.

Arabic Lullabies from Tunisia, Kuwait, Yemen, and Iraq

Perhaps the very first form of folklore that an infant child becomes aware of is the lullaby, those soothing, quiet melodies hummed or sung by mothers or wet nurses with the aim of lulling children to sleep. Some lullabies tell of riches, good fortune, and a good marriage that await the child later in life, but many lullaby traditions throughout the world include lyrics that are anything but soothing. One need look no further than the ubiquitous English lullaby "Rock a bye, baby" for an example of a very frightening image ("When the bough breaks, the cradle will fall, down will come baby, cradle and all"), and it is not uncommon to find lullaby lyrics that detail the gore of battle for boys and even the pangs of childbirth for girls. These lyrics are perhaps performed with a prophylactic intention, in the hope that by describing the evils of the world the performance will prevent their actual occurrence. Some lullaby lyrics, on the other hand, are nonsensical and are held together primarily by patterns of rhyme and rhythm, rather than the sense of the images. Still others form chains of images that might be interpreted almost as didactic songs for children, beyond their function as lullabies. Here is an Iraqi lullaby of this latter category that is formed primarily of a chain of ideas that are logically linked, almost like a children's riddling game, though with a few nonsensical references as well. The image of traveling to Mecca identifies the singer as Muslim.

> Handle of the cradle, rock, rock,
> Greet my grandparents for me,
> The grandparents have traveled to Mecca,
> They clothed me in a *thōb* [outer garment] and a sesame cake,
> And where did he hide the sesame cake?

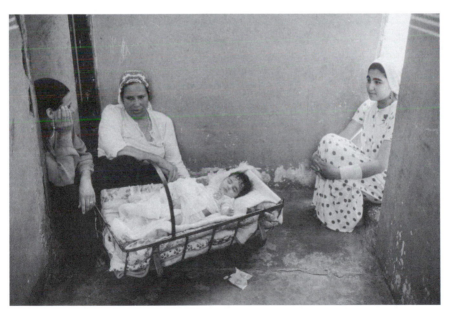

A lullaby in a Palestinian Refugee Camp. © Peter Turnley/Corbis.

He hid it inside the chest
And the chest wants a key
And the key wants a blacksmith
And the blacksmith wants money
And the bride has the money
And the bride is in the bath
And the bath wants a candle
And the candle has sunk in the well
And the well wants a rope [made of water buffalo tail hair]
And the rope wants a rope-maker
And the rope-maker wants a water buffalo
And the buffalo wants grass
And the grass wants rain
And God has the rain

(Adapted from Ferguson and Rice, 338–39)

Another version of this lullaby is the same until the image of the rope, at which point it continues:

And the rope is over the mountain,
And the mountain wants grass
And the grass wants rain
And God has the rain

In contrast, following are two Jewish Arab lullabies from Iraq, the first for a girl named Ghānī (though it could be sung to any girl since the name literally means "Dear One" or "Precious One"), and the second for a boy child. Note the difference in what the mother wishes for her daughter and her hopes for her son.

O the house of Ghānī is large and high
And higher than the mountain's tree
In it there are slaves who polish the rice
In it there is Ghānī who lets the boys play
We came to celebrate the feast, I am naked—
My dress is finished but it needs sleeves
We come to celebrate the feast under the sun's shadow—
Please tell Daddy that Ghānī is a bride
We come to celebrate the feast under the palm tree's shadow—
Please tell Daddy that Ghānī is married
She came out from the bath looking for her boy
She is the beloved of the girls, wearing an anklet
You are blessed, you cooked from the afternoon onwards
Your husband is waiting for you in the palace hall

Ghānī, you are polished silver
Shining like the Canopus star, shining in the wilderness.

(Adapted from Khayyat 1978, 18)

Welcome, O welcome!
I brought from my belly misfortune
The women took him from me
And he pushed back
Jacob, the pretty one
Rides a young horse
He is going to the palace
Play for him parade music
Drum, O drummers
Shrill from joy, O women,
Clap your hands for him, so he will dance
May his life increase, not decrease
Trill, O beloved women,
When his horse kicks his legs backward.
O children, be welcome!
Take my son with you
If you do not let him play
Cursed be your families!
Who dared to bite him
And made his tears flow?
The news reached his father
He left money and business

(Adapted from Khayyat 1978, 19)

From the southernmost region of the Arabian Peninsula, in Yemen, come the
following short lullabies sung in rhyming four- or five-verse patterns.

Lullaby to my son! And no one knows
My son is handsome and my son is a reader [reciter, i.e., of the Qur'ān]
When he reads in the house, his voice is sweet
Hearken, O my family and my neighbors!
And when he reads in the mosque, every [other] reader falls silent

Lullaby, lullaby to this daughter of mine and of her father
Prospective bridegrooms have come to her to ask for her in marriage
They seek to please her mother with two thousand (riyals),
    and they seek to please her father with two thousand (riyals),
And underneath the pillow they have forgotten two thousand!

Lullaby to my son, the son of powerful rulers
And the son of great chiefs
Who do not betray a trust
Nor deceive their neighbor

Lullaby to my son, he is sleeping
And may he who hates him, never sleep!
He who hates you, O my son,
Will redeem you and redeem me.

[Note: His death will preserve our health, like a scapegoat killed to bear sickness away.]

Yā sārī al layla wa asārī 'adan
Qul lil gharīb mā ma'a ummu min shajan
Wa hurmatu hubla wa zādat awladan
Wa jābat wulaydu wa samīnāhu hasan

O night-traveler at night, and night-travelers to Aden
Tell the absent one [the father] what sorrow his mother has!
His wife was pregnant and has added to their children,
And has brought forth an infant boy; we have named him Hasan.

(Adapted from Cline 1940, 299–301)

[Note: This lullaby is addressed to travelers to carry the news to the father, who is apparently working in the capital city of Aden, of the boy's birth and the mother's dire straits.]

Sabra Webber reports a very interesting but quite different role for lullabies related to her by a consultant in Tunisia:

A Tunisian woman of about forty described an alternate function for these lullabies quite different from that of inducing sleep. She stated that she remembers, from her childhood, young mothers using these songs in verbal duels. One example she gave was that of two mothers, living in homes with adjacent courtyards, one with a boy baby and the other with a girl, "debating" in a series of these lullabies whether it is better to be the mother of sons or daughters. As can be seen from the texts, the debates can become quite rough and might end, as she recalled, with one or the other of the young mothers running into the house in tears. (Webber in Fernea and Bezirgan 1977, 87–88)

A girl child is better than a thousand boys;
If she's far away she asks after her mother
If she's near she brings me her love
And gives me part of her food

So don't be too happy, mother of a son!
My daughter will grow up and take him.
She'll build her house on a hill far from you;
He'll earn the living, but she'll spend it! (89)

Gift! A Gift! Gift! A Gift!
A girl is better than a thousand boys,
For if my daughter lives in town,
She'll come each morning to see me;
She'll comfort me when I am ill,
And if I should die
She'll mourn for a long time (90)

Gift! A Gift! Gift! A Gift!
I say my son is better.
He brings me wheat and barley;
He brings me a granddaughter and a grandson
Who stay in my house and play together
My son wears burnooses woven with silver
Only black-eyed women are good enough for him! (90)

Finally, two lullabies from Kuwait follow, the first of which expresses the mother's hope that God will protect her child:

Lu lah lu lah
Sleep nicely on a mattress and carpet
Sleep like a deer in the wild
Sleep like your mother did when she was a child
Sleep! [For] you have a God who never sleeps,
By the honor of Moses, Jesus, and the Prophet, upon whom be peace.

(Adapted from Ghannam 1995, 77)

The second example, however, tells of a mother's fears as well as her love for her child:

While singing, a mother often expresses fears of her children's possible misbehavior in the future. She complains to her young children that after investing a long time and effort raising her child's brothers, they may not take good care of her in her old age. Still, despite her fears, the mother expresses her deep love for her baby.

I have raised you my children when you were many and small
And I fed you the tree's fruit
Now you have married and burnt my heart with fire:
Seven sons who cannot provide my supper.
The oldest son kicked me out and closed the door behind me,

Yet I love you, the fruit of my valley, and your love is my daily food,
The food of my heart,
I love you my darling, and hope that anyone who hates you will die.
I hope he will be sick and drink enough *saber* [a bitter substance] to send
   him to his death,
I hope death will come to him unawares.
I love you, sight of my eye, I love and adore you
My heart is medicine that will heal you

(Ghannam 1995, 78)

MATERIAL ARTS

The Arab world is particularly rich in its variety of material folk arts. Traditional crafts such as rug weaving, metalwork, wood carving, ceramics, jewelry making, embroidery, perfume production, ornamental tent making, basket and mat weaving, leatherwork, mother-of-pearl inlaying of boxes and furniture, and many other artistic trades are still practiced widely throughout the Middle East. Many of these art forms are familiar to Westerners since images of them can be found in almost any guidebook or picture book of the region, as well as in films and documentary television programs. In addition, however, there are also flourishing trades in products that are perhaps not so readily recognizable as "artistic" but which are of equal, if not greater, interest to the scholar of folklore due to their close relationship with the lived experience of every-day life: handmade cooking and serving utensils, storage containers of beaten tin, woven palm fronds, or adobe, agricultural tools and techniques, traditional handmade harness and tack for camels, donkeys, and horses, and, of course, vernacular architecture, the very buildings and spaces that people construct and inhabit.

Any one of these items, if studied carefully, opens up onto a whole range of cultural ideas and values. A decorated metal tray for serving food, for example, leads not only to the study of the various images and patterns engraved into the tray itself but also to the eating pattern that gives rise to such a serving technique One traditional manner of eating in the Arab world is for all present to sit cross-legged on a mat or rug on the floor with a circular tray, heaped with rice or another grain and topped with vegetables and meat, in the center. If there are guests present the men may eat alone, and the women separately in another room, but if only family members or close friends are partaking, then all will probably sit together. Each person will typically eat from the "pie wedge" space directly in front of them, serving themselves with a spoon or directly with their right hand. In some families, or in more formal settings, the male head of the household may dole out pieces of meat to all present according to their status—the largest portions go to guests, slightly smaller portions for other adults, and still smaller portions for

A seller in the Khan al-Khalili Market in Egypt displays elaborately decorated pots and pans. © Ron Watts/Corbis.

children. Where eating is done by hand, the serving tray is often closely associated with a matching pitcher and basin used for washing one's hands. A child or other member of the household will circulate around those seated placing the basin near each person in turn and then pouring water from the pitcher so that they can wash and rinse their hands. The soapy rinse water is caught in the basin and then tossed out. The decorated tray is thus tied to traditional ways of serving and eating food, to a rich set of concepts about hospitality and good "table" manners, as well as to a panoply of beliefs about which foods should be served together, which are healthy, which are not, and how they should be cooked.

In what follows, three types of material folklore are explored: first, vernacular domestic architecture in Yemen and Iraq; second, traditional "pilgrimage paintings" applied to the exterior walls of houses as decoration in Egypt and neighboring countries; and finally, the perfume traditions of women in the United Arab Emirates.

Vernacular Architecture: Arab Houses and Domestic Space

One of the most deeply rooted forms of folklore in daily life is vernacular architecture, buildings that are constructed on traditional models by local artisans, usually from readily available local materials. House forms and their furnishings represent not only a synthesis of environmental factors such as climate,

A group of men enjoy the traditional dish Quzi (roasted baby camel) in Saudi Arabia. © JTB Photo Communications, Inc./Alamy.

construction materials, and sustainable locations but also constitute a representation of many culturally specific ideas about space, family relations, gender, hospitality, health, the preparation and consumption of food, cleanliness, proper physical positions for sitting, sleeping, and other daily activities, and so forth. Although scholars of architectural history sometimes study vernacular house forms, they often do so primarily in structural and historical terms, whereas folklorists tend to bring additional perspectives to the study of houses through the study of the belief systems and patterns of habitual use that have shaped vernacular architectural traditions over the centuries.

The cultural diversity of the Arab world is readily seen in the vast number of different house types found across North Africa and the Middle East. In different regions, houses are made variously of stone, wood, oven-baked brick, adobe (sun-baked brick), palm trunks and fronds, and even marsh reeds. Some houses are organized around a central courtyard such that nearly all of the rooms in the structure open inward toward the shared open space and only one entrance gives access to the outside world. Other dwellings are more outward-looking, with no central open courtyard, with multiple entrances, and possibly benches or porches that provide an intermediary zone between the private realm within the house and the surrounding public spaces. Some regional house types place great emphasis on large spaces in a family's home for offering hospitality, whereas in other regions hospitality is traditionally relegated to shared "guesthouses" owned by extended families or clans and outsiders are only rarely invited into a family's dwelling. In some places it is common for several generations and various branches of a family (such as several brothers and their parents, wives, and children) to live in a single large home, while in others it is traditional that a groom provide a separate home for his bride upon marriage.

In the section entitled "A Unique Ramadan Tradition: The 'Brides' of al-Bakātūsh" (see Customs and Traditions) the changes that occurred in the vernacular architecture of one northern Egyptian village over the course of two decades are examined in some detail with particular reference to a local Ramadan tradition of decorating the outsides of houses. In that particular village, houses were traditionally constructed from sun-baked brick or *adobe* (a word that comes to English from Ancient Egyptian through medieval Coptic, Arabic, and finally Spanish). The traditional houses did not possess a courtyard but rather a large central hall (central room), with the *mandara* (guest room) to one side, and bedrooms and other private spaces located on the opposite side, or to the rear, of the central hall. They typically also possessed one or more mud benches along the outside walls facing the alley or street, called a *mastabā,* which provided a space for socializing and doing domestic tasks out in the sunlight since the small windows left the inside cool but dimly lit. Most older houses were only one story high, though often with one or more small rooms built on the roof for keeping birds, rabbits, and other domestic animals. In the summertime, families would spend evenings on the rooftop or even sleep there at night to enjoy the cool evening breezes, a welcome relief from the daytime heat. The introduction of a new, more modern, house type led to dramatic social and economic changes in the village, as well as the disappearance of one of the village's most distinctive Ramadan traditions.

Two additional examples of vernacular domestic architecture from the Arab world are examined in the following sections, both of which are remarkable: the ornate multistoried "tower houses" of San'a (San'ā') in northern Yemen and the fantastic structures built entirely of reeds by the "Marsh Arabs" of the Euphrates Delta in southern Iraq.

Skyscrapers of Brick and Stone in San'a (Yemen)

The houses in the old quarter of this ancient city rise from five to nine stories in height and are basically square or rectangular towers, the upper levels of which offer stunning views out over the city and its gardens. The lower one or two stories are constructed of dressed stone, but the upper levels are of exposed brickwork, embellished with ornate windows of carved gypsum trimmed on the outside with white plaster. The main door of the house is often carved or decorated, and it is secured with two heavy wooden bolts and a wooden lock. A large

A beautiful example of the ornate multi-storied "tower houses" of San'a (San'ā') in northern Yemen. Courtesy of Shutterstock.

Typical architecture for many of the multi-storied "tower houses" of San'a (San'ā') in northern Yemen. © Attar Maher/Corbis Sygma.

wooden key is used to open the lock and lower bolt, but the upper bolt can be opened or closed by the occupants from any level of the house via an ingenious system of ropes and pulleys. The combined effect of the soaring walls of stonework and red brick interspersed with elaborately carved windows trimmed with sparkling white plaster is striking, and many western visitors have commented that the city appears to be made of elaborate "gingerbread houses."

The ground floor of these tower houses is usually devoted to stalls for animals, the storage of firewood, and a lavatory. An enclosed stone staircase leads to the second floor, the primary function of which is to serve as storage space, particularly for grains such as wheat and corn but which may also include wardrooms, another lavatory, and, in larger houses, even a guardroom. The next floor is typically a multipurpose living room where the family may receive guests, take its meals, sit, relax, and even sleep. It is usually outfitted with cushions to sit on and additional cushions to use as backrests around the three walls facing the door. Some of the openings in the ornately carved windows are set with thin alabaster or stained glass and the windows themselves are placed low in the walls so that the room's occupants can comfortably look out from them while seated.

The next floor is usually the *dīwān,* which functions something like a formal parlor. Often closed unless there is a special occasion, it consists of a single large room that can be used for feasts, large family gatherings, entertaining special guests, and the far end, a place of particular importance, is also sometimes used for childbirth or funerals. One of the next floors is devoted to the kitchen, with a huge stone stove and a chimney that runs up the side of the building. The kitchen's location on one of the upper middle floors allows food to be prepared and served both downstairs in the *dīwān* and the family living spaces, and upstairs in the men's entertainment room, the *mafraj.*

The *mafraj* is one of the most distinctive features of the traditional San'a tower houses. Though one wall is typically solid to block out the cold northern winds, the remaining three walls are cut with large windows that provide remarkable views over the city and, in addition, are often fitted with window boxes filled with aromatic plants. In many houses, the *mafraj* is the most splendidly decorated and furnished space in the home, with rich carpets, embroidered cushions, and stained glass windows. Here the head of the household will entertain his male guests, smoking from large water pipes, chewing *qāt* (a mildly narcotic plant), reciting poetry, and listening to music. Social life in San'a is particularly renowned for these long afternoon sessions of composing and reciting poetry, sometimes accompanied by music, particularly the lute *(al-'ūd).*

These houses are fitted with interior wells from which, by means of long ropes, water can be drawn from several different locations within the building. The uppermost levels of the house have less usable space because they must also hold a large reservoir for water, the laundry area, and may also include some form of open terrace or courtyard as a workspace where women can do domestic chores.

The interior of a multi-storied "tower house" of San'a (San'ā') in northern Yemen. © Tiziana and Gianni Baldizzone/Corbis.

From medieval times onward, these tower houses were also cited by travelers as being remarkably free from the odors of human waste, due to the ingenious lavatory system that allows all waste to travel downwards through waterproof gypsum plaster conduits that were washed clean with a simple ladleful or two of water from a stone vessel stored in each lavatory.

The various detailed house plans published in Serjeant and Lewcock (1983) demonstrate a strong emphasis on rooms for shared social activities, with smaller chambers of various shapes and sizes that can be used for sleeping distributed throughout the remaining spaces of the building. The high point, literally, of a house, is the "room with a view," the *mafraj* (literally "place that gives release from sorrow or care"), where all of the aesthetics of visual ornamentation (carved windows with stained glass, colorful carpets, decorated brass trays, and water pipes), aural beauty (poetry and music), and even olfactory and gustatory appreciation (aromatic plants, smoking, chewing *qāt*, drinking tea, eating) are brought together in a single space.

San'a was historically also home to one of the most important Jewish Arab populations of the Arabian Peninsula. Until the establishment of the state of Israel in 1948, approximately 20 percent of the population of San'a was Jewish. As we saw in Chapter One, in ancient times Yemen was home to both significant communities of Jews and Christians. The Yemenite king Dhū Nuwās is said to have converted to Judaism, waged war against the Christians of Najrān, and then was defeated by the Abyssinian Christians who attacked from the African side of the Red Sea. With the advent of Islam, Christianity disappeared from the Arabian Peninsula, but Judaism continued to flourish in a number of urban centers. In Sanʿa, for example, one-quarter to one-third of the Jewish population was deemed wealthy by local standards. Over the centuries, Sanʿa was conquered and ruled by various outside forces including the Persians and the Ottoman Turks. In the seventeenth century, during one of its periods of independence, it was ruled by a local Zaydi dynasty (Zaydism is a branch of Shiʿite Islam found primarily in northern Yemen). There was a period of tension between the new dynasty and the Jewish community, and one Imam (ruler) ordered that the Jews of Sanʿa convert to Islam or be expelled from the city to live in the coastal region of Mawzaʿ. The vast majority refused to convert and were therefore forced to move from Sanʿa, located high in the mountains, down to the Red Sea coast. Although the expulsion lasted less than a year and the Jews were then allowed to return to Sanʿa, the brief expulsion had a long-lasting impact on the history and form of Jewish houses in the city.

First of all, the Jews were not allowed to return to the quarter they had previously inhabited in the heart of the old city, but were instead forced to build a new quarter outside the main walls. They were also not allowed to build houses of more than two stories in height. To compensate for this loss of space, most Jewish homes in the new Jewish quarter were equipped with cellars for storage (a practice not found in the homes of Muslim inhabitants of Sanʿa). Although Islamic law strictly prohibits the production and consumption of alcohol by Muslims, Jewish production of alcoholic beverages was never restricted in Sanʿa, so this activity, too, found its place in the cellars. In addition, Jewish homes had another feature that set them apart from those of their Muslim neighbors—an open courtyard in the uppermost story of the house that could be covered over with palm fronds for the weeklong celebration of Sukkōt, the Feast of the Tabernacles. This particular feature allows some of the houses in the center of the old walled city to be identified as having been built by, or owned by, Jews previous to the 1680 expulsion and their resettlement in the new Jewish quarter outside the old walls.

In these two complementary house forms we can thus see the influence of local building materials (stone and brick), climate (ventilated staircases and multiple grilled windows to provide cool interior spaces against the heat, along with solid walls without windows in the direction of the winter winds), the impact of the local urban environment (regular square houses aligned in rows), religious customs (the open court in the upper story of Jewish houses for the celebration of Sukkōt), legal restrictions (the two-story limit on Jewish homes that necessitated the addition of cellars), cultural practices (the *mafraj,* especially designed for aesthetic appreciation and entertainment), as well as health considerations (the remarkable lavatory systems), foodways (kitchens located on the second-to-highest floor to serve both the *dīwān* and the *mafraj*), and local concepts of beauty (the decorated windows, carved doors, and so forth). Houses, wherever they are found, are shaped by much more than the materials from which they are constructed.

Reed Homes and Guesthouses among the Marsh Arabs of Southern Iraq

The "Marsh Arabs," or *Ma'dan,* are one of the most distinctive communities in the Arab world. They live in the lower Euphrates river valley which constitutes one of the largest marsh areas on earth, estimated to be as much as 20,000 square miles. Although there are some semipermanent villages located on scattered mounds that rise above the water level even during periods of flood, the majority of settlements here are temporary and are constructed entirely of mud and reed. In fact, until recently the Ma'dan lived almost entirely in a world of mud and reed. From these two materials, they constructed their dwellings, shelters for their water buffalo, mats, baskets, ovens, incense burners, storage containers, cooking utensils, musical instruments, children's toys, and even jewelry. Their houses, built of reeds bundled together to form columns, arches, and cross-beams that are then covered with woven reed mats, can be disassembled rapidly and loaded onto boats to be reassembled in another location whenever need be. Their houses are sometimes constructed on land, but the Ma'dan have also perfected a remarkable technology of building on artificial islands made of layers of reed mats covered with mud. They fish with spears and maintain small herds of water buffalo, as well as some chickens and occasionally other domesticated animals. Reed products such as baskets and mats, along with dairy products from their water buffalo, are traded for grain and other staples with neighboring communities who live on the edges of the marshes but who rarely venture deep into that watery region.

The Ma'dan build a variety of structures from reeds, but the most impressive is the clan or tribal guesthouse, the *mudīf,* with its ornate facade and imposing arched roof. As Edward Ochsenschlager (2004) describes in the following section, however, it is not only the elaborate form of the guesthouse which sets it apart from a normal dwelling or even a *raba* (a structure that incorporates both a family dwelling and space for guests); the strict rules for behavior and speaking inside the guesthouse are also one of its prime characteristics. The *mudīf* is not just a piece of architecture; it is also a strictly defined social space:

A guest in a sheikh's *mudīf* will find himself surrounded by staid, stolid, older men properly dressed and on their best behavior. He should not speak unless someone speaks to him, and no matter how emotional he must speak with precision, clarity, and calmness. Conversations are considered and punctuated by silence; jokes and laughter are out of the question. In a *raba* [structure including a dwelling and a guest house] men of all

A "Marsh Arab" at work building a structure made completely out of reeds, Iraq. © Nik Wheeler/Corbis.

The interior of one of the fantastic structures built entirely of reeds by the "Marsh Arabs" of the Euphrates Delta in southern Iraq. © Nik Wheeler/Corbis.

ages, children, and even occasionally a woman are present. Conversations are loud and boisterous. Spontaneous songs and dances may provide part of the visitor's impromptu entertainment.

In the *mudif* everyone has his proper place according to his rank or status and seats himself accordingly. The sheikh or his representative will escort a guest to his proper place. When someone enters the *mudif* or the *raba* he greets everyone already there saying, "*As-salamu 'alaykum*" (peace be with you) and all assembled reply "*Wa 'alaykum is-salam*" (and peace be with you). If the person entering has higher rank than you, you must rise to your feet when you greet him. For people of significantly higher rank you should stand completely upright, for those only a little above you it is sufficient to rise a few centimeters off your haunches. All local men know the exact standing of everyone else and treat them accordingly. For an outsider it is more difficult as there is also old age status. That means that an old man with lesser social status may outrank a young man of higher social status. Modesty is not allowed. If you choose to sit in a place of lower rank, those of lower rank seated above you will abandon their positions to find a place below you.

(Adapted from Ochsenschlager 2004, 145–46)

Ochsenschlager goes on to describe in close detail the process of constructing a guesthouse from beginning to end over a period of six days (151–61). First the floor plan is laid out and a large sawhorse-like working space is created out of bundled reeds. Then the very large, tightly tied, bundles of reeds that will act as the arches are fashioned and set into holes in the ground angled slightly outward, away from what will become the interior of the guesthouse. Long cross-ribs are then made and attached horizontally to the arches. The ends of the arches are at this point, not without some difficulty, pulled toward the center and tied together to form the main structure, the backbone of the building. Tightly woven reed mats are then sewn to the sides and set in an overlapping pattern above to form the roof. Additional vertical and horizontal ribs made of thinner bundles of reeds are then sewn into place outside the mats to hold the sides and roof more securely in place. Finally, a looser latticework pattern of reeds is set in place at both ends to allow ventilation, with a single entrance at the front. Interestingly enough, guesthouse roofs typically leak the first season of their use and gradually become more and more watertight as the reeds age, alternately drying and swelling as the seasons change, and as the winds deposit dust and dirt that fill and seal the spaces between the bundled reeds. The end result is a remarkable structure, not only for its basic design but also for its obvious artistic aesthetic.

The tower houses of San'a, Yemen, and the reed houses of the Marsh Arabs in southern Iraq are but two examples of vernacular architecture from the Arab world. Each traditional structure, be it a family home, a tribal guesthouse, a dovecot, a mosque, a Sufi lodge, a saint's shrine, or a public bath, is a rich source for better understanding Arab folk culture, for each represents a complex interaction of beliefs, social customs, traditions, building techniques, and technological change.

Pilgrimage Paintings from Egypt

One of the most colorful and distinctive folk art traditions of Egypt is closely tied to vernacular architecture—the "*hajj* paintings" (pilgrimage paintings) that decorate the homes of people who have returned from making the pilgrimage to Mecca. Pilgrimage is a religious practice that permeates the Arab world and many parts of the broader Middle East, and is found among Christians, Jews, and Muslims (for lesser pilgrimages, see Customs and Traditions). One of the largest and most important pilgrimages in the world, however, is the Islamic pilgrimage to Mecca. Ideally, every Muslim who can afford to do so should undertake the pilgrimage to Mecca during their lifetime; the pilgrimage is one of the five "Pillars (or Principles) of Islam." In past centuries completing the pilgrimage to Mecca represented a journey of several weeks or even months depending upon one's point of departure. Huge caravans were organized so that pilgrims could travel together and be protected from bandits and marauding Bedouin. The Egyptian pilgrimage caravan included one element that was unique: At the head of the caravan was a large palanquin called the *mahmal,* inside of which was the ornate cloth covering (the *kiswa*) for the Ka'ba, the large cubical structure in the center of the great mosque in Mecca. For centuries it was traditional for Egyptian textile workers to weave and embroider with gold thread this elaborate covering that was replaced each year. Even though the tradition of the *mahmal* has now disappeared, it still appears in many modern *hajj* paintings.

Modern pilgrims to Mecca, of course, are more likely to travel by ship and airplane than by camel caravan and usually arrive in a matter of hours or at the most a few days. The *hajj* paintings of Egypt fully embrace these new developments and often juxtapose images of airplanes, ships, taxis, and buses alongside more historical images of camels and the *mahmal,* as well as a wide variety of religious images that symbolize the various stages of the pilgrimage. To these images are often added inscriptions that range from greetings and congratulations to the new "Pilgrim"—*hājj* (m.) or *hājja* (f.)—a title of respect that will now be used when addressing them (see Forms of Address), to verses from the Qur'ān, and verses of poetry. The decorations may consist of only one or two images beside the front door or may contain a dozen or more elements and cover the entire facade of a house. The colors are typically bright, even arresting to the eye, and the various renderings of the forms of transportation, the courtyard and minarets of the great mosque in Mecca, the Ka'ba, and the stages of the pilgrimage ritual, are produced with a wide variety of techniques and the distinctive stylistic touches of the individual painter.

The Stages of the Pilgrimage

Pilgrims travel from all over the world to the Arabian Peninsula during the annual season of the pilgrimage. The ritual consists of several parts, the first of which can be undertaken during other seasons of the year, but this "lesser *hajj*" (*'umra*) does not have the same value and merit as completing the full pilgrimage during its allotted time and does not fulfill the pilgrimage obligation. As pilgrims enter the holy sanctuary that encompasses the two cities of Medina and Mecca, they remove their worldly clothes; women wear plain clothes and men don two pieces of plain white cloth (symbolizing that all pilgrims are equal before God). The first of the major rites is the seven circumambulations of the Ka'ba, including the touching of the Black Stone if possible, first at a hurried pace and then at a more relaxed pace, in a counterclockwise direction. At this point the pilgrims declare to God: "Here I am, O God, at Thy Command, here I am!" *(labbayka Allāhumma labbayk)*. Next comes the "running" between two small hills (formerly outside but now enclosed within the great mosque): This act reenacts Hajar's frantic search for water in the desert for her son Ismā'īl (Ishmael) until an angel sent by God showed her a spring, known in Arabic as *Zamzam*. Many pilgrims drink from this well as part of their pilgrimage and bring back bottles of *zamzam* water to friends and family members as gifts. The pilgrims then leave Mecca for the town of Mina, about 5 kilometers to the east. The following day they go to the plain of Arafat and spend several hours standing until sunset—for many this is a period of deep personal contemplation and prayer. After sunset the pilgrims head to Muzdalifah to pick up pebbles that they will use over the next three days in the "stoning of the pillars" or "the stoning of the devil." This is the reenactment of an incident in the life of the Prophet Ibrāhīm (Abraham) in which the Devil appeared to him three times and the angel Gabriel each time instructed Ibrāhīm to chase him off by casting stones at him, at which point the devil finally disappeared.

At Mina the pilgrims also celebrate the Feast of the Sacrifice, which memorializes the Prophet Ibrāhīm's willingness to sacrifice his son (Ismā'īl in the Islamic tradition rather than Isaac) according to God's command. One of the main features of the celebration is the slaughter of a sheep, goat, or camel, representing the ram that God provided for Ibrāhīm to sacrifice at the last minute, rather than killing his son. Pilgrims then cut their hair or have their heads shaved, symbolizing a rebirth after the pilgrimage, and then change out of their special pilgrimage attire. At this point, they may also visit Medina where the tomb of the Prophet Muhammad is located. Whether or not they visit Medina, they eventually return to the great mosque in Mecca to perform the final "farewell" circumambulations of the Ka'ba, and with this act their pilgrimage officially comes to an end.

A mural on a village house depicts a pilgrimage to Mecca; encountered en route to the Valley of Kings, Egypt. © Earl & Nazima Kowall/Corbis.

The Hajj Paintings

While the pilgrim has been away, family and friends arrange to have his or her home decorated in celebration of their safe return. This practice is found throughout the region that extends from Libya to Syria, but is most common in Egypt, and within Egypt, is most commonly found in Upper Egypt. Here nearly every village has a talented local artisan who can be hired to design and carry out the painting, or family members may themselves undertake the task. If a painter is hired, there is usually a collaboration between the painter and the family in the selection of images and texts. Several traditional repertories make up the majority of the images seen in *hajj* paintings, but many have at least one or two images that are unique or personalized to fit the character or circumstances of the individual pilgrim.

Perhaps the single most common set of images are those associated with travel: airplanes in full flight overhead, sometimes stylized and sometimes rendered in great detail including even the name of the airline; ships crossing the Red Sea, which range from very realistic portrayals to fanciful images perhaps painted by persons who have never actually seen a large ship at sea; taxis and buses also appear, though less frequently; and, as mentioned previously, images of camels and even the now defunct *mahmal* still abound.

Nearly all *hajj* paintings also include one or more images from Mecca and Medina. The looming form of the Kaʻba draped in its black covering lavishly embroidered in gold thread is a favorite image, sometimes depicted separately and other times viewed within a larger scene that includes the surrounding great mosque, along with its arcades and minarets. To this might be added images of the pilgrim dressed in white pilgrimage garb accomplishing one of the stages of the pilgrimage or simply at prayer, sometimes in an idealized youthful form. Other favorite scenes are taken from the biblical stories to which the various rites of the pilgrimages refer: Abraham about to sacrifice his son but being stopped by the angel or Hajar with her newborn son Ismāʻīl beneath a palm tree or beside the spring of *Zamzam* (sometimes images of palm trees by themselves are used to allude to this story without actually depicting Hajar). Another common set of images depict celebrations upon the pilgrim's return complete with musicians, singers, dancers, and even microphones and loudspeakers. Amidst these primary images are often interwoven a variety of stock folk motifs including plants, flowers, animals, and so forth that help to give an overall sense of balance to the whole.

The texts that appear most frequently amidst the *hajj* imagery include religious phrases such as the word "God," "Praise be to God," "God is Great," "The messenger of God, may God bless and preserve him," and "God requires all people to make the pilgrimage if they are able," as well as other verses from the Qurʾān. Another repertory of inscriptions announces or is directed at the pilgrim—his or her name, the year of the pilgrimage, congratulations, "Accepted pilgrimage and Sin forgiven!" *(hajj mabrūr wa-dhanb maghfūr),* and other traditional well-wishings.

The images and the inscriptions turn the house itself into an object of art and serve the social function of both announcing and celebrating a major step in any Muslim's life. The pilgrimage and its folk art reflections in the *hajj* painting tradition mark a change in a person's life and a threshold crossed, both spiritually and socially.

Scents, Flavors, and Textures: Women's Arts of the United Arab Emirates

In her study *Aesthetics and Ritual in the United Arab Emirates: The Anthropology of Food and Personal Adornment among Arabian Women* (1983), Aida Kanafani points out that cultures do not equally appreciate or articulate the aesthetics of the five senses. During her fieldwork among women in the United Arab Emirates (UAE), she became increasingly aware that Western culture gives greater priority to the senses of vision and hearing over the senses of touch, smell, and taste. "Art" in the West is visual, and only secondarily auditory (music). Although foods, perfumes, and the touch of textiles all play a role in Western cultures, philosophical discussions of aesthetics or art deal only rarely with experiences of taste and almost entirely neglect the senses of smell and touch. Olfactory, tactile, and gustatory experiences are marginalized and almost never accorded the status of "art." Western languages, for example, almost all possess a highly articulated system for naming colors, but possess relatively limited resources for describing smells except perhaps in very specialized contexts such as the perfume industry. In contrast, Kanafani found that many aesthetic forms of expression among women in the UAE—their folk arts—were very much oriented to these neglected senses.

In her detailed description of the aesthetic dimensions of a women's lunch gathering *(fuāla)*, Kanafani documents in great detail the arrival of guests, the physical positions adopted by women when sitting, the washing of hands before the food arrives, the serving of the main meal, followed by fruit and sweets, after which Arabian coffee is served in a rather elaborate manner. At this point the hostess offers her guests a selection of perfumes and incense. Some are meant to be dabbed on the hair, others behind the ears and on the neck, and still others are to be applied to various places on the clothes and body. Women do not ask what type of perfume is found in each bottle as it is passed round, but instead instantly identify it by its smell according to a cultural specific categorization of which scents are appropriate for which places on the body.

The tray is removed once coffee serving is over. Then the hostess fetches the box of perfumes *(sandūg)*. The box is square, covered with felt and its glass lid is engraved with the names of God, Prophet Muhammad and the Islamic creed *(shihādah)*. It is imported from Saudi Arabia. The *sandūg* contains four to eight bottles of perfume surrounding a round plastic or glass container filled with various sorts of incense, and one or two brass bodkins [for applying the perfumes]. The perfumes are offered first, then the incense. The hostess pulls out the first bottle, uncaps it, and passes it to the first woman seated on her right, with a brass bodkin *(marwad)* to be inserted in the bottle to smear her body and clothes with. When the first woman has finished with the first bottle, the hostess hands her another one, uncovered while the first guest passes the first bottle to the next guest and so on until the last bottle has been handed around [...]

Each woman dips the bodkin in the bottle, and depending on the nature of the perfume places it either on her hair, behind her ears, on the neck and nape, on her hair-veil or on her cloak where it covers her chest, shoulders, and armpits. She repeats her gestures several times, dipping and anointing at length, obeying the exhortations of the hostess to use more of the scented oils and her own desire for a generous application. As she passes one bottle to the next woman, she receives a second bottle and perfumes her body and/or clothes with it. I have never heard any woman ask her hostess about the kind of perfume offered. Women have developed such a remarkable sensitivity to scents that however different the oil or mixture may be, all are familiar with the basic ingredients and are able to detect them individually.

(Adapted from Kanafani 1983, 23–25)

The perfumed oil dabbed behind the ears is typically a mixture of aloewood, saffron, rose, narcissus, and musk. The mixture applied to the neck usually contains the same ingredients, in different proportions, but substituting ambergris for saffron. Oils for use under the armpits are a combination of ambergris and sandalwood, and oil of aloewood alone is applied to the nostrils. For inside the ears a special mixture known as *mkhammariyah* (from the verb *khammara,* to leaven or ferment) is preferred which contains aloewood, saffron oils, civet, and a chunk of ambergris, sometimes with the addition of black musk. Finally, for the hair, a complex blend of aloewood, ambergris, saffron, jasmine oils, saffron paste, and *mkhammariyah* is used. All in all, Kanafani documents some 26 ingredients to the most common perfumed oils, all of which can be combined and recombined in various proportions. Each perfume is blended with great care, particularly the *mkhammariyah* mixture that is thought to be a sign of a woman's good taste: "After the guests have returned fragrant with [the hostess's] hospitality to their own homes, they will be asked where they have been and their hostess' performance in composing the *mkhammariyah* will be smelled and evaluated" (Kanafani 1983, 44).

Kanafani goes on to document and explore the olfactory, gustatory, and tactile world of this community of women examining their understanding and use of perfumes, spices, incense, aromatics, the texture and smell of food and clothing, as well as visual decoration such as henna dying, jewelry, and embroidery. Her study not only introduces the reader to a remarkable sense of "art" expressed in touch, taste, and smell but reminds us that in observing the folk cultures of other peoples, we can easily be blinded to some of the central artistic expressions of those cultures by our own culture's hierarchy of the senses and artistic forms.

CUSTOMS AND TRADITIONS

Much of the folklore an individual experiences in his or her daily life is found not in specific artistic fashionings (stories, songs, paintings, perfumes, etc.) but in the customs, traditions, and beliefs of their community. How we celebrate birthdays and holidays, what we think brings good or bad luck, ideas about which foods are healthy and which are not, home remedies handed down within families for everything from headaches to warts, belief in angels or jinn, how we mark births and deaths, techniques for seeing if pasta or potatoes are thoroughly cooked—all of these are part of our daily existence but are derived primarily from orally transmitted folklore rather than from our schooling or reading books. These aspects of folklore are particularly challenging to study and record because some of them are intensely private matters. In addition, there are many different levels of participation in such phenomena: Some individuals may believe wholeheartedly in a particular idea and openly participate in certain public rituals, others may publicly deny belief or participation but do so privately, and still others may behave as if they believe and participate in public rituals that they secretly do not believe in.

In the first example that follows, we examine a tradition found in only one village, a tradition that has lost any ties to specific beliefs but that may well have been tied to pagan beliefs of the past. The second example, that of spirit exorcisms, is one that many Arabs, particularly educated people, would dismiss outright as superstition, and yet at the same time they might not be 100 percent sure that the spirits do not exist. The third example, the celebration of weddings, is not only found in every nook and corner of the Arab world, but local variations in many areas are a source of pride and are often a vaunted aspect of the culture of a village, a region, or a tribe. The fourth example, saint veneration and pilgrimage, is a practice shared by Christian, Jewish, and Muslim communities in the Middle East.

A Unique Ramadān Tradition: The "Brides" of al-Bakātūsh

Until the late 1980s, a unique Ramadan ritual was practiced in the village of al-Bakātūsh in the Nile Delta of Egypt that has not been documented elsewhere. The traditional mud-brick houses of the village at that time were typically flanked by a low, earthen bench or platform called a *mastabā* (pl. *masātib*) on one or both sides of the front door. These benches provided a social space halfway between the private interiors of the houses and public gathering places such as cafés. During the morning women would sit on the benches while doing household chores such as picking rice or lentils clean for the evening meal. In the afternoon it was common to see schoolchildren sitting cross-legged on the benches while they did their homework because the lack of electricity meant that it was too dark inside for this task. But in the early evenings, when the day's agricultural work in the fields had been done, this space was occupied by adult males who would relax, often with a cup of tea, carry on conversations from one house to the next, greet passersby and offer them tea, a cigarette, or even supper.

During the fasting month of Ramadan, when adult Muslims abstain from both food and drink from sunrise to sunset, the women of the household would decorate the walls just above these benches. Combining mud, dung, and straw, they would apply a plaque to the wall that they would then decorate with bright colors and finally add at the top a small female figurine known as the *'arūsa* (lit. bride or doll), which they would adorn with a feather. Young adolescent boys who were not yet old enough to undertake the full fast (but who might be fasting part of the day or a few days of the month) would try to "steal" or "kidnap" the brides from the houses in their neighborhoods, and, when they succeeded, would run shouting through the alleyways and deliver her to the threshold of the main mosque in the village, crumbling her into dust and scattering it about in front of the main entrance. If a bride was stolen, the women of the household would then fashion another one and attach her to the wall of their house, but this time add two feathers, indicating that she had been stolen once already. These clay "brides" are used

Ramadān "Bride" of al-Bakātūsh. Photo credit: Dwight Reynolds.

in two other ritual contexts in Egypt that indicate their general association with fertility—they are sometimes affixed to bread ovens as a good omen, and they are also used as part of a folk cure for barrenness if a women is unable to conceive a child. In the latter case, a "bride" is fashioned and placed on a donkey, then led through the alleyways of the quarter with children singing *abū rīsh abū rīsh in-shalla ti'īsh* (Father of feathers, father of feathers, God willing you shall live!).

Stealing a bride was not necessarily an easy task, however, for family members, particularly the adult males, would defend their bride by shouting at the boys and threatening them with sticks or stones to drive them off. The most propitious time to steal a bride was right at sunset when the fast was being broken, for the adult family members were likely to be focused on drinking their first draught and eating their first food since dawn.

Clearly the ritual combined a number of different symbolic actions—boys who were not quite men were symbolically winning brides, demonstrating bravery or cunning by accomplishing this task despite the threats of bigger, stronger males; and when they did achieve their goal, they rendered her to a physical space that represents religious authority and community approval, that is, the entry to the mosque. In a slightly different manner we can see that this ritual game involved a complex interplay among intermediate spaces and times, "betwixt and between-ness," or what folklorists and anthropologists refer to as *liminality*. The adolescents who stole the brides were at an ambiguous age between boyhood and manhood; the space of the mud benches was located between the public and the private spheres (it belonged to the household but yet was exposed to public view); the prime time for kidnapping a bride was at the moment of breaking fast, sunset, the boundary between day and night; and the boys would take the figurines to the threshold of the mosque, the intermediate point between sacred and profane spaces.

In the late 1980s and early 1990s this ritual disappeared—but how and why? Until the 1970s nearly all of the houses of the village were built of homemade mud brick: adobe. The word *adobe* comes from the Arabic word *at-tūb*, which in turn comes from the Coptic word *tōb*, which is from Ancient Egyptian—it is a very ancient word that has traveled from Pharoanic Egypt into Arabic, then to Islamic Spain (al-Andalus) where it entered the Spanish language, and from there to the New World. In the 1970s and 1980s, however, many young Egyptian men began traveling to the Gulf or to other Arab countries as guest workers, and when they returned they would rebuild their family's old adobe houses in baked red brick. The old adobe houses had thick walls and provided good insulation from the heat of the summer and the cold of winter, and making adobe bricks cost little, but they also required constant repair, especially after heavy rains, and had to be completely rebuilt every couple of decades. When Gamāl 'Abd al-Nāsir (Nasser) built the Aswan High Dam, the Nile no longer flooded each year depositing a thick layer of rich new soil. As villagers continued to scrape away topsoil from their agricultural lands to make adobe bricks, they reached deeper, less fertile layers of topsoil, which began to affect Egypt's overall agricultural productivity. The government began to encourage building in baked red brick to save the precious fertile topsoil for farming. In addition, the red brick houses had the allure of being modern and semi-urban, whereas the traditional adobe houses came more and more to be viewed as "backward" and "rustic." The guest workers' newly acquired resources, with government encouragement, led to a nearly complete rebuilding of many villages.

The red brick houses, however, were built on a different model than the older adobe houses, and one of the differences was that they did not have benches along the outside walls. The intermediary space which the Ramadan bride ritual had occupied began to disappear. Another social change occurred as well: Young men in the village who often used to get married in their late teens now began to wait to marry until later and later in life because they spent years abroad as guest workers first. This meant that the onset of adolescence was no longer the "brink of manhood" (because full manhood was only considered to be achieved at marriage). In both spatial and temporal terms then, there was no longer a clear zone or age for the symbolic enactment of winning a bride. A final, very significant factor was the rise of Islamist interpretations of religion that have condemned such folk rituals as "un-Islamic."

Thus, in the space of less than two decades, the housing stock of the village changed dramatically, eliminating the space that the ritual had once occupied. Demographic change occurred equally as swiftly with young men waiting longer and longer to marry and often being absent from their home community for years at a time as guest workers. These two sets of changes were coupled with an equally powerful reinterpretation of Islam ("fundamentalism," though this is in many ways both an inadequate and misleading term for the complex changes of the new Islamic movements) that frowns on folk practices of many sorts. The "Brides of al-Bakātūsh" constituted a remarkable folk ritual that in modern times was found in only one village, but the many social changes that have taken place in the last few decades (including the advent of public schooling, the arrival of electricity and television, along with the changes already mentioned) all contributed to its disappearance (for more detail, see Reynolds 1994.)

Zār Rituals from Northern Sudan

The zār is a form of spirit possession that is found in a number of regions in the Middle East—in Egypt, Sudan, the Arabian Peninsula, and across the Gulf in southern Iran, as well as in a number of countries farther west along the southern rim of the Sahara. Related traditions are also found in sub-Saharan Africa. The term itself refers to both the overall belief and practice of spirit possession as well as to the spirits themselves (s. zār, pl. zayrān), and in some regions also to the ceremony in which the spirits are convoked and appeased. This ceremony is sometimes referred to in English inaccurately as an "exorcism." In a Christian exorcism. a spirit or devil is "cast out" of the human host, usually permanently; in the zār, once a person has become possessed by a spirit, that is a lifelong relationship that is never entirely severed. Like a patient suffering from a recurring disease, the possessed person must undergo periodic treatments—zār ceremonies—in which the spirit is called forth, sometimes negotiated with, and then, at least temporarily, appeased, which leads to a period of well-being for the possessed. If called out and appeased at appropriate intervals, the spirit may cause few or no problems outside the ceremonies; if ignored, however, the spirit may communicate its displeasure in many different ways ranging from uncontrollable bouts of possession and trance, to disease-like symptoms such as fever, depression, wasting away, infertility, and so on, or it may even bring about events of great misfortune.

Spirit possession has been present as a belief system in the Middle East for a very long time. Jesus, for example, is portrayed in the New Testament as casting out demons and even causing them to enter animals, and the Qur'ān speaks in many places of the jinn ("genies"), who exist in a parallel spirit world but occasionally are active in the human world as well. Thus while official Islam and Christianity may not approve of the *zār* ceremonies, it has been difficult to denounce or eradicate the belief itself since many people understand the *zār* spirits to be a form of the Qur'ānic jinn or biblical demons. In almost all regions where it is practiced, women are far more likely to be susceptible to spirit possession than men, often outnumbering male adepts by as many as 10 or 20 to 1. Various Western scholars have offered hypotheses about the causes of such possession ranging from medical reasons (vitamin deficiencies), to psychological explanations (release of anxiety, particularly over infertility), to strategic motivations (a means of demanding certain material objects as gifts or obtaining better treatment from men), to personal need (a personal need for attention or desire for an opportunity to socialize with other women). Perhaps the most widely accepted understanding currently is that individuals within a culture learn an idiom for describing physical and psychological health (cf. Western concepts such as hysteria, depression, nervous breakdowns, subconscious desires, bipolar disorder, attention deficit disorder, etc., that have come and gone over the past two centuries), and in these regions people learn the idiom of the *zār* for describing, diagnosing, and treating various forms of psychological states. In turn, it is possible that individuals with psychological disorders in different societies evince symptoms that are in part determined by their own culture's repertory of recognized psychological states.

One of the most carefully researched studies of the *zār* in recent years is Janice Boddy's *Wombs and Alien Spirits* (1989), based on fieldwork conducted in a village in northern Sudan. Following is a passage describing the first day of a several-day *zār* ceremony.

I am seated near the dancing ground, an open area *(mīdān)* bounded on three sides by palm-fiber ground mats. Here sit several dozen chanting women: the spirit possessed. Now and then one rises to her knees and begins to move her upper body in time with the sonorous beat [of the drums]. In the center of the *mīdān* stand the shaykha—*zār* practitioner or "priestess"—a forceful, brawny woman in an electric-pink pullover, *tôb* [woman's outer garment] tied loosely at her waist. She is arguing with a woman just as brash as she, who, between expletives, puffs furiously on a cigarette. I learn that the shaykha speaks not to the woman, but to her spirit, in an effort to diagnose the source of the woman's complaint. Observing from the side is a tall, very black, incongruously muscled figure clad in a [woman's] *tōb,* large wristwatch, and hairnet—the shaykha's reputedly transvestite assistant from south of Shendi. In contrast, the *'ayāna*—"sick woman" and focus of the ceremony—is frail, elderly. She rests quietly on a pillow next to the musicians, facing the front of the courtyard, arms and legs curled tight against her white-*tōb*ed body.

The shaykha concludes her discussion, sits down, and starts to drum. Using only the tips of her fingers, she beats a large earthen *dallūka* [drum] stretched with goat hide, its whitened flanks boldly adorned with mauve geometrical designs. Another *dallūka* responds in shifted accents, joined half a second later by the *nugarishan,* a tall brass mortar that rings, when struck, like a cowbell, only deeper. A fourth woman beats a complementary rhythm on an inverted aluminum washtub or *tisht.* The result is a complicated syncopation, its underlying pattern one long beat, three short. The sound is less soothing than cacophonous, yet endlessly repeated and accompanied by reiterative chants, the effect is indeed soporific. The chants, I learn, are called "threads"—*khuyūt* (a "thread," singular is *khayt*)—and when sung they are said to be "pulled."

The rhythm intensifies; the "sick woman" rises to dance. Now visible over her *tōb* is a red sash attached to a reddish waist cloth in the style of a Sam Browne belt. She is possessed, my companions say, by *Khawāja* (Westerner) spirits; a doctor, lawyer, and military officer—all of these at once. Yet it is the lattermost she appears to manifest in dance. Her *tōb* is folded cowl-like over her head, obscuring her face; she flourishes a cane—hooked, as in vaudevillian burlesque. Her dance is a slow, rhythmic walk crisscrossing a chimeric square, feet first moving side to side, then forward and back. With a leap of the imagination she is an officer of the desert corps conducting drill. Every so often she bends rigidly as the hip and, cane pressed to her forehead, bobs her torso up and down. I am told that her spirits have requested the white *tōb,* cane, cigarettes, "European" belt, and yet to be purchased, a radio.

The band takes up the chant of another *zār* [spirit]. The "sick woman" sits; the shaykha leaves her drum and starts to dance, *tōb* covering her head. Suddenly the *tōb* is thrown off. She turns on her heel, goose-steps the length of the *mīdān,* stops before me, abruptly pulls herself to attention. She salutes me three or four times, stiffly, eyes glazed and staring, a grin playing wildly on her face. Her left hand grips a sword within its sheath; with her right she grasps my own with unusual strength and pumps it "Western style" in time to the drums. I am shaken by this treatment and by thoughts of her sword. The chant sounds like a military march; I recognize the British Pasha spirit, *Abū Rīsh, Yā Amīr ad-Daysh* ("Owner of feathers, O Commander of the army"). The drums desist. At once my hand is released. The shaykha's features assume a more dignified composure and she returns to the center of the *mīdān.*

(Adapted from Boddy 1989, 125–27)

The *zār* spirits are understood to exist in an unseen world that is parallel or contiguous to ours. They are capricious, idiosyncratic, and sometimes aggressive. In general, the spirits are intrigued by the human world and seek opportunities to enter it to be entertained, to frolic about, and to obtain attention and gifts. If a possessed person's spirit or spirits are already known, those spirits can be convoked without much difficulty for they respond to specific rhythms and chants, and at times to specific material objects (such as cigarettes, clothing of a particular color, a cane, a hat of a particular sort, etc.), which then act as their "props" when they dance. Once called into being "present" in the possessed's body, that person's personality, voice, etc., temporarily disappear and are understood to be elsewhere while the *zār* spirit is in evidence. A possessed person may attend a *zār* ceremony just as regular treatment, but she may also be present because a problem or symptom has driven her to seek out the healing powers of the shaykha and the *zār* ceremony. In this case, the shaykha may speak with the spirit at length to determine what the problem is and what the spirit wants. The spirit may simply want to be allowed to dance at the *zār*, or it may have demands that have either to do with the *zār* performance itself (a prop or piece of clothing for the dance) or that have to do with the outside world (the woman must be fed duck or chicken every week, her husband must treat her better, or she is prohibited from eating a particular food, etc.). Meeting these demands and giving the spirit a chance to dance at the *zār* typically satisfies the spirit for a time and alleviates the symptoms or problem that had motivated the consultation.

These requests from the *zār* spirits have led some outsiders to understand the entire system as one in which oppressed women are able to demand changes in their lives, particularly from men, that is, they understand the *zār* as a sociopsychological "strategy." Although this may be true in some cases, the spirits' demands are sometimes not obviously to the advantage of the adept, for example, controlling what she eats by forbidding certain types of food (often foods that are considered very tasty) or prohibiting the wearing of certain colors of clothing. The symbolic world of the *zār* is so rich that it is probably not possible to capture the social function(s) it serves for all of its participants in a single term or idea, much as it would be impossible to capture the function of a religion in such blanket terminology.

One of the most fascinating aspects of the *zār* is the process of diagnosis. When a woman is possessed for the first time, or shows symptoms that people believe indicate that she may be possessed, the shaykha and her musicians run through a vast musical repertory of rhythms and chants (and sometimes the material "props" as well), seeking to call out the trouble-making spirit. When its rhythm and chant are performed, a *zār* spirit can scarcely resist manifesting itself in the movements of the possessed's body, and the "diagnosis" is confirmed by observing the movements and dance steps of the possessed's body, for each spirit has its own identifying characteristics. Thus the world of the *zār* can also be understood to be a world constructed of music—specific rhythms, chants, and dance movements are the key characteristics of the many different spirits, many of whom, incidentally are "foreigners" and not Arabs (though there are also Arab *zār* spirits). In northern Sudan, unmarried women are not usually possessed—because they have not yet had sexual intercourse, they have not yet become "open" to the spirits. The following example is an unusual case because it involves an unmarried girl; however, it gives an idea of the diagnostic process that takes place when a woman is possessed for the first time.

A piercing cry—a uniformed schoolgirl nine or ten years old has sprawled forward into the *mīdān,* upheld on all four limbs, body jerking rapidly up and down from the shoulders. Immediately, she is led off by some older women, told it is not proper for a child to behave this way at a *zār.* But she does not stop. Outside the *mīdān* the women try to calm her. Now she is sobbing and has gone quite limp. When efforts to revive her fail she is dragged, resisting, back into the center. She balks at attempts to bring her to the shaykha and is deposited before the drums. The shaykha approaches; the girl cringes. The shaykha covers her with a white *tōb,* and asks, "What do you want? Who are you?" No response.

Onlookers taunt the intrusive *zār* [spirit], trying vainly to garner its sympathies: "Ah, her father is poor! Her mother is blind! Her brother is ill!" The shaykha sends for the girl's father. He is brought into the *mīdān* and made to give his daughter's spirit ten piasters (about twenty-five cents). Still there is no word from the *zār;* the girl remains limp, appearing deeply entranced.

It is getting late. Smells of cooking waft through the *mīdān,* and laughter from the kitchen. More drumming and dancing are called for. The shaykha requests certain "threads" [chants] to test for various species of *zār* spirits, hoping the presumptuous spirit will be drawn to identify itself. She blows into the schoolgirl's ears and behind her neck; she pulls at her limbs, whips her softly with a length of rope, beats her lightly with an iron spear. She censes her, rolls her head along the girl's body. She takes the girl in her arms and dances to and fro, blowing a whistle to the incessant beat. She leads the girl around the *mīdān* and is twice successful in getting her to move briefly of her own accord. At last the girl jogs back and forth through the open space, one arm pumping like the wheel of a locomotive, the other, raised and crooked at the elbow, sounding an imaginary alarm. The shaykha blows her pipe whistle in accompaniment. The troublesome spirit is identified: Basha-t-'Adil, the *khawāja* ["foreigner"] railway engineer.

Still the episode continues. For over an hour the shaykha tries every technique in her repertoire, aiming to convince the implacable *zār* to abandon its newfound host and refrain from bothering her again until she is a woman and married. Finally the shaykha guides the girl out of the *mīdān* and out of the courtyard. The girl, now calmed and weeping softly, is brought to sit near me—a human *khawāja*—but placed with her back to the ritual.

(Adapted from Boddy, 130)

The *zār* is a fascinating world of music, dance, and symbols, an inverted world where images of local social types and foreigners are conjured up through specific bodily movements and physical props. It is also an intensely spiritual world with many medical and psychological aspects, and clearly is a reflection in other ways of the social world that exists outside the boundaries of the *zār* ceremony. Scholarly

Elaborate designs of henna decorate the hands of this bride-to-be in Morocco. Courtesy of Shutterstock.

literature on this tradition from various parts of the Middle East not only demonstrates that there are many regional variations but also that there are constant surprises even within local traditions, new spirits that have never been seen before, for example, as well as new symptoms and demands, and so forth. Only a tiny percentage of Arabs participate in this tradition, and the vast majority would reject it outright, though some larger percentage might admit that they believe in the existence of jinn, or demons, or *zār* spirits. Two intriguing aspects of folk beliefs and traditions are the varying degrees of belief and participation in a particular custom found within a given culture and the degree to which a tradition, though only supported by a small minority, may or may not influence the larger society.

Marriage and Metaphor: An Egyptian Village Wedding Song

Although life-cycle rituals marking birth, puberty, adulthood, and death are among the most powerful and oft-studied of folk traditions, perhaps none is more central to Arab culture, or more elaborately celebrated, than weddings. Weddings mark the arrival at full adulthood for the two main participants, the joining of two families, and the propagation of the community through the promise of children. Traditional weddings in some regions of the Arab world involved not only a series of ceremonial stages leading up to the actual marriage, but the final act itself was often celebrated with a week or more of festivities that featured public performances of poetry, songs, dances, a complex set of bodily rituals (bathing, shaving, the dying of hands with henna, etc.), the wearing of traditional costumes and jewelry, the preparation and offering of special foods, the exchange of gifts, and many other activities. More recently, many of these traditions have been shortened or curtailed for economic reasons or simply because the faster pace of modern life does not allow most people to spend an entire week at a celebration, even for close family members.

Following is a description of common wedding practices in a northern Egyptian village in the early 1980s:

The process of engagement and marriage in al-Bakātūsh, as in most of Egypt and the Arab world, unfolds in a sequence of ceremonial stages, often spread out over several months or even years. These include the "Reading of the *Fātiha*" *(al-fātiha)*, the "Writing of the Wedding Contract" *(katb al-kitāb)*, the "Presentation of the Dowry" *(al-shabka)*, the "Night of Henna" *(laylat al-hinna)*, the "Carrying" *(al-shayla)*, the "Procession" *(al-zaffa)*, the "Consummation" *(al-dukhla)*, and the "Morning Visit" *(al-subhiyya)*. Each of these takes place on a separate occasion and is marked by traditions and ceremonies, several of which include music in the form of traditional songs or professional entertainment. The prime context for the performance of the epic poem *Sīrat Banī Hilāl* occurs on the "Night of Henna," which is usually the largest of the public celebrations, but on occasion epic singers may be called in for the "Presentation of the Dowry" and the nights leading up to the "Night of Henna" by families who wish to make a particularly notable event of the occasion.

On the "Night of Henna" the bride and groom are separately prepared for the wedding's culminating ceremonies, which take place the following day. In their respective groups of relatives and friends, they are bathed, their hair is trimmed and coiffed, they are dressed, and each is physically adorned with henna. In the case of the groom in al-Bakātūsh, the latter is usually decorated only on the palms—in each hand he holds a lump of henna mixture which will dye his palms bright orange. Once the groom has been bathed and freshly attired, he is led outside with much festivity and seated on a chair on a platform, while relatives and friend celebrate around him. A parallel celebration takes place around the bride, though this is held indoors.

The traditional songs sung at this point of the wedding reflect not only the activities that are being carried out at that moment, but the entire complex of behaviors that are being linked with marriage. Perhaps the most common wedding song of all of Egypt, with its myriad of different verses, is "The Henna, the Henna" *(al-hinna al-hinna)*. It is most commonly sung by women as they dress and coif the bride, though it is heard and known by the men as well. The recurring interjection, "O my eye!" *(yā 'aynī)* is a reference to the eye as the seat of emotion and love in Arabic poetry (along with the heart, the soul and the liver), and the play on words at the end of the second verse is a common one because in colloquial Arabic the word *hawā* can mean either 'love' or 'a breeze':

> The henna, O the henna, O drop of dew
>> The window of my Beloved, O my eye, brings a breeze/love
> O how I fear your mother when she asks me about you,
>> I'll hide you in my eyes, O my soul, and put kohl over you.
> O how I fear your sister when she comes looking for you,
>> I'll hide you in my hair, O my eye, and pleat it over you.
> And if evil-speakers come to me and ask about you,
>> I'll put you in my breast, O my soul, and cover you with pearls.

The song refers not only to the activities of the Night of Henna (putting on kohl makeup, braiding the bride's hair, putting on jewelry), but also to the behavior demanded from the bride—that she display no emotional involvement in the proceedings. The bride must traditionally appear distant and even morose; her muted emotions must display sadness at her departure from her family home, and she must show no happiness or joy that might be construed as anticipation of the sexual act which will initiate her into womanhood. She must conceal her emotions, metaphorically described in the song as hiding her beloved.

The song also refers to traditional village ideas about public relations between men and women before marriage. If a woman does indeed love her future husband, no one must know, for it may lead to accusations of misbehavior. In front of the groom's mother and sister she should appear indifferent, hence her fears about successfully hiding her emotions. In addition, she much fear the *'awāzil* (sing. *'azūl*), who are a major concept in Egyptian folk poetry, translated here as "evil-speakers." They are people who strive to separate couples in love by creating rumors and gossip which effectively doom their chances of getting married. They do so out of jealousy, envy, and pure maliciousness. In a tightly knit society such as the village, "people's talk" *(kalām al-nās)* is a powerful social force to be reckoned with.

The imagery of the song thus indexes: (1) the intimacy and possessiveness of young love; (2) the activities involved in preparing the bride; (3) the bride's struggle to conceal her feelings and emotions and to maintain the expected passive demeanor; and, (4) the necessity of publicly dissembling any affection or desire she may feel for the bridegroom.

As the culminating portion of this celebration, when all the other ceremonies have been completed, epic poets are brought out to entertain the guests. It is a cliché in al-Bakātūsh that they should sing, "until the dawn call to prayer."

(Adapted from Reynolds 1995, 106–9)

Within a very few years of the writing of that description, epic singers were displaced as the main form of entertainment in the village, and musical groups from nearby towns who perform a repertory of urban songs using microphones, loudspeakers, and electric keyboards replaced them. By the year 2000, there were no longer any performing epic singers in the village or in the surrounding district.

An unnamed Saint's Tomb in Morocco. © Lee Frost/Robert Harding World Imagery/Corbis.

Saints, Shrines, and Pilgrimages: Shared Religious Practices

In many locations in the Arab Middle East are found graves, tombs, and shrines that are regularly visited by Jews, Muslims, and Christians. These are the burial places of "saints" or "holy persons" who are venerated both for the pious lives they led and for the miracles (Ar. *karamāt*) they continue to produce for their suppliants. The widespread veneration of saints, the visitation of their graves, the narration of saints' legends, the celebration of annual saints festivals or moulids (Ar. *mawlid* or *mūlid*), the belief in their power to intercede with God and to work miracles of their own, the concept of a spiritual power or blessing (Ar. *baraka*) that can be obtained through contact or proximity to a saint, the practice of making vows or sacrifices to saints, the composition and performance of poems and songs for the saint—all are shared practices among the three monotheist religions of the Middle East. Although the majority of these locations are sites of visitation for members of only one religion, a substantial number attract various combinations of Muslims, Jews, and Christians in a remarkable demonstration of the shared folk religiosity of the region.

In *Saint Veneration Among the Jews in Morocco* (1998), Issachar Ben-Ami studied traditions regarding 656 Moroccan Jewish saints (of whom 25 are women), and found evidence of 126 saints venerated by both Muslims and Jews (historically there has been no substantial Christian community in Morocco).

This phenomenon of shared Muslim-Jewish spirituality attracted the attention of European travelers as early as the eighteenth century, but clearly dates to a much earlier period. Similarly, the shared veneration of saints in Egypt among Christians, Muslims, and Jews has attracted notice from Western writers over the past two centuries, and Christian-Muslim veneration of saints there continues into the present, as documented in Valerie Hoffman's *Sufism, Mystics, and Saints in Modern Egypt* (1995):

Muslims have no trouble venerating Coptic saints, and attending Coptic moulids, just as, less often, Copts venerate Muslims saints and attend their moulids. The popular religious lives of the two communities often intersect. The early-nineteenth-century British observer of Egyptian life, Edward Lane, commented, "It is a very remarkable trait in the character of the people of Egypt and other countries of the East, that Muslims, Christians and Jews adopt each other's faiths. In sickness, the Muslim sometimes employs Christian and Jewish priests to pray for him: the Christians and Jews, in the same predicament, often call in Muslim saints for the like purpose." The Jewish community of Egypt has been largely driven out since the 1950's because of tensions between Jewish and non-Jewish communities engendered in Arab countries by the Arab-Israeli conflict. But Coptic-Muslim contacts often converge around saint veneration. (331–32)

Shared Christian-Muslim holy sites also exist in Palestine and have been studied by Glenn Bowman in "Nationalizing the Sacred: Shrines and Shifting Identities in the Israeli-Occupied Territories" (1993). One of the sites he documented is the Greek Orthodox monastery of Mar Elyas (the Prophet Elijah) on the road between Bethlehem and Hebron:

On the day proceeding the saint's day, local Muslims accompany Christians to Mar Elyas, a holy place on the peripheries of Bethlehem district, both to visit the monastic chapel and to join friends, family and neighbours in the ground of the nearly inoperative monastery. Outside the sixth-century building the area is bright with small groups of men, women and children picnicking under the olive trees and listening to the music of ouds (Arab lutes) and transistor radios. In front of the church is a mass of men, women and children waiting to enter the shrine, some of whom carry loaves of bread cooked with mastic, bottles of oil and candles (some three inches thick and as tall as the bearer). Once inside, the local people struggle through the priests and monks performing the divine offices specific to the coming feast day to the front of the church where those bearing gifts light their candles, leave their olive oil before the icons and hand over their loaves to a novice monk who in turn distributes bits of sanctified bread—some of which is eaten on the spot and the rest of which is given away later to family and neighbours. The donors then join the others who have gone directly to wait their turn to place a chain attached to the wall of the church around their necks, kiss it three times and step through it. In the meantime, the resident monks and the visiting members of the Greek Orthodox Brotherhood of the Holy Sepulchre struggle to amplify the Holy Word sufficiently to have it heard over the babble of thronging Palestinians and the perpetual clanking of the miraculous chain. (434)

A cave beneath the monastery is believed to be the site were Elyas fled from Jezebel (Kings 1:19), and the chain is popularly believed to be one that had bound the saint.

Of the three religions, the veneration of saints is most firmly established in the various Christian churches. Despite the lack of any clear scriptural foundation for the practice, most Christian churches early on gave official recognition to figures who had been popularly proclaimed to be saints, organizing feast days commemorating the saints into institutionalized calendars, and eventually developing the complex processes of beatification and canonization that are in use in some Churches today. In both Judaism and Islam, however, the veneration of saints has a more uneasy relationship to the larger traditions. Even in North Africa, where saint veneration was a strong part of Jewish Arab community and identity, some rabbis spoke out against the practice. In Islam, the veneration of saints and all associated practices are strongly rejected by conservative reformist movements ("fundamentalists") who not only speak out against the practice but work to eradicate it entirely. In some conservative regions such as Saudi Arabia, the veneration of saints is not tolerated.

Part of the reason that veneration of shared saints and holy sites does exist is that despite certain distinguishing characteristics, there are many commonalities among these three religions regarding the basic concepts of saint, shrine, intercession, festival, and so forth. In essence, all three religions at the popular level recognize the existence of saints or holy persons. Although the Christian concept of saint (Ar. *qiddis*), the Jewish idea of holy person (*saddiq* or *tsaddiq*), and the Islamic notion of a Sufi "friend of God" (Ar. *wali*) are not exactly the same, they are still remarkably similar. The English term *saint* will be used in this discussion for the sake of simplicity to refer to all three.

Most saints are individuals who lived pious lives and who, either while alive or after their death, are believed to have worked miracles. One distinguishing characteristic among the three traditions are that many early Christian saints were martyrs who were put to death for their faith, a category not commonly found among either Muslims or Jews. Some Muslim saints were *mujāhidīn* (warriors of the faith), such as figures who fought against the European incursions in North Africa in the sixteenth century, and others were Sufi shaykhs attached to institutionalized Sufi orders, both of which do not have exact parallels in the Christian and Jewish traditions. According to Ben-Ami, the Jewish saints of Morocco were almost never recognized as such while alive but rather only after their death, whereas the recognition of saints while still alive is relatively common among Muslims and is also known among Christians.

The power of a saint comes from a special relationship with God, particularly the saint's ability to intercede with God for supplicants at their graves or tombs. On the one hand, everything that a saint does is through God or by His will; on the other hand, there is a belief that God does as His saints request due to their great love for Him and His reciprocal love for them. The popularity of a saint is often linked to the perceived efficacy of entreating that particular figure for assistance, and the granting of such requests is one of the most common motifs of saints' legends that are narrated in a wide variety of different performance contexts. Most saints, however, are usually further associated with a body of narratives of miracles (Ar. *karamāt*) from when they were alive, or worked posthumously through visits to their tomb, dreams, and visions. Saints are credited with traveling great distances in impossibly short periods of time, knowing the future, curing the sick, making barren women fertile, appearing to people to warn them of dangers or assist them in some other manner, and similar feats. The following example is a simple narrative of assistance concerning the Egyptian saint, Sayyid al-Badawi:

Once two friends and I were visiting Tanta during the big *mulid* of Sayyid al-Badawi. Each of us had a problem. I was suffering from a pain in my lower back. One of my friends, a professor of law at Ain Shams University, was worried that his son would fail his college examinations. And the other, a physician, was bothered by debts which he could not pay. After we visited the shrine of Sayyid al-Badawi, each of us found that his problem had been resolved. I had a dream in which two doctors took me into an operating room, and when I woke up the pain was gone. And it has not bothered me since. The law professor learned that his son would receive passing marks on his examinations, even before they took place. And the doctor received an inheritance that allowed him to pay his debts.

(Reeves 1990, 66)

Other tales involve more astonishing behaviors or events, such as that told in the northern Egyptian village of al-Bakātūsh about the unusual location of a local saints' shrine in the middle of some agricultural fields: The saint was recognized as such even when he was alive, and many tales are told of miracles he worked before his death, but his status was affirmed for all to see when the men of the village tried to bear his body out to the village cemetery on a wooden bier for burial—every time they tried to turn toward the cemetery they found themselves unable to move in that direction. Even strong, able-bodied men could not force the bier in that direction, so they finally gave up and found that the body could only be carried in one direction; as long as they went that direction the bier was as light as a feather, but if they attempted to turn away from that path, the bier became too heavy to carry, until they finally arrived at the place where the shrine now stands, the place where the saint wished to be buried. Muslim, Jewish, and Christian saints' legends share many motifs and are a fascinating field for comparative study.

Although the intercession of a saint can be prayed for at any time, a request delivered in person to the saint's tomb is considered to be far more efficacious. In the Jewish tradition, saints' graves are often left simple and unadorned; in the Islamic tradition, saints' resting places are often marked over time with an increasingly large shrine (Ar. *maqām*), frequently topped with a dome (Ar. *qubba*); and in the Christian tradition, the saint's grave may be commemorated with the building of a chapel, church, or even a monastery. Personal visitations (Ar. *ziyāra*) to the grave or tomb of a saint take place all year long, but saints who have achieved a certain level of popularity are also honored with an annual pilgrimage or festival—*hillula* in the Jewish tradition and *mawlid* or *mūlid* in the Islamic and Christian traditions. In addition, some saints' shrines have weekly days for visitation. Jewish and Christian saints' festivals are usually held once a year, but many Muslim saints have two annual festivals, a greater and a lesser *mūlid*. The majority of saints' festivals are held on the date of the saint's death:

Copts and Muslims hold a common belief concerning the living reality of deceased saints and the efficacy of their intercessions, particularly for those who visit them at their tombs at the most propitious moments. Both confessional groups celebrate their saints on the day of their moulid, and although the word literally means "birthday," for both groups the moulid is celebrated on the anniversary of the saint's death. For Copts, the date of death is the date of the saint's "rebirth" into eternal life. For Muslims, the death of a saint is conceived as his or her union with God, following the pattern of a marriage consummation. For both groups, in a very real sense, the saint does not die. (Hoffman 1995, 434)

Some of the largest saints' festivals, such as that of Sayyid al-Badawī in the city of Tanta in northern Egypt, attract hundreds of thousands, even millions, of participants each year. The festival is the most common time for making requests of the saint: to be cured of illnesses, to be granted a child, protection for children or spouses, success in school or business, the safe return of a family member or loved one, and so forth are all common reasons for visiting the saint during his or her festival. These supplications are often accompanied by a vow, and indeed attendance at the festival may be part of a vow already taken. It is also widely considered good luck and a harbinger of a happy life for a boy to be circumcised at a saint's tomb or to receive his first haircut there. In the case of Christian saints, one of the central activities of the festival will be the celebration of mass, and among Muslims the communal Friday prayer may play a parallel role. But Muslim saints are often associated with Sufi orders, so the performance of *dhikr* and the singing of *inshād dīnī* (religious chant) are both prominent features of many festivals (see Musical Arts).

In the Jewish Arab tradition of Morocco, three basic song types are sung at a saint's festival: *piyyutim* (Hebrew liturgical poems) sung exclusively by men; bilingual Hebrew-Arabic *piyyutim* where only men are allowed to sing the

Hebrew sections but women often know the Arabic passages; and the *qasīda,* which is

composed entirely in Judeo-Arabic and sung principally by the women to honor the saint. It is characterized primarily by an exciting, energetic rhythm that carries celebrants away. The men also join, especially when the *qasidot* are ones that would be familiar to anyone who has participated in a *hillulah* [...] this song in Judeo-Arabic by an unknown author is a kind of general hymn of hagiographic poetry. It mentions thirteen well-known saints, although surprisingly some of the very famous ones [...] are not included:

Refrain:

O Lord! Forgive what is past!
O Lord! Provide for us in our distress!
O Lord! May our happiness never wane
Thanks to the merit of the beloved saints!

1) I started to speak in my joy
And I shall mention the beloved saint.
Whatever we ask of him he will grant
Because his name is exalted and illuminates,
The beloved Rabbi Yahya El-Khdar

2) Come, let us go, o servants!
Let us take to the distant roads
And let us offer up new prayers.
Let us visit the saints of the town,
Our dear one, Mwalin Dad.

3) The saint will be our support
And we shall come to him from far away
And we shall visit him again on the *ziyāra*
And he will make our days happy
Rabbi Eliyahu, the Master of Casablanca

4) O, my friends had you but seen
The miracles of the saint during his lifetime,
He conferred his prestige upon his family!
Happy is he who was present at the funeral
Of dear Rabbi Hayyim Pinto...

(From Ben-Ami 1998, 105–10)

Beyond those activities that are overtly performed as homage or veneration of the saint, a typical festival includes a wide variety of activities and many genres of folklore can usually be found there. Participants who have come on the visitation or pilgrimage (Ar. *ziyāra*) often spend several days at the shrine where they may picnic, listen to music, and attend performances of folk entertainments such as shadow puppet shows or storytellers, or pay to look into the "box of the world" (Ar. *sandūq al-dunyā*) in which there is a painted story-scroll that the performer turns as he narrates popular tales such as the feats of the epic heroes of the Banī Hilāl (previously examined). Many different types of foods, especially sweets and candies, are usually on sale, as well as toys for children including balloons, pinwheels, and sugar figurines of famous heroes from the epics and folktales.

FURTHER READINGS ON ARABIC ORAL POETRY

Abdel-Malek, Kamal. 1995. *Muhammad in the Modern Egyptian Popular Ballad.* Leiden: E. J. Brill.

Abu-Lughod, Lila. 1986. *Veiled Sentiments: Honor and Poetry in a Bedouin Society.* Cairo: American University of Cairo Press.

Bailey, Clinton. 1972. "The Narrative Context of the Bedouin Qasida-poem." *Folk Research Center Studies,* 3, ed. I. Ben-Ami (Jerusalem): 67–105.

———. 1981. *Bedouin Poetry from Sinai and the Negev.* Oxford: Clarendon Press.

Bohas, Georges, and Jean-Patrick Guillaume. 1985–1998. *Le roman de Baibars.* 10 vols. Paris: Sindbad.

Cachia, Pierre. 1977. "The Egyptian Mawwāl." *Journal of Arabic Literature* 8: 77–103.

———. 1989. *Popular Narrative Ballads of Egypt.* Oxford: Clarendon Press.

Caton, Steven. 1990. *"Peaks of Yemen I Summon.": Poetry as Cultural Practice in a North Yemeni Tribe.* Berkeley: University of California Press.

Connelly, Bridget. 1986. *Arabic Folk Epic and Identity.* Berkeley: University of California Press.

Fanjul, Serafín. 1976. *El mawwāl egipcio: Expresión literaria popular.* Madrid: IHAC.

Heath, Peter. 1996. *The Thirsty Sword: Sīrat 'Antar and the Arabic Popular Epic.* Salt Lake City: University of Utah Press.

Hurreiz, Sayyid H. 1977. *Ja'aliyyin Folktales: An Interplay of African, Arabian and Islamic Elements.* Bloomington: Indiana University Press.

Ingham, Bruce. 1982. *Northeast Arabian Dialects.* London: Kegan Paul.

———. 1986. *Bedouin of Northern Arabia: Traditions of the āl-Dhafīr.* London: Routledge and Kegan Paul.

Jayyusi, Lena. 1996. *The Adventures of Sayf Ben Dhi Yazan: An Arab Folk Epic.* Bloomington: Indiana University Press.

Kurpershoek, P. Marcel. 1994–2002. *Oral Poetry and Narratives from Central Arabia.* 4 vols. Leiden: E. J. Brill.

Lyons, M. C. 1995. *The Arabian Epic: Heroic and Oral Story-telling.* Cambridge: Cambridge University Press.

Marzolph, Ulrich, and Richard van Leeuwen, eds. 2004. *The Arabian Nights Encyclopedia.* Santa Barbara, CA: ABC-CLIO.

Reynolds, Dwight F. 1989. "Tradition Replacing Tradition in Egyptian Oral Epic-singing: The Creation of a Commercial Image." *Pacific Review of Ethnomusicology* 5: 1–14.

———. 1995. *Heroic Poets, Poetic Heroes: The Ethnography of Performance in an Arabic Oral Epic Tradition.* Ithaca, NY: Cornell University Press.

———. 2006b. "Sirat Bani Hilal." In *Cambridge History of Arabic Literature: Post-Classical Period,* 307–19. Cambridge: Cambridge University Press.

Richmond, Diana. 1978. *'Antar and 'Abla: A Bedouin Romance rewritten and arranged by Diana Richmond.* London: Quartet Books.

Saada, Lucienne. 1985. *"La geste hilalienne"; Version de Bou Thadi (Tunisie): Recueilli. Établie et traduite de l'arabe par Lucienne Saada.* Paris: Gallimard.

Sbait, Dirgham. 1982. "The Improvised-Sung Folk Poetry of the Palestinians." PhD diss., University of Washington.

Shryock, Andrew. 1997. *Nationalism and the Geneaological Imagination: Oral History and Textual Authority in Tribal Jordan.* Berkeley: University of California Press.

Slyomovics, Susan. 1987a. "The Death-Song of 'Āmir Khafājī: Puns in an Oral and Printed Episode of Sīrat Banī Hilāl." *Journal of Arabic Literature* 17: 62–78.

———. 1987b. *The Merchant of Art: An Egyptian Hilali Oral Epic Poet in Performance.* Berkeley: University of California Press.

Sowayan, Saad. 1985. *Nabati Poetry: The Oral Poetry of Arabia.* Berkeley: University of California Press.

'Umrān, Muhammad Ahmad. 1999. *Mūsīqā al-sīra al-hilāliyya.* Cairo: al-Majlis al-a'lā li-l-thaqāfa.

Yaqub, Nadia. 1999. "Drinking from the Well of Poetry: Tradition, Composition, and Identity in the Oral Palestinian Poetry Duel." PhD diss., University of California, Berkeley.

Yelles-Chaouche, Mourad. 1990. *Le Hawfi: Poésie feminine et tradition orale au Maghreb.* Algiers: Office de Publications Universitaires.

FURTHER READINGS ABOUT ARABIC FOLK NARRATIVES

Abdallah, Ali Lutfi. 1999. *The Clever Sheikh of the Butana and Other Stories: Sudanese Folk Tales.* New York: Interlink Books.

Abu-Lughod, Lila. 1993. *Writing Women's Worlds: Bedouin Stories.* Berkeley: University of California Press.

Bar-Itzhak, Haya, and Aliza Shenhar. 1993. *Jewish Moroccan Folk Narratives from Israel.* Detroit: Wayne State University Press.

Bushaq, Inea. 1986. *Arab Folktales.* New York: Pantheon Books.

Campbell, C. G. 1950. *Tales from the Arab Tribes: A Collection of Stories told by the Arab Tribes of the Lower Euphrates.* New York: MacMillan.

El Koudia, Jilali, and Roger Allen. 2003. *Moroccan Folktales.* Syracuse, NY: Syracuse University Press.

El-Shamy, Hasan. 1980. *Folktales from Egypt.* Chicago: University of Chicago.

———. 1999. *Tales Arab Women Tell.* Bloomington: Indiana University Press.

Ferguson, Charles A., and Frank A. Rice. 1960. "Iraqi Children's Rhymes." *Journal of the American Oriental Society* 80: 335–40.

Haddawy, Husain Fareed Ali, trans. 1990. *The Arabian Nights: Based on the Text of the Fourteenth-Century Syrian Manuscript, Edited by Muhsin Mahdi.* New York: Norton.

Han, Carolyn. 2005. *From the Land of Sheba: Yemeni Folktales.* Northhampton, MA: Interlink.

Hannoum, Abdelmajid. 2001. *Colonial Histories, Post-Colonial Memories: The Legend of the Kahina, a North African Heroine.* Portsmouth, NH: Heinemann.

Hejaiej, Mona. 1996. *Behind Closed Doors: Women's Oral Narratives in Tunis.* New Brunswick, NJ: Rutgers University Press.

Hurreiz, Sayyid H. 1977. *Ja'aliyyin Folktales: An Interplay of African, Arabian and Islamic Elements.* Bloomington: Indiana University Press.

Muhawi, Ibrahim, and Sharif Kanaana. 1989. *Speak, Bird, Speak Again: Palestinian Arab Folktales.* Berkeley: University of California Press.

Nuweihed, Jamal Sleem. 2002. *Abu Jmeel's Daughter and Other Stories: Arab Folk Tales from Palestine and Lebanon.* New York: Interlink.

Reynolds, Dwight F. 1995. *Heroic Poets, Poetic Heroes: The Ethnography of Performance in an Arabic Oral Epic Tradition.* Ithaca, NY: Cornell University Press.

———. 2006. "*A Thousand and One Nights:* A History of the Text and its Reception." In *Cambridge History of Arabic Literature: The Post-Classical Period,* ed. Roger Allen and D. S. Richards, 270–291. Cambridge: Cambridge University Press.

al-Shahi, Ahmed, and F. C. T. Moore. 1978. *Wisdom from the Nile: A Collection of Folk-Stories from Northern and Central Sudan.* Oxford: Clarendon Press.

Stevens, E. S. 1971. *Folk-tales of 'Iraq.* New York: Benjamin Blom.

Tahhan, Samir. 2004. *Folktales from Syria.* Tr. Andrea Rugh. Austin: Center for Middle East Studies, University of Texas.

Webber, Sabra. 1991. *Romancing the Real: Folklore and Ethnographic Representation in North Africa.* Philadelphia: University of Pennsylvania Press.

FURTHER READINGS ON ARABIC PROVERBS

al-Amily, Hussain M. 2003. *The Book of Arabic Wisdom: Proverbs and Anecdotes.* Oxford: New Internationalist.

Aquilina, Joseph. 1972. *A Comparative Dictionary of Maltese Proverbs.* Msida: Royal University of Malta.

Bailey, Clinton. 2004. *A Culture of Desert Survival: Bedouin Proverbs from Sinai and the Negev.* New Haven: Yale University Press.

Barakat, Robert A. 1980. *A Contextual Study of Arabic Proverbs.* Helsinki: Academia Scientiarum Fennica.

Boutarene, Kadda. 2002. *Proverbes et dictons populaires algériens.* Algiers: Office des Publications Universitaires.

Burckhardt, John Lewis. 1972. *Arabic Proverbs, or, the Manner and Customs of the Modern Egyptians Illustrated from Their Proverbial Sayings Current at Cairo.* 3rd ed. London: Curzon Press.

Elkhadem, Saad, ed. and trans. 1987. *Egyptian Proverbs and Popular Sayings.* Fredericton, NB, Canada: York Press.

Ferguson, Charles A., and John M. Echols. 1952. "A Critical Bibliography of Spoken Arabic Proverb Literature." *Journal of American Folklore* 65 (255): 67-84.

Frayha, Anis. 1953. *Modern Lebanese Proverbs.* Beirut: American University in Beirut.

Jewett, James Richard. 1893. "Arabic Proverbs and Proverbial Phrases." *Journal of the American Oriental Society* 15: 28–120.

Lunde, Paul, and Justin Wintle. 1984. *A Dictionary of Arabic and Islamic Proverbs.* London: Routledge and Kegan Paul.

Sabbagh, Isa Khalil. 1983. *As the Arabs say . . . : Arabic Quotations Recalled and Interpreted.* Washington, DC: Sabbagh Management Corporation.

Westermarck, Edward. 1980. *Wit and Wisdom in Morocco: A Study of Native Proverbs.* New York: AMS Press.

Yetiv, Isaac. 1987. *1001 Proverbs from Tunisia.* Washington DC: Three Continents.

FURTHER READINGS ON CONVERSATIONAL GENRES

Adès, Albert. 1924. *Goha the Fool,* trans. Morris Colman. New York: Albert and Charles Boni.

Ali, Abdul. 1998. *Arab Legacy to Humour Literature.* New Delhi: M.D. Publications.

Chyet, Michael L. 1988. "A Thing the Size of Your Palm: A Preliminary Study of Arabic Riddle Structure." *Arabica* 35: 267–92.

Giacobetti, P. A. 1916. *Recueil d'Enigmes Arabes Populaires.* Algiers: Imprimerie Adolphe Jourdan.

Hamidou, Abdelhamid. 1938. "Devinettes Populaires de Tlemcen." *Revue Africaine* 81: 357–72.

Jayyusi, Salma Khadra. 2006. *Tales of Juha: Classic Arab Folk Humor.* New York: Interlink.

Kishtiany, Khalid. 1985. *Arabic Political Humor.* London: Quartet Books.

Koen-Sarano, Matilda. 2003. *Folktales of Joha, Jewish Trickster.* New York: Jewish Publication Society of America.

Marsot, Afaf Lutfi al-Sayyid. 1993. "Humor: The Two-Edged Sword." In *Everyday Life in the Muslim Middle East.* Bloomington: Indiana University Press.

Marzolph, Ulrich. 1992. *Arabia Ridens: die humouristiche Kurzprosa der frühen adab-Literatur im internationalen Traditionsgeflecht.* Frankfurt am Main: V. Klostermann.

Masliyah, Sadok. 2001. "Curses and Insults in Iraqi Arabic." *Journal of Semitic Studies* 46 (2): 267–308.

al-Murtād, 'Abd al-Malik. 1982. *al-Alghāz al-sha'biyyā al-Jazā'iriyya: dirāsa fī alghāz al-gharb al-jazā'irī [Algerian Folk Riddles: A Study of the Riddles of Western Algeria].* Algiers: Dīwān al-Matbū'āt al-Jāmi'iyya.

Nesin, Aziz. 1994. *The Tales of Nasrettin Hoca,* trans. Talat Halman. Istanbul: Dost Yayinlari.

Parkinson, Dilworth. 1985. *Constructing the Social Context of Communication: Terms of Address in Egyptian Arabic.* Berlin: Mouton de Gruyter.

Quéméneur, Jean. [1944] 1997. *Énigmes tunisiennes.* Tunis: S.A.P.I. Reprint, Tunis: I.B.L.A.

Scott, Charles T. 1965. *Persian and Arabic Riddles: A Language-Centered Approach to Genre Definition.* Bloomington, IN: Mouton & Co.

Shah, Idries. 1966. *The Exploits of the Incomparable Mulla Nasrudin.* New York: Simon and Schuster.

———. 1968. *The Pleasantries of the Incredible Mulla Nadrudin.* London: Octagon.

Shehata, Samer S. 1992. "The Politics of Laughter: Nasser, Sadat, and Mubarek in Egyptian Political Jokes." *Folklore* 103 (1): 75–91.

al-Tābūr, 'Abd Allāh 'Alī. 2001. *Alghāz al-sha'biyya fī al-Imārāt [Folk Riddles from the Emirates].* UAE: Markaz Zāyid li-l-turāth wa-l-ta'rīkh.

Webber, Sabra. 1975. "It's about Our Bean-colored House: A Preliminary Look at Tunisian Riddles." Master's thesis, University of California, Berkeley.

FURTHER READINGS ON ARAB FOLK MUSIC

Cline, Walter. 1940. "Proverbs and Lullabies from Southern Arabia." *The American Journal of Semitic Languages and Literatures* 57 (3): 291–301.

Danielson, Virginia, Scott Marcus, and Dwight Reynolds, eds. 2002. *The Garland Encyclopedia of Music.* Vol. 6, *The Middle East.* New York: Routledge.

El-Mallah, Issam. 1998. *Omani Traditional Music.* 2 vols. Tutzing: Hans Schneider Verlag.

Ghannam, Farha. 1995. "Kuwaiti Lullabies." In *Children in the Muslim Middle East,* ed. Elizabeth Warnock Fernea, 77–83. Austin: University of Texas Press.

Jenkins, Jean, and Poul Rovsing Olsen. 1976. *Music and Musical Instruments in the World of Islam.* London: World of Islam Festival Publishing.

Khayyat, Shimon L. 1978. "Lullabies of Iraqi Jews." *Folklore* 89 (2): 13–22.

Marcus, Scott. 2007. *Music in Egypt: Experiencing Music, Expressing Culture.* Oxford: Oxford University Press.

Racy, A. J. 2003. *Making Music in the Arab World: The Culture and Artistry of Tarab.* Cambridge: Cambridge University Press.

Shannon, Jonathan Holt. 2006. *Among the Jasmine Trees: Music and Modernity in Contemporary Syria*. Middletown, CT: Wesleyan University Press.

Shiloah, Amnon. 1995. *Music in the World of Islam: A Socio-cultural Study*. Detroit: Wayne State University Press.

Touma, Habib Hassan. 1993. *The Music of the Arabs*. Portland, Ore.: Amadeu Press.

Waugh, Earle H. 1989. *The Munshidīn of Egypt: Their World and Their Song*. Columbia: University of South Carolina Press.

———. 2005. *Memory, Music and Religion: Morocco's Mystical Chanters*. Columbia: University of South Carolina Press.

FURTHER READINGS ON ARAB MATERIAL FOLK ARTS

Campo, Juan E. 1987. "Shrines and Talismans: Domestic Islam in the Pilgrimage Paintings of Egypt." *Journal of the American Academy of Religion* 55 (2): 285–305.

———. 1991. *The Other Sides of Paradise: Explorations into the Religious Meanings of Domestic Space in Islam*. Columbia: University of South Carolina Press.

Costa, Paolo, and Ennio Vicario. 1977. *Arabia Felix: A Land of Builders*. New York: Rizzoli.

Damluji, Salma Samar. 1992. *The Valley of Mud Brick Architecture*. Reading, UK: Garnet.

Kanafani, Aida S. 1983. *Aesthetics and Ritual in the United Arab Emirates: The Anthropology of Food and Personal Adornment among Arabian Women*. Beirut: American University in Beirut Press.

Lewcock, Ronald. 1986. *The Old Walled City of San'ā'*. Paris: UNESCO.

Lindisfarne-Tapper, Nancy, and Bruce Ingham, eds. 1997. *The Language of Dress in the Middle East*. Richmond, Surrey, UK: Curzon Press.

Ochsenschlager, Edward L. 2004. *Iraq's Marsh Arabs in the Garden of Eden*. Philadelphia: University of Pennsylvania Museum of Archaeology and Anthropology.

Parker, Ann, and Avon Neal. 1995. *Hajj Paintings: Folk Art of the Great Pilgrimage*. Washington DC: Smithsonian Institution Press.

Rathjens, Carl. 1957. *Jewish Domestic Architecture in San'a, Yemen*. Jerusalem: Israel Oriental Society.

Rugh, Andrea B. 1986. *Reveal and Conceal: Dress and Contemporary Egypt*. Syracuse, NY: Syracuse University Press.

Salim, S. M. 1962. *Marsh Dwellers of the Euphrates Delta*. London: Athlone Press.

Serjeant, R. B., and Ronald Lewcock. 1983. *San'a': An Arabian Islamic City*. London: World of Islam Festival Trust.

Thesiger, Wilfred. 1964. *The Marsh Arabs*. New York: Dutton & Co.

Young, Gavin. 1977. *Return to the Marshes*. London: Collins.

Zubaida, Sami, and Richard Tapper, eds. 2000. *A Taste of Thyme: Culinary Cultures of the Middle East*. London: Tauris Parke.

FURTHER READINGS ON ARAB FOLK CUSTOMS AND TRADITIONS

Beigman, Nicolaas H. 1990. *Egypt: Moulids, Saints, Sufis.* London: Kegan Paul International.

Ben-Ami, Issachar. 1998. *Saint Veneration among the Jews in Morocco.* Detroit: Wayne State University.

Boddy, Janice. 1989. *Wombs and Alien Spirits: Women, Men, and the Zār Cult in Northern Sudan.* Madison: University of Wisconsin Press.

Bowman, Glenn. 1993. "Nationalizing the Sacred: Shrines and Shifting in the Israeli-Occupied Territories." *Man*, New Series, Vol. 28, No. 3 (Sept. 1993), pp. 431–60.

Canaan, Tewfik. 1927. *Mohammedan Saints and Sanctuaries in Palestine.* Jerusalem: Ariel Publishing House.

Granqvist, Hilma. 1931–1935. *Marriage Conditions in a Palestinian Village.* Helsinki: Akademische Buchhandlung.

———. 1965. *Muslim Death and Burial: Arab Customs and Traditions Studied in a Village in Jordan.* Helsinki: Societas Scientiarum Fennica.

Hoffman, Valerie J. 1995. *Sufism, Mystics, and Saints in Modern Egypt.* Columbia: University of South Carolina Press.

Ismāʿīl, ʿAbd al-Rahmān. [1934] 1980. *Folk Medicine in Modern Egypt,* trans. John Walker. London: Luzac. Reprint, New York: AMS Press.

Lane, Edward. 1846. *An Account of the Manners and Customs of the Modern Egyptians.* London: C. Knight. [Reprinted in many subsequent editions]

Marcus, Scott. 2007. "*Zaffa* (Wedding Procession) Music." In *Music in Egypt,* 139–54. New York: Oxford University Press.

McPherson, J. W. 1941. *The Moulids of Egypt (Egyptian Saints' Days).* Cairo: N. M. Press.

Meri, Josef W. 2002. *The Cult of Saints among Muslims and Jews of Medieval Syria.* Oxford: Oxford University Press.

Musil, Alois. [1928] 1978. *The Manners and Customs of the Rwala Bedouin.* Reprint, New York: AMS Press.

Reeves, Edward B. 1990. *The Hidden Government: Ritual, Clientalism, and Legitimation in Northern Egypt.* Salt Lake City: University of Utah Press.

Rothenberg, Celia E. 2004. *Spirits of Palestine: Gender, Society and the Stories of the Jinn.* Landham, MD: Lexington Books.

Sbait, Dirgham. 2002. "Palestinian Wedding Songs." In *Garland Encyclopedia of World Music.* Vol. 6: *The Middle East,* 578–92. New York: Routledge.

Yaqub, Nadia. 2002. "The Palestinian Groom's Wedding Eve Celebration." In *The Garland Encyclopedia of World Music.* Vol. 6, *The Middle East,* 573–78. New York: Routledge.

Four

Scholarship and Approaches

The earliest activity of folklorists was the preservation, through collection and documentation, of examples of verbal and material art along with customs, traditions, and beliefs that they believed were on the point of disappearing and being lost forever. In Britain these concerns and activities in the late eighteenth and early nineteenth centuries were commonly referred to as *popular antiquities,* a term that highlighted the belief that these phenomena represented surviving remnants from earlier times. In 1846, W. J. Thoms coined the term *folk-lore,* which came to be used to cover all of the various genres and forms of traditional art forms, along with the beliefs and customs, of the *folk,* who were understood at that time to be the rural population and the working classes of towns and even cities. These groups were thought to possess a culture separate from that of the educated, upper classes who, although they might be familiar with folklore, did not actually participate in or transmit it. On the one hand, folklore was thought to consist primarily of traditions left over from earlier eras and to be found among the lower classes, but on the other, it was also construed as being the authentic culture of each people regardless of class, particularly by a series of continental philosophers such as Herder, Dilthey, and others. Since then, of course, scholarly ideas about the folk and folklore have changed dramatically, but the changes came over time, and as the concepts of folk and folklore changed, so did the approaches used by scholars to study them. Many of these earlier approaches are still with us in a variety of ways; not only are those earlier publications still available to be read and studied, but each new direction in scholarship built upon, or reacted against, the approaches that preceded it.

Much of the collection and documentation of folklore in the Middle East from the late eighteenth to the early twentieth century was conducted by Westerners, and this research took place within the context of the European conquest and colonization of the Arab Middle East. One of the largest and most complete ethnographic descriptions of an Arab country, for example, is the multivolume *Description de l'Egypte* that was assembled by scientists and researchers brought to Egypt by Napoleon when he invaded and briefly ruled that country beginning in 1798. The *Description* represents a fascinating encounter between the new secular rationalism championed by the French Revolution—which was coupled with the urge to assert complete control over an object of study through the compilation of an encyclopedic account of it—and a complex society with an overwhelmingly rich history reaching back more than five millennia.

The encyclopedic impulse, however, was not unique to Europe. Muslim scholars of the Middle Ages had authored universal histories of the world from the Creation to their present, as well as works that combined descriptions of the Earth's geography with history and cultural descriptions of various peoples, and a variety of other encyclopedic writings. Of particular note was the genre of *khitat* (lit. maps, plans, districts), which offered a settlement-by-settlement topographical description of a region or country and which included the history of each village, town, and city, its notable mosques and shrines, biographies of its most famous figures such as saints, scholars, and political figures, accounts of strange local customs or legends, and a wealth of other information. In the late nineteenth century, the Egyptian writer 'Alī Mubārak compiled an enormous *khitat* work, *al-Khitat al-tawfīqiyya* (1888–1889), about Egypt that makes a fascinating counterpoint to the Napoleonic *Description:* Two comprehensive accounts of a country in a single century, both of which included rich accounts of Egyptian folklore, but recounted from two dramatically different cultural perspectives.

European interest in Egypt was motivated not only by its strategic location and economic resources but also by a deep interest in the remains of the Ancient Egyptians; indeed, the culture of modern Egypt was studied primarily as a less-interesting version of a more-glorified ancient past. This orientation only intensified with Jean-François Champollion's deciphering of the Rosetta Stone in 1822 and the subsequent translation of a massive corpus of hieroglyphic texts. "Egyptomania" seized Western Europe and an astonishing fascination with all aspects of Ancient Egypt was reflected in museum exhibits, expositions, public lectures, and publications. The English poet Percy Shelley's famous poem "Ozymandias" inspired by a fallen statue of Ramses the Great, and Giuseppe Verdi's opera *Aida,* the libretto for which was written by a French Egyptologist, are but two among hundreds of possible examples of the fascination Ancient Egypt held for Europeans in the nineteenth century.

If modern Egypt was viewed by nineteenth-century Europeans as but a poor reflection of Ancient Egypt, the Holy Land was often viewed as a living museum of the Bible. In hundreds of travel accounts written by Western travelers and scholars, every aspect of Palestinian and Bedouin culture evoked from those writers' comparisons with scenes in the Bible. Palestinian folklore was at first documented and collected primarily for its value in explicating passages in the Holy Book and to bring to life biblical forebears for Christian reading publics in Europe and North America. Of particular interest to Western travelers were the various religious minorities of the region such as Samaritans, Druze, and Jews (who were at that point but a small fraction of the population), and, of course, the Eastern Christian population, who were seen as ripe candidates for conversion from their own ancient Middle Eastern churches that still celebrated their liturgies in the languages of the early Christians, to newer European and American forms of Protestantism, the majority of which were only a century or two old.

Modern tourism was born when Thomas Cook marketed the first organized "package tours" in England beginning in 1841, but soon after that Egypt and the Holy Land became the most popular foreign destinations for European travelers. One book in particular played an astonishing role in how Europeans viewed the modern Middle East—the *Thousand and One Nights*. It was quoted again and again by travelers as either the best guidebook one could read before traveling to the Middle East, or, just the opposite, they noted their intense disappointment with the real Middle East after the expectations they had constructed from reading the *Nights*. The view of most of these latter writers was that it was reality that fell short of the *Nights*, rather than that the *Nights* was a poor portrayal of reality. This curious relationship to the actual cultures of the Middle East, predetermined and defined by Westerners' fantasies *about* the Middle East, in which the fantasies were considered somehow more real than reality itself, was captured in the term *Orientalism* by Edward Said in his 1978 book of that name. Although the attitudes of many of these early writers is easily criticized, particularly their facile comparisons of life in the nineteenth-century Middle East to Ancient Egypt, the *Thousand and One Nights*, or the Bible, some of their works remain useful even today for the ethnographic data they contain and as points of historical comparison for more modern folklore studies in the Arab world.

Not all Western travelers to the Middle East in the nineteenth and early twentieth centuries, however, saw Arab folklore as a pale reflection or a mere survival from a more glorious past. One figure who devoted himself to studying the culture of modern Egypt rather than its ancient civilization was the Englishman Edward William Lane, who lived in Egypt for a number of years in the 1820s and 1830s. He eventually published *An Account of the Manners and Customs of the Modern Egyptians* (1838), a truly remarkable ethnographic account that is still widely cited today. This work includes detailed descriptions of almost all aspects of daily life in Egypt including festivals, weddings, folktales, epic performances, houses, clothing, superstitions, and a wealth of other topics. Although neither anthropology nor folklore yet existed formally as academic disciplines, Lane's work can be seen as a remarkable predecessor to both fields.

THE HISTORICAL-GEOGRAPHIC METHOD

In the later half of the nineteenth century and the early twentieth, scholars and collectors of folklore began to develop scientific comparative approaches to the study of folklore genres, particularly ballads and folktales. Western intellectual activity in the nineteenth century was in many ways dominated by the search for origins. The field of historical linguistics had made sense of the complex relationships among living languages by organizing them into "family trees" that led back to the earliest written records. Careful study had revealed processes of historical change in the sounds, grammar, and vocabulary of languages that even allowed for the creation of *proto*-languages such as proto-Indo-European—hypothetical forms created by applying those rules of change beyond the earliest written evidence. Similarly botanists and biologists were organizing all known plant and animal forms into "family trees" that expressed the relationships among species, genus, family, and so forth, based upon critical structural features, rather than simply outward similarity. Most famously, of course, Charles Darwin proposed an evolutionary model for plant and animal species, and, much as linguists had shown how languages are transformed over time into new languages, proposed a mechanism for how one species could evolve into others. All of these endeavors allowed scholars to locate and analyze what they believed to be the *Ur*-forms (original forms) of the phenomena under study. This was not, however, just historical curiosity, for in nineteenth-century Western thought, the point of origin, the *Ur*-form of a phenomenon, held a very privileged position and was understood somehow to be more significant than all of the transformations that had taken place since then. For these thinkers, the *origin* of a phenomenon embodied to a great extent its meaning and significance, regardless of how much history had unfolded since then.

As folklorists began compiling massive, carefully documented collections of ballads, folktales, proverbs, house forms, and so on, a similar approach held out the hope of making sense of the astonishing number of variations found in folkloric material. One reason that folklorists of that period wished to examine variants so carefully was that they, like their linguistic and scientific counterparts, were searching for the oldest forms of these genres. But another reason they studied variation over time and space so carefully (the *historical-geographic method*) was that they were also searching for distinctive characteristics that would demonstrate *national character*. It was deemed both possible and important to document the French, German, Italian, and other versions of "Cinderella," for example, and to determine precisely which details made the French version French, and so forth.

The nineteenth century saw the great flourishing of a new idea that we now know simply as *nationalism.* The multilingual, multiethnic kingdoms and empires of Europe were collapsing and a new concept of a separate nation-state for each and every people (usually defined as a group with a common language) became the basis for forming new nation-states. This new concept equated language, ethnicity, people, and country: Individuals who spoke the same language were believed to share the same culture and were therefore understood to be a single people, and every people deserved to have a nation-state and a government of its own. Folklore played a surprisingly powerful role in the emergence of these new peoples and states in Europe. To cite but one example, the Norwegian language was created to a great extent from folktales and folksongs collected in the field and transcribed by scholars in the mid-nineteenth century, because Norway had for centuries been ruled by Denmark and Danish had been the only written language used there up to that point. The written Norwegian language was deliberately and purposefully created out of oral Norwegian folklore. To possess their own folklore expressed in their own national language was a powerful argument that Norwegians were a distinct people who therefore deserved to be independent from Denmark and have a nation state of their own.

Although the modern study of folklore places little focus on the search for original forms or on the delineation of national character through the study of minute variations in folktales and songs, the tools that these scholars developed have remained useful to modern scholars conducting comparative research. Folklorists developed a terminology that allowed them to make comparisons across cultural boundaries, sifting through large numbers of variant forms. Two of the primary concepts that emerged were the *motif* and the *tale-type.*

The tale-type provided a means of organizing and comparing thousands of folktales collected from many different cultures. In essence, a particularly famous version of the tale ("Rumplestiltskin" or "Snow White," for example) would lend its name to the tale-type or a brief descriptive title, such as "Three Brothers Seek Riches," would be assigned to that type, and massive indices were compiled that cross-referenced all known occurrences of similar tales in various languages and cultures across the globe. The classic example of this approach was originally published in German by the Finnish scholar Antti Aarne (*Verzeichnis der Märchentypen,* 1910) but was then translated and greatly expanded by Stith Thompson and published as *The Types of the Folk-Tale: A Classification and Bibliography* (1928). This classification system allowed scholars, for example, to identify and study variants of the "Cinderella" tale from many different regions, a Palestinian version of which ("Sackcloth") was presented in Chapter Three. The Aarne-Thompson tale-type index and numbering system has been maintained by nearly all scholars afterward, and there are now tale-type indices for many different cultures including the Arab world.

Hasan El-Shamy's *Types of the Folktale in the Arab World* (2004) is currently the definitive tale-type index for the Arab folktale. The volume follows the Aarne-Thompson system that divides folktales into five main categories: (1) animal tales, (2) ordinary folktales, (3) jokes and anecdotes, (4) formula tales, and (5) unclassified tales. Within the category of ordinary folktales, for example, are found four subdivisions: (a) tales of magic, (b) religious tales, (c) novelle (romantic tales), and (d) tales of the stupid ogre. Within the first subdivision, tales of magic, are found further subdivisions for supernatural adversaries, supernatural tasks, supernatural helpers, and so forth. The very first tale-type within the category of supernatural adversaries is number 300, the dragonslayer (sacrificial maiden saved, impounded water released, imposter exposed, hero rewarded), a version of which, the Egyptian Christian folk ballad of St. George, appeared in Chapter Three of this volume. The El-Shamy index then guides us to 81 different printed versions of this tale-type from Arabic sources, many of them in translation, which could form the basis for a substantial study of the dragonslayer story in Arab culture.

A motif, on the other hand, is the smallest thematic unit in a work of folklore. In a folktale, for example, this might be a particular image, such as an egg along with its role in the tale: child hidden inside an egg; heart hidden inside an egg; hero delivers egg to sorcerer; house transformed into egg, broken egg causes death of fairy, and so forth. The first major motif index for folk literature was published by Stith Thompson under the title *Motif-Index of Folk-literature: A Classification of Narrative Elements in Folk-tales, Ballads, Myths, Fables, Mediaeval Romances, Exempla, Fabliaux, Jest-books, and Local Legends* (1932–1936). Since then motif indices for a wide variety of folk cultures around the world have been published, including Hasan El-Shamy's *Folk Traditions of the Arab World: A Guide to Motif Classification* (1995). All motif-indices are somewhat quirky tools, and they take some getting used to, but they can at times be very useful in helping to locate additional sources and variations for comparative study.

STRUCTURALISM

In the twentieth century, some scholarly focus in the field of folklore shifted from the documentation and organization of thousands of different variations and motifs to the study of the underlying *structure* of folklore forms. This new scholarly approach, known as *structuralism,* was rooted in the teachings of the Swiss linguist Ferdinand De Saussure and was later most famously developed and applied to anthropology by the French ethnographer Claude Lévi-Strauss. In folklore one of the earliest uses of this approach was Vladimir Propp's *The Morphology of the Folktale,* which was originally completed in Russian in 1928, but only translated into western European languages years later. Propp's remarkable insight was that a large number of folktales all possess a similar deep structure, no matter how different the surface details were. In his analysis, for example, the classic folktale starts out with an interdiction and its violation: If children are told to play in the garden and not to wander into the woods, they will inevitably wander into woods; if a new bride is told that she can go anywhere in her new husband's house except into the room at the end of the hall, she will of course eventually open the forbidden door. Similarly, if there are three or seven brothers or sisters, it will always be the youngest who succeeds at completing whatever task lies at the center of the tale. If the main hero or heroine meets someone in distress, he or she will always help them and in return receive a gift, which will later turn out to be indispensable for completing their quest, and so forth. For Propp it did not matter if that gift was a mirror that later magically became a lake or a comb that transformed itself into a dense forest, either was simply one of many possible gifts that later assist the main character. Note that this is a very different way of thinking about narratives than that embodied in the motif-index where the mirror and the comb would be listed entirely separately and would not be seen to be related.

In essence, the historical-geographical method postulated that analyzing the differing details in the multiple variants of a folk tale (or other genre of folklore) was critical to understanding the meaning of the tale or ballad itself. Propp's response was that the deep structure of a folktale was the significant element and that to a great degree the surface details did not matter. This was a provocative and exciting insight, but it begged the question of why, if only the deep structure of a tale mattered, cultures and individuals produced thousands of variant tellings of a single tale.

Many structuralist studies on Arabic narrative traditions have been published, but almost all of these are in Arabic. One example among many is Sa'īd Yaqtīn's *Qāla al-rāwī: al-binyā al-hikā'iyya fī al-sīra al-sha'biyya* [The Reciter Said: Narrative Structures in the Folk Epic] (1997).

FUNCTIONALISM

Another approach from the mid-twentieth century, *functionalism,* which emerged in the field of anthropology, sought to understand not so much variations in the *forms* of folklore, but rather what social function folklore served within a community or culture. The central question for functionalists such as Emile Durkheim and Bronislaw Malinowski was how communities and cultures achieved cohesion and stability, thus managing to survive over time; folkloric traditions were therefore interpreted in the context of how they contributed to social cohesion and stability. Proverbs might thus be seen as a means of storing and transmitting wisdom from one generation to another, riddles can be seen as a didactic device to educate children and sharpen their wits, folktales might be understood in part as warnings not to engage in certain activities, and so forth. Festivals, which often include strange behaviors and what might otherwise be seen as rebellious activities against the status quo (mocking local authorities, satirizing religious figures, etc.), might be interpreted as a means of releasing social tensions—"letting off steam"—and an opportunity for young people and other disenfranchised groups to make fun of the rules of behavior to which they are usually held. Paradoxically, wild behavior at festivals might therefore actually serve to maintain the existing power structures in a community by occasionally allowing that structure to be, albeit temporarily, subverted.

Western anthropologists of the Middle East in the early and mid-twentieth century documented a great deal of Arab folklore, and their ethnographic descriptions are still considered valuable, even when, in some cases, the theories that motivated their work are now criticized or even considered invalid. To give but two examples, the Finnish scholars Edvard Westermarck, who studied Morocco on several research trips undertaken between 1897 and 1904, and his student Hilma Granqvist, who studied Palestinian culture beginning in the 1920s, both published fieldwork data that are still cited today. Westermarck published a series of books including *Marriage Ceremonies in Morocco* (1914), *The Belief in Spirits in Morocco* (1920), *Ritual and Belief in Morocco* (1926), and *Wit and Wisdom in Morocco* (1931). Hilma Granqvist was particularly interested in life-cycle rituals and published a series of classic descriptions of birth, childhood, marriage, and death and burial among Palestinians: *Marriage Conditions in a Palestinian Village I* (1931), *Marriage Conditions in a Palestinian Village II* (1935), *Birth and Childhood in an Arab Village* (1947), *Child Problems among the Arabs* (1950), and *Muslim Death and Burial* (1965). One of Granqvist's major contributions was to stress the need for photographic documentation as part of ethnographic fieldwork; a selection from the nearly 1,000 photos she took of the Palestinian village of Artas was published a year before she died in a volume entitled *Portrait of a Palestinian Village* (1981). Her studies and photographs provide a fascinating account of Palestinian folk culture in the Holy Land before much of it was swept away with the creation of the Jewish state of Israel.

FOLKLORE IN CONTEXT

Much of the folkloric data collected by these early scholars was carefully recorded, but in isolated units. It was common, for example, to elicit lists of proverbs from a consultant during an interview—this had the advantage of creating a record of many proverbs, but did not allow scholars to understand how people actually used proverbs in their daily lives. In the second half of the twentieth century a major shift in basic ethnographic methods and analysis took place in the field of folklore with a strong new emphasis on studying folklore in context. Scholars began to abandon the collection and documentation of isolated items of folklore and began to focus on understanding folklore in the specific context in which it occurred. It became clear that what might at first appear to be the same piece of folklore (a proverb, a tale, a custom, or a belief) could in fact mean different things if cited or performed by different individuals at different times. Folklore studies began to include detailed information about the persons from whom the collector had gathered materials as well as copious information about the context in which that information was gathered: Was it a naturally occurring performance to which the fieldworker had been invited? Or was this a recollection of earlier performances that only came to be recorded because the researcher had been asking questions about that topic? Or was this a performance that had been undertaken simply to please the visiting scholar and adapted to what the performer perceived as the scholar's expectations? The process of collecting and documenting folklore began to meld with the broader scholarly practice of ethnography. The two had always been closely related, but the emphasis on bringing contextual elements to bear on the analysis of individual performances or traditions of folklore further strengthened this bond. It came to be considered more and more necessary to conduct a comprehensive ethnography of a community to understand the place of various folklore genres within it.

PERFORMANCE STUDIES

By the 1970s a new focus of research had emerged with the twin concepts of *performance* and the *ethnography of communication.* Drawing on the writings of Richard Bauman, Charles Briggs, Dell Hymes, and anthropologists such as Victor Turner, folklorists developed a concept of *performance* as a special mode of communicative activity, one that asks those present to interpret what is being said or enacted in a way different from the way they might interpret normal, everyday conversation. Scholars noted that many performances are framed with traditional phrases ("Once upon a time..." or "Have you heard the one about...") understood by members of that community to signal that a performance is about to take place, that someone is about to recount a story, tell a joke, sing a song, or present some other genre of performance. It also became clear through careful analysis that performed communication is often of a different texture than ordinary speech, either in the actual words or in the way the words are delivered, in such a way that these communications are deemed *artistic* or *aesthetic* to some degree, so that one can say, for example, that so-and-so is a good joke teller or tells good stories or sings well. Audiences can and do evaluate performances on aesthetic criteria. One critical feature of performance came to be understood as the *assumption of aesthetic responsibility,* meaning that when performing a story, a song, or a joke, individuals usually try to render it both correctly and well (concerns that do not usually enter into normal conversation). In short, it appears that much of what we term folklore is *performed communication.* From these insights also came a flood of new ideas about the interaction between the performer and the other participants in a *performance event,* and the various ways in which performed communication differs from everyday communication.

While the historical-geographic method had understood the minute variations in folklore to be marks of its history or of its rootedness in a particular regional culture, and the structuralists had seen those variations as relatively unimportant, scholars of performance studies came to understand small changes from performance to performance as critical to understanding how a performer situated a particular piece of folklore in the context of that moment. The changing details came to be seen as one of the means by which a performer adapts well-known patterns and makes them relevant to a specific audience—even elements that were not previously conceived of as part of the tale (framing comments by the performer before the tale begins, explanatory asides to the audience during the telling, the inclusion of references to audience members or local situations within the tale, etc.) were now included in the analysis as part of the broader performance. To some degree, for performance scholars, the variations in performance provide the link between the traditional material and the current audience and give folklore its ability to feel both familiar and yet new at the same time. Although the larger pattern or structure may be well known, it is often the distinctive characteristics of a particular performer or a particular telling, that make that pattern entertaining and meaningful time and time again.

Many studies of Arab folklore published in English from the 1980s onward use performance as a central concept (see, for example, Abu-Lughod 1986, Caton 1990, Reynolds 1995, and Slyomovics 1987b).

ORAL COMPOSITION IN PERFORMANCE

From a different area of scholarship came a powerful set of new ideas that greatly influenced many studies in the field of folklore. Milman Parry and his student Albert Bates Lord were classicists who were interested in the question of how lengthy epic poems such as the *Iliad* and *Odyssey* attributed to Homer might have been composed and transmitted before the widespread use of writing. To understand what the technical possibilities were, they traveled to the former Yugoslavia in the 1930s and studied living epic singers. This was a remarkable and even radical idea—choosing to study modern traditions to better understand the processes of composition, performance, and transmission of the past. During their fieldwork, they carefully documented how these modern epic singers learned their craft, how they remembered their material, the degree to which their performances differed from one rendition to another, and the degree to which they were capable of generating new materials. To their surprise, Parry and Lord discovered that Yugoslavian epic singers did not memorize the poems they sang, at least not in the sense of word-for-word memorization, but rather learned a special *epic language* that helped them retell these lengthy tales by relying on short stock phrases, which Parry and Lord termed *oral formulae,* and joining them into larger units of stock scenes and sequences—all the while respecting the meter and verse structure of the epic song form. The most accessible summary of those findings is Lord's masterwork, *The Singer of Tales* (1960), which had a tremendous impact on studies of many different oral traditions around the world. The twin concepts of *oral-formulaic composition* and *composition in performance* were soon recognized as major breakthroughs in our understanding of how certain oral traditions function and also provided explanations for previously mystifying characteristics of some ancient texts. John Foley's *Oral-Formulaic Theory and Research: An Introduction and Annotated Bibliography* (1985) gives an overview of the thousands of books and articles that have addressed the concept of oral-formulaic composition in traditions from dozens of different languages. Studies of Arabic epic poetry have been deeply influenced by the work of Parry and Lord, but their findings have also been applied to early pre-Islamic Arabic poetry (Abu-Deeb 1975, Monroe 1972, Zwettler 1978), as well as modern Bedouin oral poetry (Alwaya 1977), medieval Arabic poetry (Hamori 1969), modern Tunisian oral poetry (Sioud 1976), and other types of Arabic poetry, with varying results.

Parry and Lord's work demonstrated that folklorists could not study transcribed oral performances as if they were texts that had been composed in writing but rather would have to take into account the techniques of memory, composition, and transmission found within each tradition to understand those transcribed performances fully. Variation in performance, it turns out, is not solely a product of a performer making aesthetic choices before an audience but rather is also a function of oral performance in and of itself.

CONTEMPORARY APPROACHES

It has become less and less common in recent years for scholars to rely upon a single approach or method when documenting and analyzing folkloric materials. Fewer and fewer works are now entirely structuralist, or functionalist, or oral-formulaic in their approach, and more and more studies combine insights from a variety of different fields. Additional analytic resources are constantly applied so that folklorists can study aspects of identity formation, race, gender, sexuality, political and economic power, and other dimensions of folklore. And yet, in the end, the study of folklore retains a special and distinctive voice amidst the many different scholarly approaches now used in studying human culture. Folklore tends to retain a strong focus on the artistic product itself, appreciating and celebrating the aesthetic impulses and tastes of individuals and communities, and recognizing that the everyday experience of these traditions is one of the most powerful means by which we learn about, and then express, who we are. Folklore as an academic endeavor strives through its emphasis on direct person-to-person communication and the transmission of traditions from generation to generation to understand the what, why, and how of being a person, a member of a family, a resident in a neighborhood, and a member of a community. Within that endeavor lies a simple but powerful message: Books and the media teach us much about the wider world, but the folklore of everyday life is often how we learn to be ourselves.

Five
Contexts

Looking back over the history of human culture, we can see that folklore has typically been created in environments that are primarily oral and often in face-to-face performance contexts or, in the case of the material arts, through one-by-one individual production, rather than by machine or mass production. But folklore's role within many cultures has not been restricted to those small face-to-face performances because it has also been recorded in a variety of ways both in past centuries and in the modern world. If a folktale gets written down and then circulates among literate readers, is it still folklore? Some scholars would argue that if the tale has been faithfully recorded in writing, then it should be considered folklore because the tale itself is the product of the folk worldview, the oral traditional processes of a community, and is thus folklore in its own right. Other scholars, however, would argue that when the tale is written down it is decontextualized, removed from the interactive feedback loops of the performance process through which an audience expresses its approval or disapproval at the very moment of its performance, and it therefore needs to be understood as something completely different. When a teller tells a tale orally, he or she typically makes changes (whether they are aware of it or not) according to who the audience members are and may even choose to tell a particular tale as a reaction to a specific social situation (for example, a mother telling a story to two fighting children to get them to stop fighting or an epic poet adjusting the evening's performance to comment on political problems in the village); the tale may therefore carry a lesson or be a means of social action rather than just a form of entertainment. The written tale, however, is frozen and does not change according to the reader or the situation. So, can it be folklore if it is no longer in the living tradition? And what if the written text is not a faithful rendition of an oral performance but has been deliberately altered by an author in style or content? What are we to call stories that have moved from oral tradition to written literature, been altered by the "author" and perhaps turned into "children's literature," but which then re-enter oral tradition because parents after reading the story in a book, retell the tales orally to their children and, over time, develop their own versions of the tales that are told and retold, perhaps over several generations, within the same family? What relationship to folklore does a TV cartoon or a movie version of an artistically reworked tale have, particularly if the tale has been translated through several languages before reaching the film studio? Should Disney's animated film *Aladdin* be thought of as Arab folklore?

These are some of the many issues that scholars of folklore deal with when they study folklore in performance in the here and now and when they study the impact folklore has had through its written forms in past centuries and in modern times through film, television, theater, the internet, and other media. Orally performed forms of folklore have over the centuries inspired a wide variety of literary, musical, and artistic creations; though these may not be the original forms of folklore, they are often the only records left to study in later periods, long after the oral performances have disappeared.

ORALITY IN EARLY ARAB CULTURE

In many cultures, the earliest written texts in a language are closely related to that culture's verbal art (or *oral literature*), but over time, written texts then develop styles, genres, and structures of their own, growing further and further away from oral ways of expression and eventually becoming *literature*. So the early literature of a culture often offers fascinating glimpses of the verbal art of that period. In addition, however, it is common for written literatures to cull the riches of verbal art over time; sometimes this results in texts that attempt to record or document oral traditions, and other times an oral performance has inspired an author to produce a written text that bears little resemblance to the folk original. All of these processes are evident in the history of Arabic literature, which make it a rich source for researching the history of Arab folklore.

Many of the earliest works of Arabic literature are either drawn directly from or have their origins in oral traditions and were only set down in writing after being transmitted for decades or even centuries after their first creation. The structures of oral composition, transmission, and performance had a tremendous impact on early Arabic literature, and many of these now *classic* texts should be read with an understanding of their oral roots to understand and appreciate them fully. This fundamentally oral nature was true not only of materials that might be classified as folklore (oral histories, poems, narratives, fables, proverbs, etc.) but also of the foundational texts of the Islamic religion: The Qur'ān was revealed, transmitted, and preserved primarily through oral recitation. Although the text of the Qur'ān was eventually committed to writing, most early Muslims knew it primarily as an *aural text,* or what in French would be called an *objet sonore* (lit. sound object), rather than through its written form. There is, even today, a sense that the Qur'ān is the orally recited–aurally perceived text and that the written version is not the Qur'ān itself but rather a transcription of the actual Qur'ān (see Nelson 2001). In this view, the oral/aural version is the real thing and the written version is a copy.

The next most-authoritative source in the Islamic religion after the Qur'ān is the *hadīth* (sayings), a body of literature that includes quotations from the Prophet Muhammad as well as testimony from his closest companions about his *sunna* (actions). These materials were transmitted orally for several generations before they were committed to writing and eventually gathered into large, thematically organized collections. The texts, even today, have a structure that makes their oral origins very clear. Following, for example, is one text from the *hadīth*:

'Abd Allāh ibn 'Umar—may God be pleased with him—transmitted to 'Abd Allāh ibn Shihāb who transmitted to 'Uqayl, who transmitted to al-Layth, who transmitted to Yahyā ibn Bukair who transmitted to us that the Messenger of God [Muhammad]—may God bless and preserve him—said: A Muslim is a brother of another Muslim, so he should not oppress him, nor should he hand him over to an oppressor. Whoever fulfills the needs of a brother, God will fulfill his needs; whoever has brought his (Muslim) brother out of a discomfort, God will bring him out of the discomforts of the Day of Resurrection; and whoever has protected a Muslim, God will protect him on the Day of Resurrection.

(Adapted from al-Bukhārī 1977, 373)

Thus along with the words of the Prophet are preserved the complete chain of transmission *(isnād)* of how this quotation had been passed on through the generations until it was written down. Early Muslim compilers of *hadīth* were also greatly concerned with determining if the figures in question could indeed have met (by comparing their ages and checking to see whether they had ever been in the same place at the same time, for example) and whether they were all respected and pious figures who could be trusted to have transmitted the saying reliably.

All this is not to suggest that the Qur'ān or the *hadīth* was, or is, in any way folklore, but rather to highlight the fact that orality was the primary channel through which early Arab culture was transmitted, whether that was high culture such as religious texts, or folk culture such as poetry, folk tales, and so forth. It is otherwise far too easy for those of us who live in highly literate societies to forget this basic fact and to assume that cultures and literatures are created and transmitted primarily through written texts. For most of human history (and to a great extent even today) what is written constitutes only bits of flotsam and jetsam from the enormous sea of oral culture in which we live our everyday lives.

FROM ORAL TO WRITTEN: FOLKLORE IN MEDIEVAL ARABIC LITERATURE

Some of the earliest oral poems and historical tales of the pre-Islamic Arab tribes were eventually compiled into written collections known as the *Ayyām al-'arab* (The Days of the Arabs). The events recounted in these texts occurred between the late fifth and early seventh centuries, but they were not written down until the late eighth century, and the versions that are most widely known today were re-worked as late as the tenth through thirteenth centuries. The title comes from the way the collections were organized with historical narratives and poems grouped around a single "day," often a battle or a raid, which forms the culmination of that sequence of events. As we saw earlier, these early oral histories alternated between prose accounts and the accompanying poetry, which both confirmed the veracity of the prose account and embellished the performance (see Oral Poetry in Tribal Contexts in Chapter Three). Although no society is static and remains unchanged over time, the modern Bedouin tribes of the Arabian Peninsula lived in a remarkably similar environment to that of their pre-Islamic forebears at least until the end of the nineteenth century, and the form, style, and imagery of their traditional poetry are highly reminiscent of those of the "Days of the Arabs" texts. Many scholars have found it instructive to compare these early oral poems with modern oral poems from the same regions and thus to allow our understanding of one corpus to enrich our understanding of the other. It must be said, however, that because many Arabs are used to thinking of these ancient poems as being classical literature rather than as oral poems that were written down long ago, some might reject the idea that they are a genre of folklore. The same debate, however, might easily be held over the nature of Homer's epics—are they classical literature or examples of Greek folklore? Or both? Much of the Classical Arabic poetry up to the eighth century or so can just as easily be studied as oral folk poetry that was later committed to writing and which only seems classical to us moderns because their language is archaic and difficult to understand.

As early as the eighth century and certainly by the ninth, literacy had made remarkable advances in Arabo-Islamic culture, and the imprint of orality becomes less and less obvious on most literary works; in short, a culture of writing, books, and written composition had emerged. At the same time Arabic had spread out from the Arabian Peninsula and was suddenly being spoken across a vast territory that extended from Spain to China and only a small percentage of those speakers were native speakers of the language. As time went by, the regional dialects grew further and further apart and the written, classical form of the language became more and more removed from the language of everyday life. This meant that if an author wished to write down a story he had heard in the marketplace, for example, he basically could not write it down exactly as he had heard it, but would have to "retell" the story in Classical Arabic, altering some of the words and grammatical features of the original. Some differences between the spoken and written forms of language exist in nearly every culture, but in Arabic this distinction is much more pronounced and is referred to by scholars as *diglossia* (double-tongued), referring to the two levels of the language (although in reality there is something more like a spectrum ranging from very slangy to very formal rather than just two distinct levels). So it is difficult to call the tales, romances, and other folk materials found in Arabic written texts "folklore" because they are couched in the classical language. We might consider calling these materials "popular literature" or "written folklore" (see Reynolds 2006). The problem of language aside, however, it is clear that Arabic medieval literature has preserved a vast and rich body of tales, songs, poems, proverbs, shadow plays, and so forth that originated in oral folklore.

For a fascinating survey of some of these materials from tenth-century Baghdad, we can examine the *Catalogue* (Fihrist) of the bookseller Ibn Nadīm (d. 990) who kept a written record of every book he saw or heard of during his career. One of his chapters (Ibn Nadīm 1970, 2:712–24) deals specifically with materials that are folk or popular in nature and is divided into three sections: (1) stories and tales; (2) works on magic; and (3) books on various leisure-time activities including sex, fortune-telling, horsemanship, chess, falconry, joke books, wisdom literature and proverbs, and so on.

The section on stories and tales starts out with the statement that the first people to set stories and tales down in writing were the ancient Persians and then offers a legendary account of Alexander the Great ordering that tales "which would make him laugh" be collected and written down (though Ibn Nadīm carefully notes that he did so not for mere entertainment, but to preserve the wisdom of the tales). He then discusses the three great "frame tale" collections of his day: the *Thousand and One Nights, Kalīla wa-Dimna,* and *Sendebar,* all three of which were later transmitted from Arabic into European languages, some via Hebrew translations of the Arabic. The Arabic *Kalīla wa-Dimna,* for example, was translated into Latin, Spanish, Greek, Syriac, and Hebrew, and a thirteenth-century Hebrew version then generated versions in Italian, German, English, and Dutch. The impact of these and other translations from the Arabic can be seen in the works of European authors such as Boccaccio, Chaucer, Petrus Alfonsi, Juan Manuel, Juan Ruiz, Ramon Llull, and others.

Ibn Nadīm also includes a brief vignette about another collection that offers a glimpse of how such works were assembled. He notes that a certain Abū

'Abd Allāh al-Jahshiyārī (d. 942) was inspired by the *Thousand and One Nights* to create an even larger collection in which each "night" consisted of a single story (rather than one story being told over several nights). To do so he hired oral storytellers to perform for him and selected what most pleased him from their repertories and wrote that down, but he also read all of the available written collections of tales and selected what he liked from them as well. Sadly he had completed only the first 450 nights of his work when he died, and the text has not survived to modern times.

Ibn Nadīm then goes on to list the titles of over 200 works of folk and popular narrative. Almost none of these appear to have survived, at least under the titles he has given them in his list, but from those titles it can be seen that there are several large categories or types of tales represented. Some are legendary historical tales of ancient peoples, others are romances or the tales of pairs of famous lovers, and still others appear to be related to typical folktales and bear titles such as "The Book of the Youth and the Woman Who Threw the Pebble" or "The Book of the Egyptian Man and the Meccan Woman." In addition, there are titles of joke books, books about "fools" (including about Juhā—see Chapter Three), books of humorous anecdotes about sex, wisdom literature, collections of proverbs, and many others that can be identified as folklore. Written versions of folklore were clearly a prominent field of literature in tenth-century Baghdad.

In later centuries folk materials of many different genres continued to find their way into the written record. The folk epics begin to be written down in the eleventh to thirteenth centuries, and by the eighteenth century there are manuscript versions of these tales that are thousands of pages long. Joke books, collections of humorous anecdotes, proverb collections, and religious legends all multiply and are found in nearly every corner of the Arab world throughout this period. One fascinating corpus of folk literature was produced by the Muslims who remained in northern Spain once it had been conquered by the Christians. As these *Mudéjars* (Muslims living under Christian rule) began to lose their Arabic and became native speakers of Spanish over time, they produced a remarkable body of literature in Spanish but written in Arabic script (called *aljamiado* literature), so that the texts could not be read by Christians. These texts include a fascinating body of religious and historical legends including tales that have not been preserved in Arabic, such as an account of the death of Moses and an important version of the Alexander romance. In the sixteenth century Muslims living under Christian rule were forced to convert to Christianity and were thereafter referred to as *Moriscos;* to avoid detection, or sometimes as they fled Spain for Muslim lands, they sometimes hid these texts in secret places in their houses or elsewhere, and these hidden texts are still being found today as historic buildings are demolished or renovated.

FOLKLORE IN MODERN ARAB
LITERATURE AND CINEMA

Arab folklore has influenced modern Arabic literature and the arts in a variety of ways, including inspiring artistic versions of folk narratives as short stories, novels, plays and films. In addition, literary works and artistic creations that are not based on folk narratives often include references to and portrayals of folk narratives or practices. Only a small portion of these works is available to non-Arabic speaking readers and audiences, however. Following are a handful of sample works available in English translation that include depictions of Arab folk traditions.

The Seven Days of Man, by 'Abd al-Hakīm Qāsim, is a beautiful and moving novel set in the Egyptian countryside. The life of the main character unfolds through a series of accounts of an annual Sufi saint's festival, each taken from a different period of his life. Together these accounts give a detailed portrait of the role of a Sufi brotherhood in the life of an Egyptian village and how those Sufi practices relate to the modern, urban lifestyle of a young man who leaves the village to go live in the city.

Wild Thorns, by Sahar Khalifeh, is a powerful novel that recounts the lives of Palestinians under the Israeli occupation of the Palestinian West Bank and Gaza Strip. Woven into the stories of the lives of a number of different individuals are frequent references to Arab folklore, particularly to Abū Zayd, one of the central heroes of the epic of the Banī Hilāl.

The collection of short stories, *The Wedding of Zein,* by the Sudanese writer Tayeb Salih, includes one classic story that explores the conflict between local tradition and government-sponsored modernization ("The Doum-tree of Wad Hamid"), and the title story provides a memorable and paradoxical account of the sometimes unclear boundaries between the figures of saint and fool, similar in some ways to Dostoyevsky's *The Fool.*

Daughter of Damascus, by Siham Tergeman, provides an almost ethnographic portrait of life in the Syrian capital filled with references to a wide variety of customs, traditions, and practices.

Autobiography is another genre of literature that often includes references to and descriptions of folklore of many types. Taha Hussein's moving account of his childhood, *Egyptian Days,* for example, tells of his early life in a village in southern Egypt before he traveled to Cairo to study at the al-Azhar University. Equally engaging is Jabra Ibrahim Jabra's *The First Well: A Bethlehem Boyhood,* which provides similar glimpses of Palestinian folk culture.

Perhaps most prominent among Arab films available with English subtitles is *Wedding in Galilee,* directed by Marcel Khleifi (1987), which offers a complex and rich portrait of a Palestinian family attempting to celebrate a wedding under the supervision of the Israeli military. Palestinian wedding traditions are deftly woven into this metaphorical treatment of a people struggling to maintain their culture and identity.

The study of Arab folklore is a field that is expanding in many directions. There remain many forms of folk art, poetry, narrative, belief, and practice in the Arab world that have scarcely been documented or studied, so there is much basic ethnographic work still to be done. The folklore of social groups such as clubs, organizations, student associations, and so forth (a direction in folklore research that is only a few decades old in Europe and North America) has barely begun in most Arab countries. In addition, the redeployment of folklore in new contexts—or "mediated folklore"—is leading scholars to study its occurrence in a plethora of other media including literature, film, drama, television, music videos, videogames, and the Internet. Although the study of folklore remains rooted in the study of person-to-person communication, these other media offer a powerful reminder that the influence of art forms, customs, and beliefs created in more traditional contexts can extend far beyond their original usage. Finally, the study of Arab folklore also feeds directly into one of the most pressing cultural needs of our time, the need to promote a more balanced and complete understanding of Arab culture in other parts of the world. Knowledge of any culture based purely in politics and economics will be hopelessly skewed and distorted if it is not complemented by knowledge of the culture of everyday life and the artistic forms of communication that build and maintain our cultural identities.

Glossary

ʿĀdāt wa-taqālīd. lit. "customs and traditions"

Alghāz (s. lughz). riddles, puzzles, conundrums

al-ʿūd. See *ʿūd*

Amthāl (s. mathal). proverbs, adages, exempla

al-Andalus. Arabic term for Muslim Spain

Arghūl. a folk double clarinet of the Arab world with fingerholes on only one tube (cf. *mizwij*)

ʿArūbī. a genre of music performed in the western Algerian city of Tlemcen

ʿArūsa. lit. "bride" or "doll"; also a figurine attached to the outer walls of houses as part of a Ramadān tradition in northern Egypt

Ayyām al-ʿarab. lit. "Days of the Arabs"; the oldest historical accounts in Arabic, told in alternating prose and poetry, transmitted orally for about two centuries, then written down in the eighth and ninth centuries

Bālah. a short, improvised form of poetry performed by men at weddings in Yemen

Baladī. lit. "local" or "folk"; name of an Arab rhythm in four beats, also known as *masmūdī saghīr*

Bandīr. round frame drum

Banī/Banū Hilāl. lit. "Sons of Hilāl"; name of a Bedouin tribe whose exploits are chronicled in the epic poem *Sīrat Banī Hilāl*

Baraka. lit. "blessing"; the charismatic supernatural power believed to be possessed by "saints" or "holy persons"

Bilād al-Sūdān. lit. "Lands of the Blacks"; the Arabic term referring to the region of the southern Sahara, from which English derived the name "Sudan"

Buzuq. a long-necked lute common in Lebanon, related to the Greek *bouzouki*

Damma. lit. "gathering"; a genre of music in Port Said, Egypt

Darbukka. See *tabla*

Dhikr. (also pronounced *zikr*). Sufi ritual of remembrance in which participants often chant the name of God, sometimes accompanied by coordinated body movements and by music

Dirbakki. See *tabla*

Dīwān. term with many meanings in Arabic; in the early Islamic period a "registry," associated with the phrase "poetry is the *dīwān* (registry) of the Arabs"; in traditional houses in Yemen, a large communal living room

Dumm. syllable used by Arab musicians to represent the low, deep tone of the drum when struck in the center of the skin (cf. *takk*)

Duyak. an Arab rhythm

Fuāla. lunchtime gathering among women of the United Arab Emirates

Gamāl ʿAbd al-Nāsir. President of Egypt from 1954 to 1970, referred to in English as "Nasser"

Ghinnāwa. a sung poetic genre performed by Bedouin women of the western desert region of Egypt

Guimbrī. a long-necked lute common in Morocco

Hadhramī/Hadhramawt. the Hadhramawt is a region in southern Yemen; a person or thing from that region is *Hadhramī*

Hajj. the Islamic pilgrimage to Mecca; *hājj*, with long vowel, is a term of respect used in addressing persons who have completed the *hajj*, lit. "pilgrim"; note that "pilgrimages" to saints' shrines are referred to by another term, *ziyāra*, which literally means a "visit"

Hakawātī. storyteller, often a professional storyteller who performs in cafés or other public venues

Harf. in Standard Arabic a "letter" such as a letter of the alphabet, but in Yemen, used to refer to a hemistich, a half-line of poetry

Hawfi. a form of sung women's poetry from the western Algerian city of Tlemcen

Hawzī. a song genre from Tlemcen, in western Algeria, related to the classical Andalusian song tradition but with lyrics composed in the local dialect of Tlemcen

Henna/Hinna. a plant-based dye applied to the hands as decoration at weddings; also applied to the hair

Hijra. the flight of the Prophet Muhammad from Mecca to Medina that marks the beginning of the Islamic calendar, hence the term "*Hijri* calendar," abbreviated as A.H. (for example, "in the year 990 A.H.")

Hikāya. story, tale, folktale

Ibn Nadīm. tenth-century Bagdadi bookseller whose catalogue of books offers an encyclopedic view of medieval Islamic culture

Ifrangī. lit. "foreign" or "western"; derived in medieval times from the word "Frank"

Imruʾ l-Qays. famous pagan Arab poet of the pre-Islamic period whose daughter and wealth were protected by the Jewish Arab al-Samawʾal ibn ʿĀdiyāʾ

Inqilābāt. a song genre from Tlemcen, Algeria, closely related to the classical Andalusian song tradition, with lyrics in classical Arabic in the Andalusian style, but composed by local poets, rather than transmitted from medieval Muslim Spain

Inshād dīnī. lit. "religious chant," a song genre associated with Sufi rituals and other contexts, the primary theme of which is praise to the Prophet Muhammad

Iqāʿ (pl. iqāʿāt). rhythmic cycles in Arab music

Jāhiliyya. lit. "Age of Ignorance" (i.e., of true religion); Arabic term for the pre-Islamic era

Jank. medieval harp of the Arabo-Islamic world; no longer extant

Jawzeh. four-stringed bowed fiddle common in Iraq

Jazīra. the Arabic term for the Arabian Peninsula (cf. English "AlJazeera")

Jim. conch shell wind instrument played in Oman

Kaʿba. the large, cube-like structure in Mecca that is the focal point of the Islamic pilgrimage

Kalām manzūm. lit. "organized words" or "strung words"; ancient Arabic term for poetry still in use today

Kalām manthūr. lit. "scattered words"; ancient Arabic term for prose still in use today

Karamāt. miracles, particularly those worked by "saints" or "holy persons"

Khitat. lit. "plans" or "maps"; a genre of Arabic literature giving a topographical description of a country or region

Kiswa. elaborately embroidered covering for the *Kaʿba* in Mecca

Kwitra. short-necked lute found in Algeria

Laʿna (pl. laʿanāt). curse, imprecation, malediction

Lēwa. genre of dance in Oman

Lughz (pl. alghāz). riddle, puzzle, conundrum

Maʿdan. the "Marsh Arabs" of southern Iraq

Madīh. praise poetry or song, particularly of the Prophet Muhammad

Mafraj. lit. "place that gives relief from cares"; the top floor of traditional tower houses in Sanʿa, Yemen, used for entertaining male guests

Maghrib (also Maghreb). lit. "place where the sun sets"; Arabic term for western North Africa, and more specifically, Morocco

Mahmal. a palanquin that used to carry the *kiswa* (embroidered covering for the *Kaʿba*) from Egypt to Mecca during the pilgrimage

Mālid. genre of religious song in Oman, usually performed on the birthday of the Prophet Muhammad

Maqām (pl. maqāmāt). melodic modes in Arab music

Maqsūm. an Arab rhythm in four beats, also known as *duyak*

Mashriq. lit. "place where the sun rises"; Arabic term for the eastern Mediterranean Arab countries (Palestine, Lebanon, Jordan, Syria, and sometimes Iraq)

Masmūdī saghīr. slow, deliberate Arab rhythm in four beats, also known as *baladī*

Mastabā. an adobe brick bench along the outside walls of traditional houses in Egypt

Mathal (pl. amthāl). proverb, adage, exemplum

Mawlid (also mūlid). a saint's festival

Mawwāl (pl. mawāwīl). a poetic song genre with a complex rhyme scheme, often ending in wordplays and puns

Mizmār. folk oboe

Mizwij (also mijwiz). a folk double clarinet with fingerholes on both tubes (cf. *arghūl*)

Mudīf. guesthouse

Mūlid. See *mawlid*

Munshid (pl. munshidīn and munshidūn). singer of *inshād dīnī*

Muruwwa. manhood, bravery, stalwartness

Muwashshah. a poetic song genre with complex rhyme schemes that originated in medieval Muslim Spain *(al-Andalus)*

Naqīb. one of the terms for the overseer or supervisor of the *dhikr* ceremony

Nawādir (s. nādira). lit. "rare things" in the sense of unusual occurrences; anecdotes

Nāy. reed flute used in classical Arab music traditions

Nukat (s. nukta). jokes

Piyyūt (pl. piyyūtīm). genre of Jewish liturgical poetry

Rabāb. Arab bowed fiddle; first bowed string instrument to enter Europe; the term was adopted into Spanish as *rabel* and then into French and English as *rebec*

Rahmānī. type of drum closely associated with Omani identity

Razha. genre of sung poetry and saber dancing in Oman

Qabīlī. lit. "tribal"; used to describe a man who maintains tribal mores and behavior

Qarāqib. large metal "clackers" played in Morocco

Qasaba. a folk reed flute

Qasīda (also qasīd). a classical poetic form in which every verse has the same end rhyme and each verse is split into two equal hemistichs; often translated as "ode"

Qāt. a plant whose leaves, when chewed, give a slightly narcotic effect; consumed in Yemen

Qiddīs. a Christian saint

Qissa (pl. qisas). story, tale, folktale

Qubba. lit. "dome"; a saint's tomb or shrine

Qur'ān. the Koran, holy book of Islam understood to be the word of God revealed to the Prophet Muhammad primarily through the Angel Gabriel; first taught orally to early Muslims and later written down and assembled into a single text

Raba. among the "Marsh Arabs" of southern Iraq, a reed house combined with space for entertaining male guests

Rai. lit. "my opinion" or "my way"; a modern popular music form from the region of western Algeria, particularly the port city of Oran (Wahrān)

Rāwī. reciter or transmitter; in pre-Islamic times he memorized, performed publicly and transmitted to others the poetry of a master poet; in the folk epic tradition the term is used to mean the "narrator" of the story (not the performing poet)

Ramadān. fasting month in Islam, during which Muslims are to abstain from all food and drink from sunrise to sunset

Riqq. tambourine

Sa'ālīk. early Arabian poets of the pre-Islamic period who left their tribes to fend for themselves in the wilderness; sometimes translated as "outcast" or "brigand" poets

Saddiq (also Tsaddiq). a Jewish "saint" or "holy person"

Saffēn. lit. "two rows"; the two groups of men who act as the chorus during the performance of *bālah* poetry in Yemen

Salamiyya. a folk reed flute

Salfeh. story, tale, folktale, legend

al-Samaw'al ibn 'Ādiyā'. Jewish Arab of the pre-Islamic period proverbially famous for keeping his oath to the poet *Imru' l-Qays*

Sandūq al-dunya. lit. "box of the world"; a large box equipped with view-holes and a painted scroll inside that the narrator turned while telling the tale depicted on the scroll

Sha'bī. in Standard Arabic "folk" or "of the people"; in Algeria, a form of urban popular music from the mid-twentieth centuries with roots in Tlemcen, though it achieved its greatest success in Algiers

Shabbāba. a folk reed flute

Shā'ir. poet

Shalla. verse of poetry sung during the performance of *razha* dancing in Oman

Sharīf. lit. "noble"; a descendant of the Prophet Muhammad; also the ruler of Mecca

Shatā'im (s. shatīma). insults

Shaykh. an old man, a respected figure, a political or religious leader, a tribal chief, also spelled *sheikh*

Simsimiyya. a folk lyre found in the regions of the Suez Canal and the Red Sea

Sīra. in Classical Arabic literature a "biography"; in popular literature an epic poem

Sukkōt. Jewish feast of the Tabernacles

Tabla. goblet-shaped drum; also known as *darbukka* and *dirbakki*

Taghrība. westward journey; the central section of the epic of the Banī Hilāl that recounts the tribe's journey toward, and conquest of, North Africa from the Arabian Peninsula

Takk. syllable used by Arab musicians to represent the high, sharp tone of a drum when struck on the edge of the skin (cf. *dumm*)

Tanbūra. term used for several different instruments, among them, a large folk lyre

Taqālīd. lit. "things which are imitated"; customs or traditions

Tarīqa. a Sufi "brotherhood" or "order"

'Ūd. Arab short-necked lute; origin of the English word "lute"

'Ukāz. a marketplace in Arabia famous in the pre-Islamic period for the public recitation of poetry

Walī. lit. "someone close to God"; a Muslim "saint"

Zāmil. a poetic genre used primarily in solemn contexts in Yemen, such as tribal gatherings and processions

Zamzam. a spring in Mecca, believed to be the well where the biblical Hagar found water for her son Ismāʿīl (Ishmael)

Zār. the belief in, and practice of, spirit possession; a term for a spirit; also the ceremony at which spirits possessing humans are called forth and appeased

Zāwiya. a Sufi "lodge" or gathering place, often the site of the *dhikr* ritual

Zikr. See *dhikr*

Ziyāra. lit. "visit" or "visitation"; a pilgrimage to a saint's tomb or shrine, distinct from the *hajj,* the Muslim pilgrimage to Mecca

Bibliography

Aarne, Antti. 1910. *Verzeichnis der Märchentypen.* Helsinki: Suomalainen tiedeakatem-ian toimituksia.

Abdallah, Ali Lutfi. 1999. *The Clever Sheikh of the Butana and Other Stories: Sudanese Folk Tales.* New York: Interlink Books.

Abdel-Malek, Kamal. 1995. *Muhammad in the Modern Egyptian Popular Ballad.* Leiden: E. J. Brill.

Abu-Deeb, Kamal. 1975. "Towards a Structural Analysis of Pre-Islamic Poetry." *International Journal of Middle Eastern Studies* 6: 148–84.

Abu-Lughod, Lila. 1986. *Veiled Sentiments: Honor and Poetry in a Bedouin Society.* Cairo: American University of Cairo Press.

———. 1993. *Writing Women's Worlds: Bedouin Stories.* Berkeley: University of California Press.

Adès. Albert. 1924. *Goha the Fool,* trans. Morris Colman. New York: Albert and Charles Boni.

Alcalay, Ammiel. 1993. *After Arabs and Jews: Remaking Levantine Culture.* Minneapolis: University of Minnesota Press.

Ali, Abdul. 1998. *Arab Legacy to Humour Literature.* New Delhi: M.D. Publications.

Ali, Muhsin Jassim. 1981. *Scheherazade in England: A Study of Nineteenth-Century English Criticism of the Arabian Nights.* Washington DC: Three Continents Press.

Allen, Roger. 2000. *An Introduction to Arabic Literature.* New York: Cambridge University Press.

Alwaya, Semha. 1977. "Formulas and Themes in Contemporary Bedouin Oral Poetry." *Journal of Arabic Literature* 8: 48–76.

al-Amily, Hussain M. 2003. *The Book of Arabic Wisdom: Proverbs and Anecdotes.* Oxford: New Internationalist.

Aquilina, Joseph. 1972. *A Comparative Dictionary of Maltese Proverbs.* Msida: Royal University of Malta.

Bailey, Clinton. 1972. "The Narrative Context of the Bedouin Qasida-poem." *Folk Research Center Studies,* ed. I. Ben-Ami (Jerusalem), 3:67–105.

———. 1981. *Bedouin Poetry from Sinai and the Negev.* Oxford: Clarendon Press.

———. 2004. *A Culture of Desert Survival: Bedouin Proverbs from Sinai and the Negev.* New Haven: Yale University Press.

Barakat, Robert A. 1980. *A Contextual Study of Arabic Proverbs.* Helsinki: Academia Scientiarum Fennica.

Bar-Itzhak, Haya, and Aliza Shenhar. 1993. *Jewish Moroccan Folk Narratives from Israel.* Detroit: Wayne State University Press.

Beigman, Nicolaas H. 1990. *Egypt: Moulids, Saints, Sufis.* London: Kegan Paul International.

Ben-Ami, Issachar. 1998. *Saint Veneration among the Jews in Morocco.* Detroit: Wayne State University Press.

Ben-Amos, Dan. [1969] 1976. "Analytical Categories and Ethnic Genres." *Genre* 2 (September): 275–301. Reprint, *Folklore Genres,* ed. Dan Ben-Amos, 215–42. Austin: University of Texas Press.

Boddy, Janice. 1989. *Wombs and Alien Spirits: Women, Men, and the Zār Cult in Northern Sudan.* Madison: University of Wisconsin Press.

Bohas, Georges, and Jean-Patrick Guillaume. 1985–1998. *Le roman de Baïbars.* 10 vols. Paris: Sindbad.

Boutarene, Kadda. 2002. *Proverbes et dictons populaires algériens.* Algiers: Office des Publications Universitaires.

Bowerstock, G. W. 1983. *Roman Arabia.* Cambridge, MA: Harvard University Press.

Bowman, Glenn. 1993. "Nationalizing the Sacred: Shrines and Shifting Identities in the Israeli-Occupied Territories." *Man,* New Series, Vol. 28, No. 3 (Sept. 1993), pp. 431–60.

al-Bukhārī, Muhammad. 1977. *The Translation of the Meanings of Sahīh al-Bukhārī: Arabic-English,* trans. Muhammad Muhsin Khan. Chicago: Kazi Publications.

Burckhardt, John Lewis. 1972. *Arabic Proverbs, or, the Manner and Customs of the Modern Egyptians Illustrated from Their Proverbial Sayings Current at Cairo.* 3rd ed. London: Curzon Press.

Bushaq, Inea. 1986. *Arab Folktales.* New York: Pantheon Books.

Cachia, Pierre. 1977. "The Egyptian Mawwāl." *Journal of Arabic Literature* 8: 77–103.

———. 1989. *Popular Narrative Ballads of Egypt.* Oxford: Clarendon Press.

Cambridge History of Arabic Literature. 1983–2006. 5 vols. Cambridge: Cambridge University Press.

Campbell, C. G. 1950. *Tales from the Arab Tribes: A Collection of Stories Told by the Arab Tribes of the Lower Euphrates.* New York: MacMillan.

Campo, Juan E. 1987. "Shrines and Talismans: Domestic Islam in the Pilgrimage Paintings of Egypt." *Journal of the American Academy of Religion* 55 (2): 285–305.

———. 1991. *The Other Sides of Paradise: Explorations into the Religious Meanings of Domestic Space in Islam.* Columbia: University of South Carolina Press.

Canaan, Tewfik. 1927. *Mohammedan Saints and Sanctuaries in Palestine.* Jerusalem: Ariel Publishing House.

Caton, Steven. 1990. "Peaks of Yemen I Summon." In *Poetry as Cultural Practice in a North Yemeni Tribe.* Berkeley: University of California Press.

Chyet, Michael L. 1988. " 'A Thing the Size of your Palm': A Preliminary Study of Arabic Riddle Structure." *Arabica* 35: 267–92.

Cline, Walter. 1940. "Proverbs and Lullabies from Southern Arabia." *The American Journal of Semitic Languages and Literatures* 57 (3): 291–301.

Conant, Martha Pike. 1908. *The Oriental Tale in England in the Eighteenth Century.* New York: Columbia University Press.

Connelly, Bridget. 1986. *Arabic Folk Epic and Identity.* Berkeley: University of California Press.

Costa, Paolo, and Ennio Vicario. 1977. *Arabia Felix: A Land of Builders.* New York: Rizzoli.

Damluji, Salma Samar. 1992. *The Valley of Mud Brick Architecture.* Reading, UK: Garnet.

Danielson, Virginia, Scott Marcus, and Dwight Reynolds, eds. 2002. *The Garland Encyclopedia of Music.* Vol. 6, *The Middle East.* New York: Routledge.

Elias, Jamal. 1999. *Islam.* Upper Saddle River, NJ: Prentice-Hall.

El Koudia, Jilali, and Roger Allen. 2003. *Moroccan Folktales.* Syracuse, NY: Syracuse University Press.

Elkhadem, Saad, ed. and trans. 1987. *Egyptian Proverbs and Popular Sayings.* Fredericton, NB, Canada: York Press.

El-Mallah, Issam. 1998. *Omani Traditional Music.* 2 vols. Tutzing: Hans Schneider Verlag.

El-Shamy, Hasan M. 1980. *Folktales of Egypt: Collected, Translated, and Edited with Middle Eastern and African Parallels.* Chicago: Chicago University Press.

———. 1995. *Folk Traditions of the Arab World: A Guide to Motif Classification.* Bloomington: Indiana University Press.

———. 1999. *Tales Arab Women Tell and the Behavioral Patterns They Portray.* Bloomington: Indiana University Press.

———. 2004. *Types of the Folktale in the Arab World: A Demographically Oriented Tale-type Index.* Bloomington: Indiana University Press.

Fanjul, Serafín. 1976. *El mawwāl egipcio: Expresión literaria popular.* Madrid: IHAC.

Ferguson, Charles A., and John M. Echols. 1952. "A Critical Bibliography of Spoken Arabic Proverb Literature." *Journal of American Folklore* 65 (255): 67–84.

Ferguson, Charles A., and Frank A. Rice. 1960. "Iraqi Children's Rhymes." *Journal of the American Oriental Society* 80: 335–40.

Foley, John. 1985. *Oral-Formulaic Theory and Research: An Introduction and Annotated Bibliography.* New York: Garland.

Frayha, Anis. 1953. *Modern Lebanese Proverbs.* Beirut: American University in Beirut.

Fromkin, David. 1990. *A Peace to End All Peace: The Fall of the Ottoman Empire and the Creation of the Modern Middle East.* New York: Avon Books.

Gerber, Jane. 1994. *The Jews of Spain: A History of the Sephardic Experience*. New York: Free Press.

Ghannam, Farha. 1995. "Kuwaiti Lullabies." In *Children in the Muslim Middle East*, ed. Elizabeth Warnock Fernea, 77–83. Austin: University of Texas Press.

Giacobetti, P. A. 1916. *Recueil d'enigmes arabes populaires*. Algiers: Imprimerie Adolphe Jourdan.

Gossen, Gary H. 1971. "Chamula Genres of Verbal Behavior." *Journal of American Folklore* 84: 145–67.

Granqvist, Hilma. 1931–1935. *Marriage Conditions in a Palestinian Village*. 2 vols. Helsingfors: Akademische Buchhandlung.

———. 1947. *Birth and Childhood in an Arab Village*. Helsingfors: Soderstrom.

———.1950. *Child Problems among the Arabs: Studies in a Muhammadan Village in Palestine*. Helsingfors: Söderström.

———. 1965. *Muslim Death and Burial: Arab Customs and Traditions Studied in a Village in Jordan*. Helsinki: Societas Scientiarum Fennica.

———. 1981. *Portrait of a Palestinian Village: The Photographs of Hilma Granqvist*, ed. Karen Seger. London: Third World Centre for Research and Pub.

Haddawy, Husain Fareed Ali, trans. 1990. *The Arabian Nights: Based on the Text of the Fourteenth-Century Syrian Manuscript, Edited by Muhsin Mahdi*. New York: Norton.

Hahn, Franz. 2002. *François Pétis de la Croix et ses Mille et un jours*. Amsterdam: Rodopi.

Hamidou, Abdelhamid. 1938. "Devinettes Populaires de Tlemcen." *Revue Africaine* 81: 357–72.

Hamilton, Terrick. 1820. *Antar, a Bedoueen Romance*. London: J. Murray.

Hamori, Andras. 1969. "Examples of Convention in the Poetry of Abū Nuwās." *Studia Islamica* 30: 5–26.

Han, Carolyn. 2005. *From the Land of Sheba: Yemeni Folktales*. Northhampton, MA: Interlink.

Hannoum, Abdelmajid. 2001. *Colonial Histories, Post-Colonial Memories: The Legend of the Kahina, a North African Heroine*. Portsmouth, NH: Heinemann.

Hassan, Scherazade Qassim. 2002. "Musical Instruments in the Arab World." In *The Garland Encyclopedia of World Music*. Vol. 6, *The Middle East*, 401–23. New York: Routledge.

Heath, Peter. 1996. *The Thirsty Sword: Sīrat 'Antar and the Arabic Popular Epic*. Salt Lake City: University of Utah Press.

Hejaiej, Mona. 1996. *Behind Closed Doors: Women's Oral Narratives in Tunis*. New Brunswick, NJ: Rutgers University Press.

Hoffman, Valerie J. 1995. *Sufism, Mystics, and Saints in Modern Egypt*. Columbia: University of South Carolina Press.

Hourani, Albert. 2002. *A History of the Arab Peoples*. Cambridge, MA: Belknap Press of Harvard University Press.

Hoyland, Robert G. 2000. *Arabia and the Arabs: From the Bronze Age to the Coming of Islam.* New York: Routledge.

Hurreiz, Sayyid H. 1977. *Ja'aliyyin Folktales: An Interplay of African, Arabian and Islamic Elements.* Bloomington: Indiana University Press.

Ibn Nadīm, Abū l-Faraj Muhammad. 1970. *The Fihrist of al-Nadīm: A Tenth-Century Survey of Muslim Culture,* ed. and trans. Bayard Dodge. New York: Columbia University Press.

Ingham, Bruce. 1982. *Northeast Arabian Dialects.* London: Kegan Paul.

———. 1986. *Bedouin of Northern Arabia: Traditions of the āl-Dhafīr.* London: Routledge and Kegan Paul.

Irwin, Robert, ed. 2002. *Night and Horses and the Desert: An Anthology of Classical Arabic Literature.* New York: Anchor Books.

Ismā'īl, 'Abd al-Rahmān. [1934] 1980. *Folk Medicine in Modern Egypt,* trans. John Walker. London: Luzac. Reprint, New York: AMS Press.

Jayyusi, Lena. 1996. *The Adventures of Sayf Ben Dhi Yazan: An Arab Folk Epic.* Bloomington: Indiana University Press.

Jayyusi, Salma Khadra. 2006. *Tales of Juha: Classic Arab Folk Humor.* New York: Interlink.

Jenkins, Jean, and Poul Rovsing Olsen. 1976. *Music and Musical Instruments in the World of Islam.* London: World of Islam Festival Trust.

Jewett, James Richard. 1893. "Arabic Proverbs and Proverbial Phrases." *Journal of the American Oriental Society* 15: 28–120.

Kanafani, Aida S. 1983. *Aesthetics and Ritual in the United Arab Emirates.* Beirut: American University in Beirut Press.

Kennedy, Hugh. 2004. *The Prophet and the Age of the Caliphates: The Islamic Near East from the Sixth to the Eleventh Century.* Harlow, England, U.K.: Pearson/Longman.

Khayyat, Shimon L. 1978. "Lullabies of Iraqi Jews." *Folklore* 89 (1): 13–22.

Kishtiany, Khalid. 1985. *Arabic Political Humor.* London: Quartet Books.

Koen-Sarano, Matilda. 2003. *Folktales of Joha, Jewish Trickster.* New York: Jewish Publication Society of America.

Kurpershoek, P. Marcel. 1994–2002. *Oral Poetry and Narratives from Central Arabia.* 4 vols. Leiden: E. J. Brill.

Lamb, David. 2002. *The Arabs: Journeys Beyond the Mirage.* New York: Vintage Books.

Lane, Edward. 1846. *An Account of the Manners and Customs of the Modern Egyptians.* London: C. Knight.

Lewcock, Ronald. 1986. *The Old Walled City of San'ā'.* Paris: UNESCO.

Lindisfarne-Tapper, Nancy, and Bruce Ingham, eds. 1997. *The Language of Dress in the Middle East.* Richmond, Surrey, U.K.: Curzon Press.

Lord, Albert Bates. 1960. *The Singer of Tales.* Cambridge: Harvard University Press.

Lunde, Paul, and Justin Wintle. 1984. *A Dictionary of Arabic and Islamic Proverbs.* London: Routledge and Kegan Paul.

Lyons, M. C. 1995. *The Arabian Epic: Heroic and Oral Story-telling.* Cambridge: Cambridge University Press.

Mahdi, Muhsin, ed. 1984–1994. *The Thousand and One Nights* [Alf Layla wa-Layla] *from the Earliest Known Sources.* 3 vols. Leiden: E. J. Brill.

Mansfield, Peter. 2004. *A History of the Middle East.* New York: Penguin Books.

Marcus, Scott. 2007. *Music in Egypt: Experiencing Music, Expressing Culture.* Oxford: Oxford University Press.

Marsot, Afaf Lutfi al-Sayyid. 1993. "Humor: The Two-Edged Sword." In *Everyday Life in the Muslim Middle East.* Bloomington: Indiana University Press.

Marzolph, Ulrich. 1992. *Arabia Ridens: Die humoristiche Kurzprosa der frühen adab-Literatur im internationalen Traditionsgeflecht.* Frankfurt am Main: V. Klostermann.

Marzolph, Ulrich, and Richard van Leeuwen, eds. 2004. *The Arabian Nights Encyclopedia.* Santa Barbara, CA: ABC-CLIO.

Masliyah, Sadok. 2001. "Curses and Insults in Iraqi Arabic." *Journal of Semitic Studies* 46 (2) (Autumn): 267–308.

McPherson, J. W. 1941. *The Moulids of Egypt* [Egyptian Saints' Days]. Cairo: N. M. Press.

Meri, Josef W. 2002. *The Cult of Saints among Muslims and Jews of Medieval Syria.* Oxford: Oxford University Press.

Miller, W. Flagg. 2007. *The Moral Resonance of Arab Media: Audiocassette Poetry and Culture in Yemen.* Cambridge, MA.: Harvard Center for Middle East Studies.

Monroe, James. 1972. "Oral Composition in Pre-Islamic Poetry." *Journal of Arabic Literature* 3: 1–53.

Muhawi, Ibrahim, and Sharif Kanaana. 1989. *Speak, Bird, Speak Again: Palestinian Arab Folktales.* Berkeley: University of California Press.

al-Murtād, 'Abd al-Malik. 1982. *al-Alghāz al-sha'biyyā al-Jazā'iriyya: dirāsa fī alghāz al-gharb al-jazā'irī* [Algerian Folk Riddles: A Study of the Riddles of Western Algeria]. Algiers: Dīwān al-Matbū'āt al-Jāmi'iyya.

Musil, Alois. [1928] 1978. *The Manners and Customs of the Rwala Bedouin.* New York: American Geographical Society. Reprint, New York: AMS Press.

Nelson, Kristina. 2001. *The Art of Reciting the Qur'an.* Cairo/New York: American University in Cairo Press.

Nesin, Aziz. 1994. *The Tales of Nasrettin Hoca,* trans. Talat Halman. Istanbul: Dost Yayinlari.

Newby, Gordon Darnell. 1988. *A History of the Jews of Arabia: From Ancient Times to Their Eclipse under Islam.* Columbia: University of South Carolina Press.

Nicholson, Reynold A. 1930. *A Literary History of the Arabs.* Cambridge: Cambridge University Press.

Nuweihed, Jamal Sleem. 2002. *Abu Jmeel's Daughter and Other Stories: Arab Folk Tales from Palestine and Lebanon.* New York: Interlink.

Ochsenschlager, Edward L. 2004. *Iraq's Marsh Arabs in the Garden of Eden.* Philadelphia: University of Pennsylvania Museum of Archaeology and Anthropology.

Pacini, Andrea, ed. 1998. *Christian Communities in the Arab Middle East: The Challenge of the Future*. New York: Oxford University Press.

Parker, Ann, and Avon Neal. 1995. *Hajj Paintings: Folk Art of the Great Pilgrimage*. Washington DC: Smithsonian Institution Press.

Parkinson, Dilworth. 1985. *Constructing the Social Context of Communication: Terms of Address in Egyptian Arabic*. Berlin: Mouton de Gruyter.

Propp, Vladimir. 1968. *Morphology of the Folktale*. Austin: University of Texas Press.

Quéméneur, Jean. [1944] 1997. *Énigmes tunisiennes*. Tunis: S.A.P.I. Reprint, Tunis: I.B.L.A.

Racy, A. J. 2003. *Making Music in the Arab World: The Culture and Artistry of Tarab*. Cambridge: Cambridge University Press.

Rathjens, Carl. 1957. *Jewish Domestic Architecture in San'a, Yemen*. Jerusalem: Israel Oriental Society.

Reeves, Edward B. 1990. *The Hidden Government: Ritual, Clientalism, and Legitimation in Northern Egypt*. Salt Lake City: University of Utah Press.

Reynolds, Dwight F. 1989. "Tradition Replacing Tradition in Egyptian Oral Epic-singing: The Creation of a Commercial Image." *Pacific Review of Ethnomusicology* 5: 1–14.

———. 1995. *Heroic Poets, Poetic Heroes: The Ethnography of Performance in an Arabic Oral Epic Tradition*. Ithaca, NY: Cornell University Press.

———. 2006a. "A Thousand and One Nights: A History of the Text and Its Reception." In *Cambridge History of Arabic Literature: The Post-Classical Period*, eds. Roger Allen and D. S. Richards, 270–91. Cambridge: Cambridge University Press.

———. 2006b. "Sirat Bani Hilal." In *Cambridge History of Arabic Literature: The Post-Classical Period*, eds. Roger Allen and D. S. Richards, 307–19. Cambridge: Cambridge University Press.

Richmond, Diana. 1978. *'Antar and 'Abla: A Bedouin Romance: Rewritten and Arranged by Diana Richmond*. London: Quartet Books.

Rothenburg, Celia E. 2004. *Spirits of Palestine: Gender, Society and the Stories of the Jinn*. Landham, MD: Lexington Books.

Rugh, Andrea B. 1986. *Reveal and Conceal: Dress in Contemporary Egypt*. Syracuse, N.Y.: Syracuse University Press.

Saada, Lucienne. 1985. *"La geste hilalienne"; Version de Bou Thadi (Tunisie): Recueillé. Établie et traduite de l'arabe par Lucienne Saada*. Paris: Gallimard.

Sabbagh, Isa Khalil. 1983. *As the Arabs Say .... Arabic Quotations Recalled and Interpreted*. Washington, DC: Sabbagh Management Corporation.

Said, Edward. 1978. *Orientalism*. New York: Pantheon Books.

Salim, S. M. 1962. *Marsh Dwellers of the Euphrates Delta*. London: Athlone Press.

Sbait, Dirgham. 1982. "The Improvised-Sung Folk Poetry of the Palestinians." PhD diss., University of Washington.

———. 2002. "Palestinian Wedding Songs." In *The Garland Encyclopedia of World Music*. Vol. 6, *The Middle East*, 578–92. New York: Routledge.

Schippmann, Klaus. 2001. *Ancient South Arabia: From the Queen of Sheba to the Advent of Islam.* Princeton, NJ: Markus Weiner.

Scott, Charles T. 1965. *Persian and Arabic Riddles: A Language-Centered Approach to Genre Definition.* Bloomington: Mouton & Co.

Seifert, Lewis C. 1996. *Fairy Tales, Sexuality, and Gender in France 1690–1715: Nostalgic Utopias.* Cambridge: Cambridge University Press.

Sells, Michael A. 1987. *Desert Tracings: Six Classic Arabian Odes.* Middletown, CT: Wesleyan University Press.

———. 1999. *Approaching the Qur'ān: The Early Revelations.* Ashland, Ore.: White Cloud Press.

Serjeant, R. B., and Ronald Lewcock. 1983. *San'a': An Arabian Islamic City.* London: World of Islam Festival Trust.

Shah, Idries. 1966. *The Exploits of the Incomparable Mulla Nasrudin.* New York: Simon and Schuster.

———. 1968. *The Pleasantries of the Incredible Mulla Nadrudin.* London: Octagon.

al-Shahi, Ahmed, and F. C. T. Moore. 1978. *Wisdom from the Nile: A Collection of Folk-Stories from Northern and Central Sudan.* Oxford: Clarendon Press.

Shannon, Jonathan Holt. 2006. *Among the Jasmine Trees: Music and Modernity in Contemporary Syria.* Middletown, CT: Wesleyan University Press.

Shawqi, Yusuf. 1994. *Dictionary of Traditional Music in Oman.* Wilhelmshaven: F. Noetzel/New York: C.F. Peters Corp.

Shehata, Samer S. 1992. "The Politics of Laughter: Nasser, Sadat, and Mubarek in Egyptian Political Jokes," *Folklore* 103 (1): 75–91.

Shiloah, Amnon. 1995. *Music in the World of Islam: A Socio-cultural Study.* Detroit: Wayne State University Press.

Shryock, Andrew. 1997. *Nationalism and the Geneaological Imagination: Oral History and Textual Authority in Tribal Jordan.* Berkeley: University of California Press.

Sioud, Hèdi. 1976. "La Poésie orale tunisienne: structure formulo-orale." *Revue tunisienne de science sociale* 46: 153–92.

Slyomovics, Susan E.. 1987a. "The Death-Song of 'Āmir Khafājī: Puns in an Oral and Printed Episode of *Sīrat Banī Hilāl.*" *Journal of Arabic Literature* 17: 62–78.

———. 1987b. *The Merchant of Art: An Egyptian Hilali Oral Epic Poet in Performance.* Berkeley: University of California Press.

Sowayan, Saad. 1985. *Nabati Poetry: The Oral Poetry of Arabia.* Berkeley: University of California Press.

Stevens, E. S. 1971. *Folk-tales of 'Iraq.* New York: Benjamin Blom.

al-Tābūr, 'Abd Allāh 'Alī. 2001. *Alghāz al-sha'biyya fi al-Imārāt* [Folk Riddles from the Emirates]. UAE: Markaz Zāyid li-l-turāth wa-l-ta'rīkh.

Tahhan, Samir. 2004. *Folktales from Syria,* trans. Andrea Rugh. Austin: Center for Middle East Studies, University of Texas, Austin.

Thesiger, Wilfred. 1964. *The Marsh Arabs.* New York: Dutton & Co.

Thompson, Stith, ed. and trans. [1910] 1928. *The Types of the Folk-tale: A Classification and Bibliography*. Helsinki: Suomalainen Tiedeakatemia. Originally written by Antti Aarne and published as *Verzeichnis der Märchentypen*.

―――. 1932–1936. *Motif-Index of Folk-literature: A Classification of Narrative Elements in Folk-tales, Ballads, Myths, Fables, Mediaeval Romances, Exempla, Fabliaux, Jest-books, and Local Legends*. Helsinki: Suomalainen Tiedeakatemia.

Touma, Habib Hassan. 1993. *The Music of the Arabs*. Portland, OR: Amadeu Press.

'Umrān, Muhammad Ahmad. 1999. *Mūsīqā al-sīra al-hilāliyya* [Music of the Hilālī epic]. Cairo: al-Majlis al-a'lā li-l-thaqāfa.

Waugh, Earle H. 1989. *The Munshidīm of Egypt: Their World and Their Song*. Columbia: University of South Carolina Press.

―――. 2005. *Memory, Music and Religion: Morocco's Mystical Chanters*. Columbia: University of South Carolina Press.

Webber, Sabra. 1975. "It's about Our Bean-colored House: A Preliminary Look at Tunisian Riddles." Master's thesis, University of California, Berkeley.

―――. 1977. "Four Tunisian Lullabies." In *Middle Eastern Muslim Women Speak*, eds. E. Fernea and B. Bezirgan, 87–93. Austin: University of Texas Press.

―――. 1991. *Romancing the Real: Folklore and Ethnographic Representation in North Africa*. Philadelphia: University of Pennsylvania Press.

Westermarck, Edward. 1914. *Marriage Ceremonies in Morocco*. London: MacMillan.

―――. 1920. *The Belief in Spirits in Morocco*. Abo: Abo Akademi.

―――. 1926. *Ritual and Belief in Morocco*. London: MacMillan.

―――. 1931. *Wit and Wisdom in Morocco: A Study of Native Proverbs*. New York: Liveright Press.

Yaqtīn, Sa'īd. 1997. *Qāla al-rāwī: al-binyā al-hikā'iyya fī al-sīra al-sha'biyya* [The Reciter Said: Narrative Structures in the Folk Epic]. Beirut: al-Markaz al-Thaqāfī al-'Arabī.

Yaqub, Nadia. 1999. "Drinking from the Well of Poetry: Tradition, Composition, and Identity in the Oral Palestinian Poetry Duel." PhD diss., University of California, Berkeley.

―――. 2002. "The Palestinian Groom's Wedding Eve Celebration." In *The Garland Encyclopedia of World Music*. Vol. 6, *The Middle East*, 573–78. New York: Routledge.

Yelles-Chaouche, Mourad. 1990. *Le Hawfi: poésie feminine et tradition orale au Maghreb*. Algiers: Office de Publications Universitaires.

Yetiv, Isaac. 1987. *1001 Proverbs from Tunisia*. Washington DC: Three Continents.

Young, Gavin. 1977. *Return to the Marshes*. London: Collins.

Zubaida, Sami, and Richard Tapper, eds. 2000. *A Taste of Thyme: Culinary Cultures of the Middle East*. London: St. Martin's Press.

Zwettler, Michael. 1978. *The Oral Tradition of Classical Arabic Poetry: Its Character and Implications*. Columbus: Ohio State University Press.

Web Resources

ANCIENT ARABIA

General History:
http://www.livius.org/ap-ark/arabia/arabia.html
http://www.saudiaramcoworld.com/issue/196501/inside.arabia.felix.htm

King Dhū Nuwās of Yemen:
http://www.jewishencyclopedia.com/view.jsp?artid=319&letter=D

The Medina Charter:
http://www.constitution.org/cons/medina/con_medina.htm

EGYPT

General Folklore:
http://www.cultnat.org/Folk/folklore_about.html

MOROCCO

Museums of Morocco:
http://www.maroc.net/museums

Tangiers Museum of Moroccan Arts:
http://www.maroc.net/museums/tang1.html

Chechaouen Ethnographic Museum:
http://www.maroc.net/museums/chefchaouen1.html

Tetouan Ethnographic Museum:
http://www.maroc.net/museums/tetouan2.html

Meknes Dar Jamai Museum:
http://www.maroc.net/museums/meknes1.html

Rabat Oudaias Museum:
http://www.maroc.net/museums/rabat1.html

Fez Dar Batha:
http://www.maroc.net/museums/fez1.html

Marrakesh Bert Flint Museum:
http://www.maroc.net/museums/marrakesh3.html

Assaouira Sidi Mohamed Ben Abdallah Museum:
http://www.maroc.net/museums/essaouira1.html

Moroccan Music:
http://www.mincom.gov.ma/english/gallery/music/music.html (downloadable
    examples of a wide variety of Moroccan musical traditions)

OMAN

Oman Centre for Traditional Music
http://www.octm-folk.gov.om (photos and downloadable examples of several genres
    of Omani folk music)

PALESTINE

Palestinian Folklore:
http://www.barghouti.com/folklore (examples of Palestinian folksongs, proverbs and
    stories)

Palestinian Folklore Center:
http://www.inash.org/accomplishments/folklore.html

Palestinian Heritage Center (Bethlehem):
http://www.palestinianheritagecenter.com

Artas Folklore Center:
http://www.palestine-family.net/index.php?nav=223–222&cid=534&did=1046
http://www.geocities.com/artas_heritage/aboutartasfolklorecentergen.html

SAUDI ARABIA

Review article on Arab Gulf and Saudi Arabian music:
http://fp.arizona.edu/mesassoc/Bulletin/campbell.htm

SYRIA

General site including performing arts, handicrafts, folk traditions and food:
http://www.medinaproject.net/syria/pages/home.php?ID_Lang=1

Al-Azem Palace Folk Museum, Damascus:
http://www.syriagate.com/Syria/about/cities/Damascus/azem.htm

Index

About the Author

DWIGHT F. REYNOLDS is Professor of Religious Studies at the University of California, Santa Barbara. His previous books include *Interpreting the Self: Autobiography in the Arabic Literary Tradition* (2001), and *Heroic Poets, Poetic Heroes: The Ethnography of Performance in an Arabic Oral Epic Tradition* (1995).

**Recent Titles in
Greenwood Folklore Handbooks**

Folk and Fairy Tales: A Handbook
D. L. Ashliman

Campus Legends: A Handbook
Elizabeth Tucker

Proverbs: A Handbook
Wolfgang Mieder

Myth: A Handbook
William G. Doty

Fairy Lore: A Handbook
D. L. Ashliman

South Asian Folklore: A Handbook
Frank J. Korom

Story: A Handbook
Jacqueline S. Thursby

Chicano Folklore: A Handbook
María Herrera-Sobek

German Folklore: A Handbook
James R. Dow

Greek and Roman Folklore: A Handbook
Graham Anderson

The Pied Piper: A Handbook
Wolfgang Mieder

Slavic Folklore: A Handbook
Natalie Kononenko